Great Thinkers in Economics

Series Editor
A.P. Thirlwall
School of Economics
University of Kent
Canterbury, UK

D1602850

"An intellectual historian discussing an eminent figure in social theory must not only be sensitive to the subtle nuances of that theorist's own contributions, he must be able to relate those nuances to the complex, shifting intellectual fashions against which that theorist was rebelling. Peter Boettke's skillful treatment of Hayek's intellectual journey brilliantly and provocatively succeeds in achieving this standard of excellence. This is a book that will be recognized as path-breakingly important for many decades to come."

—Israel M. Kirzner, *New York University, USA*

"Among mid-twentieth century economists, only Hayek's work enabled us to understand what I found truly astonishing. People in my market experiments quickly discovered the efficient equilibrium outcomes hidden in their dispersed knowledge of individual item values that I had assigned them privately. For Hayek, prices convey the coordinating information that incentivizes performance by harnessing dispersed knowledge like no other known system. Boettke brings this towering intellect into your own thinking. Hayek's deep insights extend far beyond economics and into jurisprudence, social and political philosophy. Read Boettke's Hayek and soar."

—Vernon L. Smith, *Nobel Laureate Chapman University, USA*

"Boettke advocates a humane and cosmopolitan liberalism as an antidote to the nationalist and populist enthusiasms so evident today on the left and the right. Hayek fought the same battles, of course, against similar foes. Boettke deftly brings Hayek's main contributions in the areas of economics, political economy, and social philosophy into conversation with current concerns and recent writers. On the way he corrects some egregious misreadings. It is a fine achievement."

—Bruce Caldwell, *Duke University, USA*

The famous historian, E.H. Carr once said that in order to understand history it is necessary to understand the historian writing it. The same could be said of economics. Famous economists often remark that specific episodes in their lives, or particular events that took place in their formative years attracted them to economics. Great Thinkers in Economics is designed to illuminate the economics of some of the great historical and contemporary economists by exploring the interaction between their lives and work, and the events surrounding them.

More information about this series at
http://www.palgrave.com/gp/series/15026

Peter J. Boettke

F. A. Hayek

Economics, Political Economy and Social Philosophy

palgrave
macmillan

Peter J. Boettke
Department of Economics
George Mason University
Fairfax, VA, USA

F. A. Hayek Program for Advanced Study
in Philosophy, Politics and Economics
Mercatus Center, George Mason University
Fairfax, VA, USA

Great Thinkers in Economics
ISBN 978-1-137-41159-4   (hardcover)   ISBN 978-1-137-41160-0   (eBook)
ISBN 978-1-349-68175-4   (softcover)
https://doi.org/10.1057/978-1-137-41160-0

Library of Congress Control Number: 2018946249

This Palgrave Macmillan imprint is published by the registered company Springer Nature Limited
The registered company address is: The Campus, 4 Crinan Street, London, N1 9XW, United Kingdom

Pictured left to right: Jack High, Don Lavoie, F. A. Hayek, John Egger, Karen Vaughn, Thomas DiLorenzo, and Richard Fink. At George Mason University in 1983

To Richard Fink, Karen Vaughn, and in memory of Donald Lavoie

Acknowledge Permission to Utilize Content From

Boettke, Peter. 1990. The Theory of Spontaneous Order and Cultural Evolution in the Social Theory of F. A. Hayek. *Cultural Dynamics* 3 (1): 1–11.

———. 2007. Hayek and Market Socialism. In *Cambridge Companion to Hayek*, 51–66. Cambridge: Cambridge University Press.

———. 2016. Friedrich August von Hayek (1899–1992). In *Handbook on the History of Economic Analysis Volume I: Great Economists Since Petty and Boisguilbert*, ed. Gilbert Faccarello and Heinz D. Kurz, 557–567. Cheltenham: Edward Elgar Publishing.

———. 2018. Economic Policy of a Free Society. *The Review of Austrian Economics*, forthcoming.

Boettke, Peter, and Liya Palagashvili. 2016. The Comparative Political Economy of a Crisis. In *Studies in Austrian Macroeconomics*, Advances in Austrian Economics, ed. Steven Horwitz, vol. 20, 235–263. Bingley: Emerald Group Publishing Limited.

Boettke, Peter, and Rosolino Candela. 2017. The Intellectual Context of F. A. Hayek's The Road to Serfdom. *The Journal of Private Enterprise* 32 (1): 29–44.

Boettke, Peter, Vlad Tarko, and Paul Aligica. 2016. Why Hayek Matters: The Epistemic Dimension of Comparative Institutional Analysis. In *Revisiting Hayek's Political Economy*, Advances in Austrian Economics, ed. Peter Boettke and Virgil Henry Storr, vol. 21, 163–185. Bingley: Emerald Group Publishing.

Preface

It is a great honor to be asked to write a book on F. A. Hayek for the *Great Thinkers in Economics* series. For this opportunity, I owe my thanks to series editor Tony Thirlwall of the University of Kent. In his introduction to the general series, he writes: "The famous historian, E.H. Carr, once said that in order to understand history it is necessary to understand the historian writing it. The same could be said of economics. Famous economists often remark that specific episodes in their lives, or particular events that took place in their formative years, attracted them to economics. This new series, *Great Thinkers in Economics*, is designed to illuminate the economics of some of the great historical and contemporary economists by exploring the interaction between their lives and work, and the events surrounding them." Hayek certainly lived an eventful life—one filled with up close witnessing of man's inhumanity in World War I, the economic ruin of the Great Depression, and a dangerous game of brinkmanship with respect to Western civilization itself, with the rise of fascism and communism in the 1930s and 1940s; of meteoric professional success and crushing defeats that he often seemed to barely acknowledge as he continued on with the honing of his craft as an economist, political economist, and social philosopher; of personal relations torn asunder, as well as lasting and loyal intellectual and personal friendships. How all this impacts a thinker is for a historian to glean through devotion to archival work and placing thinkers and their ideas in proper context.

This book, however, is *not* a proper intellectual history. Part of this relates to the fact that as I embarked on this project, I did a survey of the intellectual landscape in what could be termed "Hayek studies." A literal explosion in this field has taken place since 1975 and I document this in material in the appendices and in the "Living Bibliography of Works on Hayek" (https://ppe.mercatus.org/essays/living-bibliography-works-hayek) that provides bibliographic details on books, articles, dissertations, and citations. It is also the case that I have been working with, and writing on, Hayek's ideas since the mid-1980s and have carved out a certain interpretative niche myself in this literature. So, the principle of comparative advantage kicked in as this project took shape the same way that it kicks in all our endeavors. As the epigraph to Philip Wicksteed's brilliant *The Common-Sense of Political Economy* (1910) states, "we are all doing it, though none of us knows we are doing it." Well, sometimes we economists are more conscious of when our behavior conforms to our theories than the average person. Still, it might make sense to first explain what not to expect from this book.

As already stated, it is *not* a proper intellectual history of Hayek—for that I recommend the works of Bruce Caldwell and in particular, not only his excellent *Hayek's Challenge* (2004), but the various editorial introductions that Caldwell has written for the *The Collected Works of F. A. Hayek*, as well as his own ongoing research in a historical biography forthcoming on Hayek. Nor have I written a popular introduction to the essential ideas of Hayek for economic and social understanding, the best book for that in my judgment being my colleague and good friend Don Boudreaux's *The Essential Hayek* (2015)—and the multimedia educational tools that go with it. Don is a master communicator of the basic principles of economics and he captures Hayek's work on the price system and the political, legal, and social order in as readable and as concise a treatment as is humanly possible. My book is not an effort at attention grabbing among lay readers either—for that, we have Alan Ebenstein's two works *Friedrich Hayek* (2001) and *Hayek's Journey* (2003). I do not have the singularity of praise for Ebenstein's work as I do for Caldwell and Boudreaux's books, but I do recognize that there is much value to be found in his books; I just think there are some subtle issues in philosophy and technical economics that are ill-treated in such an effort at popularization. Writing to a general audience always has this risk associated with it, but those gaps in Ebenstein's work have marred, for me, what I otherwise would deem a valiant effort to communicate Hayek's ideas to a new audience and his relevance to a new time. Finally, my book, while dealing with the critical debates that Hayek engaged in throughout his long career of a methodological, analytical, and practical political economy nature, is *not* a proper history of economic controversy—for that, I simply point the reader to my colleague Lawrence H. White's *The Clash of Economic Ideas* (2012).

So, enough telling you what my book is not; let me tell you what it actually is, and how it fits into *The Great Thinkers in Economics* series. *The book seeks to clarify refinements in economics, political economy, and social philosophy that Hayek was led to make during his career because of the context of times and context of the argument.* In the process, it is my hope to clear up some general misconceptions about Hayek's ideas that have, in my humble opinion, served to block understanding the full implications of his arguments. While stressing the context—both historical and intellectual—the story I am weaving together will be one-sided and not one seeking balance between the contending perspectives. This is a story of the evolution of *a perspective* of economic, political economic, and social philosophic thought about how the world works. Hayek, in short, is given several bites of the apple in developing his argument in relationship to the central issues in economic theory, political economy, and social philosophy. The book that my book resembles the most would be Gerald O'Driscoll's *Economics as a Coordination Problem* (1977), but obviously, I have my own twist. That twist turns on what I term in this book *epistemic institutionalism*.[1] The various debates in which Hayek was embroiled during the 1930–1960 period led in economics and political economy to a renewed focus on the institutional framework, but primarily to the role that framework played in structuring the *incentives* that economic actors faced. While this *incentive institutionalism*, in the hands of Armen Alchian, James Buchanan, Ronald Coase, Harold Demsetz, Milton Friedman, Leonid Hurwicz, Douglass North, Mancur Olson, Vincent and Elinor Ostrom, Gordon Tullock, Oliver Williamson, and others played a significant role in forcing a major rethinking in economic science

---

[1] See this discussion at *Liberty Matters* initiated by my lead essay, "Hayek's Epistemic Liberalism" (September 2017) http://oll.libertyfund.org/pages/lm-hayek.

and political economy post-1950, and even though many of these think-ers stressed information and even some used the word "knowledge," they do not fully address themselves to Hayek's argument about the contextual nature of knowledge; the knowledge of time and place; the tacit domain of our knowledge, and therefore they do not (with the notable exception of the Ostroms) address the discovery and learning aspect of alternative institutional arrangements as was the emphasis in Hayek.

If indeed the "curious task of economics is to demonstrate to men how little they really know about what they imagine they can design," then the central question of economics becomes one about the institutional pre-requisites required for learning and error correction among individuals in society (Hayek 1988, 76). It is Hayek's deepening exploration of the *epis-temic properties of alternative institutional arrangements* that is the primary focus of this book, and then, the drawing out of the implications of that focus for methodology of the social sciences, analytical economics, and practical public policy that I hope readers will see. I believe Hayek is of continuing relevance not because of the man Hayek, and not because of the critical role he played in intellectual debates during his career, but because of what his ideas still have to say to us in our context and in our debates to this day and where they may be going.

I think of Hayek's intellectual journey as consisting of four phases, none of which are actually clearly distinct from one another. He begins his journey pursuing questions of a theoretical nature dealing with inter-temporal coordination, and in particular, monetary and capital theory. Hog farmers, for example, are currently making investments in the main-tenance of livestock that will only yield returns in the future. How is it possible that these farmers make this investment decision rationally?

Understanding how the assessment of the future demand for bacon guides the investment decisions in hog farming today is critical to answer-ing the question of the coordination of economic activity through time. In developing his understanding of the "imputation problem," Hayek emphasized the role that interest rates play in investment decisions, and the role that prices play in production decisions. He was working in the grand tradition of the first and second generation of Austrian School economists.

Hayek and his fellow Austrian economists were consciously articulating a particular branch of early neoclassical economics grounded in both subjective utility theory and the economic calculus of individual decision-making on the margin. But several things separated the Austrians from Carl Menger to Hayek from others in the neoclassical approach that would only become increasingly evident in the coming years: namely, a thoroughgoing subjectivism that would encompass not just value, but costs and expectations; incorporating the passage of real time in the analysis of exchange and production; the uncertainty of the economic environment and ignorance of the decision-maker must be acknowledged in the analysis of the choice calculus; the non-neutral nature of money so that distortions of the monetary unit can result in distortions in the patterns of exchange, production, and distribution; and the heterogeneous nature of capital goods that possess multiple specific uses. Steel, for example, can be used to build not only bridges and buildings, but steel is not all that critical in the production of ham sandwiches. Again, how do economic actors figure out the best way to extract iron ore, the best method to produce steel, the most valued use of that steel by others in the market, and in what amount and at what quality would best satisfy the uncertain and future demand for steel? The perennial economic questions of how, what, and for whom have to be answered and answered anew everyday by critical decision-makers scattered throughout the economy.

The *economic answer* provided by the Austrian School of economics placed prices at the center of the analysis of the economic system. Or, as we will see, they actually placed *property*, *prices*, and *profit-and-loss* in a position of prominence in their theoretical explanation of the coordination of economics activities. The production plans of some, to put this simply, must mesh with the consumption demands of others. Otherwise, scarce resources will be wastefully utilized and economic frustration among suppliers and demanders will result, and wealth-creating opportunities will be passed over. It is the function of property, prices, and profit-and-loss to structure incentives, mobilize information, discover and utilize the knowledge that is dispersed throughout the economy, and provide the spur for innovation and the feedback on bad decision-making that is necessary for economic actors to coordinate their plans, and in so doing realize the mutual benefits of productive specialization and peaceful social cooperation.

This theoretical articulation of the continual process of the coordination of economic activity through time, and the adjustments and adaptations to changing circumstances guided by property, prices, and profit-and-loss can be found in the writings of Carl Menger, Eugen Bohm-Bawerk, Friedrich Wieser, Joseph Schumpeter, and Ludwig Mises, and we must always remember that this formed the common bases for the continued theoretical refinement of this analytical approach by Hayek and his generation of theoretical economists in Vienna: Fritz Machlup, Oskar Morgenstern, and Gottfried Haberler. This *market process theory* and *theory of the institutional framework* is the common core of the Austrian School of economics from its founding to today. And in my reading, Mises and Hayek were responsible for the greatest refinements of this contribution to scientific economics and the art of political economy.

I have belabored this first phase of Hayek's career because it is from this common core that all the other phases of his career emerge. This first phase can be termed, for our purposes, **Economics as a Coordination Problem** and can be roughly dated 1920–1945. It is in this phase that Hayek makes many, if not all, of his most original contributions to economic science. As Hayek developed these various contributions, he first encountered acceptance by other leading economists, for example, his appointment at the London School of Economics in the early 1930s. However, as the decade of the 1930s progressed, his ideas met with greater resistance. This resistance came in the form of both a philosophical rejection of his approach and an analytical rejection of his theory of the market process and the theory of the institutional framework.

Hayek's brilliance, I contend, was to see the philosophical and analytical rejection as interrelated. This led naturally to the second phase of his career, which was labeled by him as **The Abuse of Reason Project**, which I date as running between 1940 and 1960. In my reading, the culmination of this project was not only Hayek's *The Counter-Revolution of Science* (1952), but *The Constitution of Liberty* (1960) and his critique of the rational constructivism of the administrative state. Viewed in this way,

Hayek's third phase of his career also seems to follow naturally from the previous two.

In the period between 1960 and 1980, Hayek transitioned to a third phase of intellectual inquiry, **The Restatement of the Liberal Principles of Justice**. Here, Hayek articulates the importance of general rules—a theme of course that a careful reading of *The Road to Serfdom* (1944) would also reveal as key to his analysis of the institutional framework. As Hayek developed these ideas in more depth, he sharpened his critique of the modern theory and practice of democratic society. Crucial to Hayek's work during this period is the contrast between the liberal principles of justice and the demands of social justice.

The interconnection between Hayek's first three phases of his career is reflected throughout his work, and as I said, as a matter of historical record, it is near impossible to draw distinct boundaries around the different phases. He was always working as a technical economist concerned with the problem of economic coordination through time, and he was always a political economist who cared about the institutional infrastructure within which economic activity took place. And he was always a social philosopher who thought seriously about the liberal order. As Erwin Dekker (2014) has recently argued, we must understand the contributions of Hayek, and his fellow Austrian School economists, as the product of "students of civilization." This was always the subtext even in the most technical of discussions about money, capital, interest, and the price system. And this discussion animated the seminars and discussion groups that made up the various intellectual circles in interwar Vienna. And it was this discussion that animated Hayek's later efforts with the Mont Pelerin Society. As Hayek (1967, 123) argued in his essay "The Dilemma of Specialization," the social sciences are in a different position than the natural sciences. "The physicist who is only a physicist can still be a first-class physicist and a most valuable member of society. But nobody can be a great economist who is only an economist—and I am even tempted to add that the economist who is only an economist is likely to become a nuisance if not a positive danger."

Post-1980, Hayek's work turned to what I would term **Philosophical Anthropology and the Study of Man**, the last phase of his intellectual journey, ending with his death in 1992. The culmination of this phase in his career was *The Fatal Conceit* (1988). His work during this time is a challenge not only to the development in economic thinking by John Maynard Keynes and Oskar Lange, but broad social theorists such as Karl Marx, Sigmund Freud, and Karl Polanyi. The arguments that Hayek develops in this phase of his career will not be treated with the depth they deserve in this book. It is my hope that future scholars will find the ideas I discuss in these pages to be intellectually enticing and promising so they will want to apply them to the contemporary intellectual debate in moral economy and social economy.

In what follows, we will mainly focus on the intellectual evolution of the first three phases in Hayek's career, and try to highlight as I have said is my purpose—the refinement and articulation of Hayek's *epistemic institutionalism*. It is important for my narrative to understand that Hayek never abandoned the first phase of his journey. From 1920 to 1980, his work consistently and persistently is grounded in his "Austrian" understanding of the coordination of economic activity through time. But he was compelled to explore the underlying philosophical reasons why his fellow economists were resistant to his analysis of the coordination problem. As he said on various occasions, figuring out why others did not find conclusions he thought logically followed from the economic calculus and market theory was of utmost importance to him, and a great stimulus for his work. Why did economists in the 1930s–1960s seem to overlook not only the insights of the Austrian economists from Menger to Mises, but the teachings of the classical political economists such as David Hume and Adam Smith? Why did they overlook the institutional framework that the classical and early neoclassical theorists had taken as given? What happened to the basic understanding that economists and political economists shared concerning property, prices, and profit-and-loss? And since he believed he put his finger on the philosophical culprit, how can we restate the foundations of our scientific discipline and discuss the political economy of a free people once we overcome this intellectual detour?

The structure of the book will follow this chronological and intellectual order I have just presented. After a chapter identifying what I think are the greatest misconceptions about Hayek in the secondary literature, and a brief biographical chapter, I proceed with a chapter addressing money, capital, and business cycles, followed by a chapter on market theory and the price system. I then turn to Hayek's battle with socialism in two chapters, and then turn to his development of a genuine institutional economics. The ideas Hayek developed through his first two phases of his career—1920–1960—culminate in his version of institutional economics, but I would argue that his institutional economics must be read back in an explicit way into his earlier writings to truly understand Hayek's scientific contributions and the revolutionary implications for the practice of the science of economics and the art of political economy.

Just as Hayek, after his battle with Keynes and macroeconomics, and his battle with market socialists and *The Road to Serfdom*, turned his attention (at least in part) to the rejuvenation of the liberal project, so do I turn to this project. I do not provide a full history of the Mont Pelerin Society (MPS), but it is obvious that MPS played a major role in Hayek's career and life. But MPS, to Hayek, I would argue, was understood as a scholarly project and not an ideological or public policy project as it is often portrayed by skeptics of MPS and the liberal project. I would contend that MPS is a debate and discussion society headlined by Hayek, Milton Friedman, and James Buchanan. Of course, the society can also boast as members several other Nobel Prize economists, such as George Stigler, Gary Becker, and Vernon Smith, but I think in painting with a broad brush describing the society's intellectual culture with reference to Hayek, Friedman, and Buchanan is quite accurate. MPS was never a Davos for neoliberal economists as critics have continually sought to depict it as, but has always been a debate and discussion society concerned with foundational issues facing the liberal society. And this was actually the purpose starting actually with the Walter Lippmann Colloquium in 1938, which would inspire Hayek to found MPS in 1947. The rejuvenation of liberalism in Hayek's time and in our time is the subject of Chaps. 8, 9, and 10.

The book concludes with a discussion of what I view as the progressive research program in the social sciences and humanities of Hayek's legacy. Here again, I hope the reader will find insight and inspiration on how to think seriously about fundamental issues in economic science, political economy, and social philosophy.

In working on this book, I benefited greatly from the financial support from the Earhart Foundation and the John Templeton Foundation, as well as the general academic support from the Mercatus Center and the Department of Economics at George Mason University. Through this support, I was able to make research trips to the archives at the Hoover Institution on War, Revolution and Peace, where Hayek's papers are located; the London School of Economics, where Lionel Robbins's papers are located; Grove City College, where Mises's papers are located; the Library of Congress and Abba Lerner's papers; the University of Vienna, and the ongoing work in establishing the collection of papers of James M. Buchanan at George Mason University. Numerous people helped me with this background research and I want to especially thank Rosemary Boettke, Emily Skarbek, and Roland Fritz. I have relied on several research collaborators throughout my years of writing on Hayek; these include: Paul Aligica, William Butos, Rosolino Candela, Christopher Coyne, Daniel D'Amico, Steve Horwitz, Roger Koppl, Peter Leeson, Jayme Lemke, Adam Martin, Kyle O'Donnell, Liya Palagashvili, Ennio Piano, David Prychitko, Emily Skarbek, Dan Smith, Nicholas Snow, Virgil Storr, Vlad Tarko, and Karen Vaughn. Thank you to all of them for how much I have learned in the process of working with them to try to make sense of Hayek's ideas and their evolutionary potential. As this project took shape, I also benefited from the critical feedback and suggestions from Solomon Stein—a talented intellectual historian of economic ideas, who happens to love archival research and the contextualization of ideas, so he was a great sounding board as this project was working through the various steps along the way. I also need to express a great intellectual debt to Rosolino Candela—a very talented economist who cares passionately about ideas and has been a constant source of inspiration and assistance throughout. I also benefited greatly from a faculty lunch organized by my colleague Jayme Lemke where I got critical feedback on the project from my colleagues at the F. A. Hayek Program for Advanced Study in Philosophy, Politics and Economics: Paul Aligica, Don Boudreaux, Tyler Cowen, Chris Coyne, Stefanie Haeffele, Roberta Hertzberg, Peter Leeson, Virgil Storr, Richard Wagner, and Lawrence White. Throughout the project, I was helped in a variety of ways by a team of graduate students: Caleb Fuller, Aidan Harkin, Ennio Piano, Scott King, Andrew Humphries, Kaitlyn Woltz, Bryan Cutsinger, Nathan Goodman, John

Kroencke, and Jordan Lofthouse. And none of this would be possible without the constant intellectual and administrative support I received from Eric Celler and Stephen Zimmer. I also would be very remiss if I did not acknowledge the great assistance I have received through the years in building our research and educational program here at GMU and Mercatus from Peter Lipsey. To say his contributions have been indispensable would be an understatement for they have been the very meaning of the term "mission critical". I cannot thank him enough for what he has helped me do here at GMU/Mercatus. I must also thank Tyler Cowen, Brian Hooks, and Dan Rothschild for their leadership at the Mercatus Center and for their general support of our research and graduate educational programs at GMU. Finally, as this manuscript was going through the final edits, I benefited greatly from comments from Tony Thirlwall, Chris Coyne, Rosolino Candela, and the excellent editorial suggestions of my colleagues at Mercatus McKenzie Robey and Erica T Celler, as well as both Clara Heathcock and Laura Pacey at Palgrave Macmillan. I would also like to thank Production Project Manager Dhanalakshmi Jayavel for her attention to detail in guiding this project through its final stages. Of course, the usual caveat holds.

Much of the story that you will encounter here has appeared in one form or another through the years, starting with my first published papers in the 1980s. During that course of time, of course I have accumulated a great debt to such scholarly mentors as James Buchanan, Warren Samuels, Israel Kirzner, and Mario Rizzo, and a list of fantastic PhD students whom I have had the privilege to work with so closely in developing my ideas at both NYU and GMU. Chris Coyne, Peter Leeson, and Virgil Storr were once students of mine in name, but in reality, they have always been my closest collaborators, cherished friends, and professional colleagues, who I am lucky enough to work with at GMU to build our research and educational programs. But my biggest debt actually goes to the individuals directly responsible for my professional career in economics and how they shaped that—Richard Fink, Don Lavoie, and Karen Vaughn. In the 1980s, they established the Center for the Study of Market Processes at George Mason University, and along with the Center for Study of Public Choice formed the core of a new PhD program in economics. I was in one of the first classes of PhD students in that program beginning in 1984 and finishing in 1988. They created the

intellectual space in academia where the ideas of Hayek were treated neither as sacred texts to be memorized with great care and uncritical acceptance, nor as a closed chapter in the history of economic thought. Instead,
they insisted that we treat Hayek's texts as an invitation to inquiry into
the yet unwritten chapters of a progressive research program in the social
sciences and humanities. That vision still inspires me today, and the institutional infrastructure that Rich, Don, and Karen created at George
Mason University has made possible our efforts to translate that earlier
inspiration to an aspiration to ultimately a realization in our research and
graduate education initiatives at the F. A. Hayek Program for Advanced
Study in Philosophy, Politics and Economics at the Mercatus Center at
George Mason University. It is with that acknowledgment in mind that I
dedicate this book to Richard Fink and Karen Vaughn, and in the memory of Don Lavoie.

Department of Economics   Peter J. Boettke
George Mason University
Fairfax, VA, USA
F. A. Hayek Program for Advanced Study
in Philosophy, Politics and Economics
Mercatus Center, George Mason University
Fairfax, VA, USA

Bibliography

Boettke, Peter J. 2017. Hayek's Epistemic Liberalism. *Liberty Matters: An Online Discussion Forum.*
Boudreaux, Donald. 2014. *The Essential Hayek.* Vancouver: Fraser Institute.
Caldwell, Bruce J. 2004. *Hayek's Challenge: An Intellectual Biography of F. A. Hayek.* Chicago: University of Chicago Press.
Ebenstein, Alan. 2001. *Friedrich Hayek: A Biography.* Chicago: University of Chicago Press.
———. 2003. *Hayek's Journey: The Mind of Friedrich Hayek.* London: Palgrave Macmillan.
Hayek, F.A. 1944. *The Road to Serfdom.* Chicago: University of Chicago Press.

————. 1967. The Dilemma of Specialization. *Studies in Philosophy, Politics, and Economics*.

————. 1988. *The Fatal Conceit: The Errors of Socialism, the Collected Works of F. A. Hayek, W. W. Bartley, III*. Chicago: University of Chicago Press.

O'Driscoll, Gerald P. 1977. *Economics as a Coordination Problem: The Contributions of Friedrich A. Hayek*. Kansas: Sheed Andrews and McMeel Retrieved Liberty Fund's Online Library of Liberty.

Wicksteed, Philip. 1910. *The Common Sense of Political Economy*. London: Routledge & Kegan Paul Limited.

White, Lawrence H. 2012. *Clash of Economic Ideas: The Great Policy Debates and Experiments of the Last Hundred Years*. Cambridge, MA: Cambridge University Press.

Contents

List of Figures

1

Clarifying Some Misconceptions About Hayek

F. A. Hayek is a lightning-rod figure in the social and policy sciences. He is often criticized, along with Milton Friedman, as the architect of a neo-liberal conspiracy that somehow hijacked the twentieth century and created tensions and conflicts that plague the twenty-first century. I will not be able to fix those interpretative issues in this book. If you are expecting an effort to counter Naomi Klein or Corey Robin and their attempt to scandalize Hayek and his project, this book is not where to look. There are two reasons for this. First, I believe the writings of Naomi Klein and Corey Robin are actually not that challenging to a serious student of Hayek's work; they are, instead, musings of ideological ax-grinders who appeal to those who already believe as they do. I would like to avoid that entire "intellectual" enterprise.[1] If you want to read legitimate scholarship that finds serious flaws in Hayek's writings and actions in this area of the scandalous, I recommend, instead, the works of Andrew Farrant and Edward McPhail (2014). For a more empathetic discussion of Hayek, I

---

[1] See my 2017 Liggio Lecture "Context, Continuity and Truth," https://www.atlasnetwork.org/news/article/context-continuity-and-truth-theory-history-and-political-economy for a discussion of what I believe to be the intellectual bankruptcy of the "hermeneutics of suspicion" in the history of ideas, and how this is a problem for both the left and the right. Science and scholarship, I would contend, advance in a culture of criticism, not as often portrayed in a culture of skepticism for this very reason.

© The Author(s) 2018
Peter J. Boettke, *F. A. Hayek*, Great Thinkers in Economics,
https://doi.org/10.1057/978-1-137-41160-0_1

would recommend Bruce Caldwell and Leonidas Montes (2015). Second, my purpose throughout this book is not to defend Hayek the man, but to discuss the evolution of Hayekian ideas. In this regard, I believe an extended discussion about Hayek, his efforts with the Mont Pelerin Society, and his purported relationship with political figures such as Pinochet, Reagan, or Thatcher is simply tangential to my purposes except as it relates to the focus on the evolution of Hayekian ideas.

F. A. Hayek, like all of us, was a flawed man. He was, in a strange way, thrust into public view early in his career, then again in the middle of the career, and finally, at the end of his career—with long lapses of general disinterest in what he had to say by the intellectual elite and general public. He fought with John Maynard Keynes, he fought with a variety of socialists such as Oskar Lange, and he fought in general with an intellectual *zeitgeist* that he struggled to fully grasp. Hayek, the man, demonstrated the same confusions and frustrations in trying to make sense of it all that all flesh-and-blood human beings do, and in the process, said and did things, I am sure, in hindsight he would regret.

No doubt some of the remarks he said about the situation in Thatcher's England or Pinochet's Chile would qualify as such remarks. But his relationships with those in political power was remote at best as Hayek was *never* a political consultant to any leader in power; he was always a critical scholar who tried to speak truth to power from the outside. While I have no desire to defend Hayek, the man, I still have to ask—as Michel Foucault in *Power/Knowledge* (1980, 135) taught—what in those texts of Hayek that supposedly were developing an argument for true liberalism might make possible authoritarian regimes?[2] Hopefully, the reader will find my exposition of Hayekian liberalism in the later parts of this book

---

[2] See along these lines not only Farrant and McPhail's (2014) discussion of "transitional dictatorship," but Meadowcroft and Ruger (2014) and the discussion of the relationship between liberty and democracy in the works of Friedman, Hayek, and Buchanan. In these discussions, however, we must always keep in mind that there exists an "institutional possibility frontier" that any historically situated society also must take as a given constraint in time that consists of the existing stock of human capital and technology. There are, in essence, constraints on the constraints of our choosing. This makes for some very complicated issues in the historical examination of pathways to political and economic development. See Boettke et al. (2005) and the references therein, but also the work by North et al. (2009) and Acemoglu and Robinson (2004). As my colleague Pete Leeson likes to say, the rules in any given society might tell us what is permissible, but the constraints tell us what is possible.

as a sufficient beginning to this necessary conversation on the nature and significance of the liberal project for our times.

Hayek, the man, witnessed first-hand the inhumanity of World War I (WWI) and was dismayed by the lack of understanding among his London School of Economics (LSE) colleagues of the developments in Germany during the 1930s (see Hayek [1963] 1995, 62). Thus, his over-arching concerns were the institutional setting of economic life and how that institutional setting could be destroyed by unrestrained government (whether democratic or not). Hayek's articulation of Hayekian liberalism was incomplete, and thus, the Hayekian argument needs to be continually worked on so as to realize a better understanding of the institutional infrastructure of a political order of a free people: a political order that exhibits neither discrimination nor dominion. Hayek was in many ways a revolutionary, but strictly in the intellectual sense and not in the political sense.

Unfortunately, Hayek suffered the fate of an intellectual revolutionary in two ways. He was misunderstood by foes and falsely appropriated by friends as a result of the intellectual prejudices of the times. In the practical policy realm, this meant that his books such as *The Road to Serfdom* ([1944] 2007)[3] and *The Constitution of Liberty* (1960) were not read, but displayed. His arguments were not wrestled with, but reduced to slogans. In the realms of methodology and analytics, Hayek's bold ideas were either incorrectly translated into the preferred language of the day—the very language he was trying to get folks to break out of—or they were outright dismissed as either incomprehensible or relics of an earlier age that science had progressed beyond. I recently wrote in an article for the *Journal of the History of Economic Thought* that: "Mises was a sophisticated nineteenth-century thinker and Hayek was a sophisticated twenty-first-century thinker, but in both instances the twentieth century didn't know how to deal with their arguments about methodology, analytic methods, and the political economy import of their analysis of socialism, interventionism, and radical liberalism" (2015, 84). This thesis will be repeatedly

---

[3] Keynes famously commented on Hayek's *The Road to Serfdom* in a letter dated June 28, 1944, reprinted in John Maynard Keynes, *Activities 1940–1946: Shaping the Post-War World: Employment and Commodities, The Collected Writings of John Maynard Keynes Vol. 27* (1980, 385).

stressed as we study the evolution of Hayekian ideas concerning *epistemic institutionalism* and attempt to clarify a variety of misconceptions about Hayek's argument along the way.

So, putting aside the ideological misconceptions that are embedded in the critique of neoliberalism, the main scientific misconceptions are:

1. Hayek's methodological individualism was based upon atomistic actors who were *perfectly rational.*
2. Hayek saw the price system as *perfectly efficient.*
3. Hayek was *categorically opposed* to government action.
4. Hayek presented a *slippery slope argument* toward totalitarianism in *The Road to Serfdom.*
5. Hayek saw something being the product of spontaneous order as a *normative approval* of that order.
6. Hayek's resistance to formal modeling and statistical testing was based on old-fashioned methodological ideas that led to *dogmatic stances* rather than scientific progress.
7. Hayek's evolutionary arguments developed late in his career about group selection constituted an *abandonment* of his earlier *methodological individualism.*
8. Hayek's ideas on monetary theory and the price system *never evolved* throughout his career.
9. Hayek's ideas were *roundly defeated* by Keynes with respect to macroeconomics, and by Lange-Lerner with respect to the market socialism.
10. Hayek effectively *abandoned economics* after the publication of *The Pure Theory of Capital* ([1941] 2007) and retreated to political theory, legal theory, and public intellectual work.

It is my hope to counter each of these ten claims throughout this book. I will make judicious use of quotes from Hayek's body of work, which challenge each of these claims so the reader can see that these misconceptions are a product of efforts to pigeonhole a thinker who defies easy characterization. They are not, however, *the* topic of focus in the chapters to come, but they will all be challenged in the material I present. It is my sincere intent to demonstrate that Hayek's ideas went through critical refinement throughout his long career, and that there is a fundamental coherence in those refinements in his capacity as an economic theorist, a practitioner of political economy, and as a social philosopher.

Hayek did not shift topics and fields to run away from perceived intellectual defeats. Rather, he sought to deepen our understanding of the nature of the economic problem that modern societies must confront and the demands of a truly liberal order. He became an economist in his late teens and early 20s and he remained an economist into his 90s, but in order to appropriately place his intellectual innovations in economics, he had to situate those ideas in various intellectual and institutional contexts—not unlike the Scottish Enlightenment Philosophers who he took so much inspiration from: David Hume and Adam Smith. His technical economics bumped into his political economy, and his political economy bumped into his yet broader social philosophy, but that social philosophy also feeds back into a deeper understanding of his technical economics. As Hayek himself has put it, "the task of economic theory was to explain how an overall order of economic activity was achieved which utilized a large amount of knowledge which was not concentrated in any one mind but existed only as the separate knowledge of thousands or millions of different individuals," but "only through a re-examination of the age-old concept of freedom under the law, the basic conception of traditional liberalism, and of the problems of the philosophy of the law which this raises, that I have reached what now seems to be a tolerably clear picture of the nature of the spontaneous order of which liberal economists have so long been talking" (1967: 91–92).

Karen Vaughn (1999) once published a paper on "Hayek's Implicit Economics," where she tries to articulate the underlying economics that can be found in his later writings. This book is completely consistent with that spirit. Moreover, it also asks the reader to think seriously about "Hayek's Implicit Political Economy and Social Philosophy" that provided the institutional background even as he developed his most technical economics in the 1920s and 1930s. By weaving back and forth between the implicit background and the explicit foreground of analysis in Hayek's career as divided from the 1920s to the 1940s, and then from the 1950s to 1980s, what is implicit in both will become explicit and thus capable of serving as building blocks for something altogether new in the twenty-first-century practice of economics, political economy, and social philosophy.[4]

As a matter of historical fact, the critical period for the development of Hayekian ideas is from 1930 to 1950, though there was continuous development after 1950, and foundational developments in the 1920s.[5] But for the period I see as critical, one must always remember Lionel Robbins's (1971, 129) warning that "the historian of the future, if he wishes to treat of the relations between London and Cambridge during this period … that any generalizations that he may wish to make must fit facts of considerable complexity if they are not seriously to misrepresent the situation." Indeed, the disputes of these times that sharpened Hayek's thinking were complex. They took place during economic crisis in the UK and the USA, and political crisis in Germany and elsewhere in Continental Europe, and would eventually result in World War II (WWII). These disputes, in other words, were more than just purely academic exercises.

To put things in historical context, it is useful to look at a few charts and figures that might give us a window into the everyday world that an economic and social thinker confronted during Hayek's formative years as a researcher of consequence. The changes during Hayek's life are nothing short of monumental. Figure 1.1 illustrates the 20-year period of unemployment rates in Germany, the UK, and the USA, each of which was unable to escape the macroeconomic consequences of the Great Depression, and address the economic situation that was the historical background against which Hayek developed his economic ideas. Figure 1.2 is meant to illustrate roughly the standard of living in the countries where Hayek was working throughout his career—Austria

[4]On the analytical importance of thinking about background and foreground and how shifting those results in radical shifts in perspective, see Richard Wagner's brilliant *Mind, Society and Human Action* (2010, 1–26) and his idea of bivalent logic for economic inquiry.
[5]"When I look back to the early 1930s, they appear to me much the most exciting period in the development of economic theory during this century." It was, Hayek continues, "a high point and the end of one period in the history of economic theory and the beginning of a new very different one." He is referring there to ascendancy of Keynesian macroeconomics that treated "the economic process in terms of aggregates" rather than focus on the "structure of relative prices," and thus was unable to provide an explanation of "changes in relative prices or their effects." This would require, Hayek suggests, economists to someday go back to the 1930s and "take up where we left off then" to make progress in economic theory once again ([1963] 1995, 49; 60; 49).

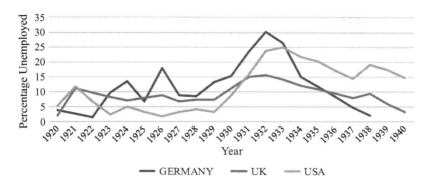

Fig. 1.1 Unemployment rate in Germany, UK, and USA, 1920–1940. Source for UK and Germany: Mitchell (1998a). Source for USA: Mitchell (1998b)

Fig. 1.2 Real GDP per capita. (Source: Bolt et al. (2018))

(1920), the UK (1930s–1940s), the USA (1950s), and Germany (1960s–1980s). In the same countries and during the same period Fig. 1.3 illustrates the growth of government as a percentage of Gross Domestic Product (GDP) due to the rise of the welfare state, particularly after WWII. And, it is critical to always keep in mind, as illustrated in Fig. 1.4, the experienced inhumanity that thinkers of this time were forced to process during the first half of the twentieth century. To capture this, look at the death toll from WWI, Soviet Communism, Nazi Germany, and WWII.

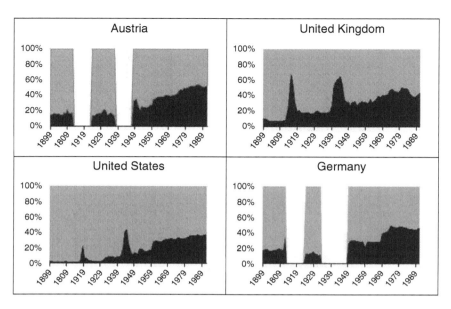

Fig. 1.3 Government expenditure as a % of GDP. (Source: IMF (2016))

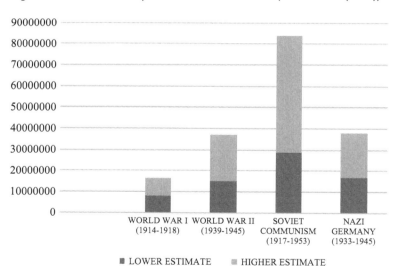

Fig. 1.4 Number of deaths. Sources: WWI lower estimate (Source: Haythornthwaite (1992)). WWI higher estimate (Source: White (2011)). WWII lower estimate (Combat deaths) (Source: Rummel (1994a)). WWII Higher estimate (Combat deaths) (Source: White (2011)). Communist Russia lower estimate (Source: White (2011)). Communist Russia higher estimate (Source: Rummel (1994b)). Nazi Germany lower estimate (Source: White (2011)). Nazi Germany higher estimate (Source: Rummel (1994c))

It is against this historical backdrop of economic and political turmoil that social science was being developed in the 1930s and 1940s. These grand debates in economics and political economy were taking place to understand the prior causes that resulted in the macroeconomic instability of the Great Depression, the problems and difficulties of socialist planning, and the future of a humane and civil social order. As Hayek wrote to his good friend Fritz Machlup in June 21, 1940, the work he was doing on *The Abuse and Decline of Reason* constituted a very important challenge to the prevailing wisdom of the day and was, in his judgment "the best I can do for the future of mankind."[6] The disputes were not merely abstract academic discussions, but addressed the bridging of the gap between high theory and practical policy in a very fundamental sense. The cutting edge of academic research was meant to address the pressing needs of public policy, since the stakes were to be found in Western civilization itself. The disputes were fundamental, but they were also personal and cut very close to the bone.

To give an example of the sort of impression one gets from commentators even as skilled as Robert Skidelsky, consider this summary judgment that Hayek did not engage Keynes after *The General Theory* (1936) was published because "Hayek did not want to expose himself to another mauling from the Keynesians," and that as a result, he became by the late 1930s a "bystander as the Keynesian Revolution unfolded" (1992, 456–459). Even Hayek's closest associate at the LSE, Lionel Robbins, recanted his intellectual affinity to the Austrian school and argued that his trouble was purely intellectual. He "had become the slave of theoretical constructions which, if not intrinsically invalid as regards logical consistency, were inappropriate to the total situation which had then developed and which therefore misled my judgment" (1971, 153). Robbins would put his change of mind in a very dramatic form, arguing that:

> Now I still think that there is much in this theory as an explanation of a *possible* generation of boom and crisis. But, as an explanation of what was going on in the early '30s, I now think it was misleading. Whatever the

---

[6] This letter can be found in the Fritz Machlup papers at the Hoover Institution Box 43, Folder 15 and is reprinted in Volume 13 of Hayek's *Collected Works* (2010, 312–313).

genetic factors of the pre-1929 boom, their *sequelae*, in the sense of inappropriate investments fostered by wrong expectations, were completely swamped by vast deflationary forces sweeping away all those elements of constancy in the situation which otherwise might have provided a framework for an explanation in my terms. The theory was inadequate to the facts. Nor was this approach any more adequate as a guide to policy. Confronted with the freezing deflation of those days, the idea that the prime essential was the writing down of mistaken investments and the easing of capital markets by fostering the disposition to save and reducing the pressure on consumption was completely inappropriate.

To treat what developed subsequently in the way which I then thought valid was as unsuitable as denying blankets and stimulants to a drunk who has fallen into an icy pond, on the ground that his original trouble was overheating. (Robbins 1971, 154)

This led Robbins to conclude that: "I shall always regard this aspect of my dispute with Keynes as the greatest mistake of my professional career, and the book, *The Great Depression*, which I subsequently wrote, partly in justification of this attitude, as something which I would willingly see be forgotten" (Robbins 1971, 154).

Interestingly enough, we do not see a similar recanting of Robbins's *Economic Planning and the International Order* (1937). But more importantly, his recanting of the monetary theory of the trade cycle was *not* a logical refutation in the same way that Keynes claimed that Hayek's *Prices and Production* was "muddled." As Robbins himself stated, he *never* refuted Hayek's theory itself, only its applicability to the particular time and place—namely, the Great Depression of the 1930s. Therefore, our understanding of Robbins's position would be better appreciated as a question of application and policy pragmatics.

Robbins and Hayek represented a formidable research and educational team in the 1930s. Both had been deeply influenced by Ludwig von Mises in the 1920s, and in particular, Mises's *Socialism* ([1922] 1981). They sought, as described in Dahrendorf's *LSE: A History of the London School of Economics and Political Science, 1895–1995*, to develop an international flavor to teaching and scholarship at the LSE that featured the work of the Austrian school economists (1995, 222). Syllabi and seminars reflected this, as well as the constant stream of visitors. In most histories, folks date this to after Hayek's arrival, but the facts are that Robbins was an Edwin Cannan student, and was influenced by Mises and knew him personally from the mid-1920s and had developed a warm personal relationship with Mises. Mises had, in fact, visited the LSE on numerous occasions as well as interacted with Robbins at European conferences of economists. The influence of these ideas were not limited to Robbins and Hayek, but permeated the intellectual climate of the department in the 1920s and 1930s. Arnold Plant, W. H. Hutt, Ronald Coase, Nicholas Kaldor,[7] Ludwig Lachmann, and G. L. S. Shackle would all, in one way or another, pick up various bits and pieces of these ideas and develop them throughout their careers as teachers and scholars.

The misconceptions of Hayek's ideas lead to an inability to see the varied streams of thought that developed in the 1930s, and which had their base within the blended traditions of the Austrian school and its British counterparts, such as Wicksteed, or its US counterparts, such as Knight. In Dahrendorf's history of the LSE, for example, he actually describes Hayek as a "classical 'a-social' individualist" (1995, 515), a position that could really only be held if one never reads Hayek in any depth, but only reads the slogans associated with Hayek, such as Thatcher's "There is no such thing as society." A closer reading of Hayek (and Thatcher, for that matter) will reveal that he was far from being an atomistic thinker. His theory of social cooperation under the division of labor was not only critical to his economics, his political economy, and his social philosophy, but also inconsistent with methodological atomism.

Hopefully, this gives the reader a clear picture of how I will proceed and what purpose I have in mind. Once we see the Hayekian emphasis on *epistemic institutionalism* as the critical development in response to the disputes of the 1930s against Keynes, against market socialists, and against philosophical movements in the philosophy of science, then the unfolding of Hayek's career will come into sharp relief. The questions he asked, the answers he offered, and most importantly, the continuing promise and relevance of the Hayekian research program will be better

---

[7] Well known as a Keynesian, Nicholas Kaldor had begun his career working within the Austrian tradition. His first published paper in 1932 was an "Austrian" interpretation of the trade cycle in "The Economic Situation of Austria," *Harvard Business Review* 11(10): 23–34. He later translated, with Honor Croome, Hayek's *Monetary Theory and the Trade Cycle* in 1933. See also Klausinger, Hansjörg. 2011. "Hayek and Kaldor: Close Encounter at LSE." *History of Economic Ideas* 19 (3): 135–163.

understood. Economics is about the coordination problem that society must confront. The solution to that coordination problem is found in the competitive entrepreneurial market process of discovery and learning through time. But the effectiveness of that process of discovery and learning is a function of the institutional framework within which economic activity is played out. The knowledge that is necessary to guide and discipline decisions is institutionally contingent—it literally does not exist unless within a certain institutional environment.

What this ultimately means for economics, political economy, and social philosophy will hopefully be what will unfold in the following chapters as we talk about the following: the nature of a capital-using economy; the role of money in such an economy; what function interest rates serve in intertemporal coordination; how prices guide production; what function property rights serve; why socialist planning faces an insurmountable knowledge problem; the political consequences of pursuing socialist economic planning; why the rule of law and the generality norm in politics provide the background for a discussion of the appropriate institutional infrastructure for a vibrant and creative economy and society; and what a political order that exhibits neither discrimination nor dominion would look like and whether it holds promise for us today in our world. It is my belief that this approach is the best way to communicate to a new generation what Hayek's ideas have to offer. We must first clarify these ideas and then eliminate some of its most egregious misconceptions so that we can judge the evolutionary potential of these ideas for social science and the humanities.

Let's begin.

Bibliography

Acemoglu, Daron, Simon Johnson, and James Robinson. 2004. *Institutions as the Fundamental Cause of Long-Run Growth*. The National Bureau of Economic Research, NBER Working Paper No. 10481.

Alves, André Azevedo, and John Meadowcroft. 2014. Hayek's Slippery Slope, the Stability of the Mixed Economy and the Dynamics of Rent Seeking. *Political Studies* 62 (4): 843–861.

Boettke, Peter J. 2015. The Methodology of Austrian Economics as a Sophisticated, Rather than Naïve, Philosophy of Economics. *Journal of the History of Economic Thought* 37 (1): 79–85.

———. 2017. *Context, Continuity and Truth*. Atlas Network, November 9.

Boettke, Peter J., Christopher Coyne, Peter Leeson, and Frederic Sautet. 2005. The New Comparative Political Economy. *Review of Austrian Economics* 18 (3–4): 281–304.

Bolt, Jutta, Robert Inklaar, Herman de Jong, and Jan Luiten van Zanden. 2018. Rebasing 'Maddison': New Income Comparisons and the Shape of Long-run Economic Development. *GGDC Research Memorandum 174*.

Caldwell, Bruce J., and Leonidas Montes. 2015. Friedrich Hayek and His Visits to Chile. *The Review of Austrian Economics* 28 (3): 261–309.

Dahrendorf, Ralf. 1995. *LSE: A History of the London School of Economics and Political Science, 1895–1995*. Oxford: Oxford University Press.

Farrant, Andrew, and Edward McPhail. 2014. Can a Dictator Turn a Constitution into a Can-Opener? F.A. Hayek and the Alchemy of Transitional Dictatorship in Chile. *Review of Political Economy* 26 (3): 331–348.

Foucault, Michel. 1980. *Power/Knowledge: Selected Interviews and Other Writings 1972–1977*. Ed. Colin Gordon. New York: Pantheon Books.

Hayek, F.A. 1933. *Monetary Theory and the Trade Cycle*. Trans. Nicholas Kaldor and Honor Croome. London: Jonathan Cape.

———. [1941] 2007. The Pure Theory of Capital. In *The Collected Works of F.A. Hayek Vol. 12*, ed. Lawrence H White. Chicago: University of Chicago Press.

———. [1944] 2007. *The Road to Serfdom*. Chicago: University of Chicago Press.

———. 1960. *The Constitution of Liberty*. Chicago: University of Chicago Press.

———. [1963] 1995. The Economics of the 1930s as Seen from London. In *The Collected Works of F. A. Hayek: Contra Keynes and Cambridge: Essays, Correspondence Vol. 9*, ed. Bruce Caldwell. Chicago: University of Chicago Press.

———. 1967. Kinds of Rationalism. In *Studies in Philosophy, Politics, and Economics*, ed. F.A. Hayek. Chicago: University of Chicago Press.

———. 2010. *The Collected Works of F. A. Hayek: Studies on the Abuse and Decline of Reason Vol. 13*. Ed. Bruce Caldwell. Chicago: University of Chicago Press.

Haythornthwaite, Philip J. 1992. *The World War One Source Book*, 382–383. London: Arms and Armour.

International Monetary Fund. 2016. Government Expenditure, Percent of GDP % of GDP. *Fiscal Affairs Departmental Data*. http://www.imf.org/external/datamapper/exp@FPP/USA/FRA/JPN/GBR/SWE/ESP/ITA/ZAF/IND?year=2011. Data Accessed 5 July 2018.

Kaldor, Nicholas. 1932. The Economic Situation of Austria. *Harvard Business Review* 11 (10): 23–34.

Kalusinger, Hansjörg. 2011. Hayek and Kaldor: Close Encounter at LSE. *History of Economic Ideas* 19 (3): 135–163.

Keynes, John Maynard. 1936. *The General Theory of Employment, Interest and Money*. London: Palgrave Macmillan.

———. 1980. *Activities 1940–1946: Shaping the Post-War World: Employment and Commodities*. The Collected Writings of John Maynard Keynes Vol. 27, ed. Elizabeth Johnson and Donald Moggridge. Cambridge: Cambridge University Press.

Meadowcroft, John, and William Ruger. 2014. Hayek, Friedman, and Buchanan: On Public Life, Chile, and the Relationship Between Liberty and Democracy. *Review of Political Economy* 26 (3): 358–367.

Mises, Ludwig. von. ([1922] 1981). *Socialism: An Economic and Sociological Analysis*. Indianapolis: Liberty Fund.

Mitchell, B.R. 1998a. *International Historical Statistics: Europe, 1750–1993*. London: Macmillan.

———. 1998b. *International Historical Statistics: The Americas, 1750–1993*. London: Macmillan.

North, Douglas, John J. Wallis, and Barry A. Weingast. 2009. *Violence and Social Orders: A Conceptual Framework for Interpreting Recorded Human History*. Cambridge: Cambridge University Press.

Robbins, Lionel. 1937. *Economic Planning and International Order*. London: Macmillan.

———. 1971. *Autobiography of an Economist*. London: Palgrave Macmillan.

Rummel, R.J. 1994a. *Death by Government*, 25. New Brunswick: Transaction Publishers.

———. 1994b. *Death by Government*, 83. New Brunswick: Transaction Publishers.

———. 1994c. *Death by Government*, 111. New Brunswick: Transaction Publishers.

Skidelsky, Robert. 1992. *John Maynard Keynes Volume 2: The Economist as Savior, 1920–1937*. New York: Penguin.

Vaughn, Karen I. 1999. Hayek's Implicit Economics: Rules and the Problem of Order. *Review of Austrian Economics* 11 (1–2): 129–144.

Wagner, Richard E. 2010. *Mind, Society, and Human Action: Time and Knowledge in a Theory of Social Economy*. New York: Routledge.

White, Matthew. 2011. *Source List and Detailed Death Tolls for the Primary Megadeaths of the Twentieth Century*. http://necrometrics.com/20c5m.htm. Accessed 5 July 2018.

2

Hayek: An Overview of His Life and Work

Introduction

Though I have stated that this work is not a proper biography, some biographical information is not only unavoidable, but also appropriate. Let us begin with an overview of Hayek's life and work. F. A. Hayek passed away on March 23, 1992, at the age of 92. His first academic publication was in the 1920s and his last was in the late 1980s. Bruce Caldwell's intellectual biography of Hayek, *Hayek's Challenge* (2004), focuses on the various critical points of contestation that Hayek faced in developing his unique contributions to economics, political economy, and social philosophy. Caldwell does an outstanding job of discussing the *methodenstreit*, the marginalist revolution, the emergence of macroeconomics, the development of formal modeling and sophisticated statistical testing, and Hayek's complicated role in all these professional disputes. Hayek, indeed, faced huge intellectual challenges during his long career. But as Bruce Caldwell has put it, this also creates a challenge for those writing about Hayek and his ideas:

> The volume of Hayek's work provides another daunting challenge for interpreters. Hayek lived from 1899 to 1992, and his writings span seven

© The Author(s) 2018
Peter J. Boettke, *F. A. Hayek*, Great Thinkers in Economics,
https://doi.org/10.1057/978-1-137-41160-0_2

decades. Worse, he was incredibly prolific. Even worse, he did not restrict himself to economics, making contributions in fields as diverse as psychology, political philosophy, the history of ideas, and social-science methodology. (Caldwell 2004, 4)

Hayek's depth and breadth was probably unmatched among twentieth-century economists, and was more in keeping with the grand tradition of moral philosophy and political economy as it was practiced from Adam Smith to John Stuart Mill. There is certainly little doubt that Hayek was among the most prodigious classical liberal scholars of the twentieth century. Though his 1974 Nobel Prize was in Economic Science, his scholarly endeavors extended well beyond economics. At the time of his death, he had published 130 articles and 25 books on topics ranging from technical economics to theoretical psychology, from political philosophy to legal anthropology, and from the philosophy of science to the history of ideas. Hayek was no mere dabbler; he was an accomplished scholar in each of these fields of inquiry. On Google Scholar, his article "The Use of Knowledge in Society" (1945) has been cited over 11,000 times, while his classic works in political economy *The Road to Serfdom* (1944), *The Constitution of Liberty* (1960), and *Law, Legislation and Liberty* (1973, 1976, 1979) all have over 5000 citations each. Finally, his work in theoretical psychology, *The Sensory Order* (1952a), has also received close to 1000 citations. Moreover, in a study by David Skarbek (2009) on the Nobel Prize lectures, Hayek was the second most cited author by the other Nobel Prize winners in their own official Nobel lectures.[1]

Hayek was born into a family of intellectuals in Vienna on May 8, 1899. During the early years of the twentieth century, the theories of the

---

[1] Kenneth Arrow is the most cited. Also see Boettke (1999, xiv–xv), where I compare the general citation pattern of Hayek with his peers and argue that his analytical impact in modern economics is less than what it should be. Though in this citation study, the pattern does show an increasing interest in Hayek from relative neglect in the 1970s (Social Science Citation Index (SSCI) citations less than 100 per year) to extreme interest in the late 1980s and 1990s (SSCI citations in the 200–300 range per year). But those citations are more likely in the broad social science journals rather than the main scientific journals of economics. See the appendix A, where an updated citation study is provided, and appendix B, where the list of the 20 most influential articles in the *American Economic Review (AER)* are listed and "The Use of Knowledge in Society" is among those selected. Also see the Living Bibliography on Hayek that I collected in the process of researching this book with the assistance of my graduate students (Boettke 2018).

Austrian School of Economics, sparked by Menger's *Principles of Economics* ([1871] 1953), were gradually being formulated and refined by Eugen von Böhm-Bawerk, his brother-in-law, Friedrich Wieser, Joseph Schumpeter, and Ludwig von Mises. Hayek's grandfather was an academic colleague and friends with Böhm-Bawerk and Wieser. His father was a physician and botanist. Hayek grew up in an atmosphere of science and scholarship. "Hayek would later say," Caldwell writes, "that he grew up thinking that being a university professor was the highest of all callings" (2004, 135). His initial academic interests, like those of his father, were in biology. However, the economic and political consequences of WWI, particularly the breakdown of the Austro-Hungarian Empire, drew his interests away from the natural sciences to the social sciences. Outside of his academic interests, his hobbies were mountain climbing and skiing (Hayek [1978] 1983, 397).

Economics at the University of Vienna was integrated with the study of law. Hayek began his studies at the University of Vienna in November 1918, earning his first doctorate in law in 1921, and his second doctorate in political economy in 1923. As a student, Hayek studied law, psychology, and economics, before specializing in economic theory. He recalled attending one of Ludwig von Mises's classes as a student, but found Mises's anti-socialist position too strong for his liking. Friedrich Wieser, who was more or less a Fabian socialist, and a very distinguished professor, offered an approach that was more attractive to Hayek at the time, and Hayek became his pupil. Hayek would eventually do his first original work in economic theory dealing with the problem of imputation under the guidance of Wieser. Yet, ironically, it was Mises, through his devastating critique of socialism published in 1922, who became his mentor throughout the 1920s and set Hayek on the research path he would pursue in philosophy, politics, and economics throughout his long career.[2]

---

[2] It is important to realize that at this time, as Hayek has stressed, the Austrian school of economics was not at all understood in an ideological sense. The Menger/Böhm-Bawerk/Mises branch was well known for its liberalism, but that was not seen as essential to the scientific contributions of the school, which were not tied to any political philosophy, but were, instead, focused on marginal utility analysis. See Hayek's preface to the 1981 edition of *Socialism* (Mises [1922] 1981) for its impact on him (and others of his generation). Lionel Robbins in the UK would be similarly impacted upon reading Mises's *Socialism* in 1923 and began efforts to secure the translation of Mises's work in to English at that time. See Lionel Robbins, *Autobiography of an Economist* (1971, 106) and Susan

After graduating in 1921, Hayek was hired by Mises via an introduction from Wieser to work in a government office set up for the primary purpose of the settlement of prewar private debts between nations as part of the Treaty of Versailles of 1919. Hayek worked under Mises's direct supervision in this office until 1927, interrupted only by his visit to the USA. In 1927, Mises helped Hayek establish the Austrian Institute for Business Cycle Research, which Hayek directed. When Hayek left for the LSE in 1931, Oskar Morgenstern assumed the directorship until he himself emigrated to the USA.

The best way to understand Hayek's vast contributions to economics and classical liberalism is to view them in light of the study of social cooperation laid out by Mises. Mises, the great system builder, provided Hayek with this research program. Hayek became the great dissector and analyzer. His life's work can best be appreciated as an attempt to make explicit what Mises had left implicit, to refine what Mises had outlined, and to answer questions Mises had left unanswered. Of Mises, Hayek stated: "There is no single man to whom I owe more intellectually" (1978, 17).

The Misesian connection is most evident in Hayek's work on the problems with socialism. But the insights derived from the analysis of socialism permeate the entire corpus of his work—from business cycles to the origin of social cooperation. Hayek stressed how working in close collaboration with Mises was a great stimulus for original thought when he agreed strongly with the conclusions that Mises reached, but not necessarily the analysis used to reach these conclusions. As Hayek put it: "I was always influenced by Mises's answers, but not fully satisfied by his arguments. It became very largely an attempt to improve the argument, which I realized led to correct conclusions. But the question of why it hadn't persuaded most other people became important to me; so I became anxious to put it in a more effective form....Being for ten years in close contact with a man with whose conclusions on the whole you agree but whose arguments were not always perfectly convincing to you, was a great stimulus" ([1978] 1983: 13; 176).

Howson's *Lionel Robbins* (2011, 135) for a description of Robbins's enthusiasm for this "revolutionary" work on the economic problems of socialism.

In 1923, Hayek traveled to the USA to observe and study the latest statistical techniques that were being developed to study industrial fluctuations. Hayek spent time both at New York University (NYU) and at Columbia. At NYU, Hayek worked as a research assistant to Jeremiah Jenks and submitted work toward earning a PhD. At Columbia, he visited Wesley Clair Mitchell, who was pioneering the empirical approach to business cycles that would define the early National Bureau of Economic Research (NBER) approach. However, Hayek's financial situation had deteriorated over the year, and news of a much-needed fellowship from the Rockefeller Foundation that would have enabled him financially to stay in the USA failed to reach him in time, so almost destitute, he boarded a ship to return to Europe. Upon his return to Vienna, Hayek continued his work with Mises, and they established the Austrian Institute for Business Cycle Research. During his trip to the USA, Hayek had already begun to draft "The Monetary Policy of the United States After the Recovery from the 1920s Crisis" ([1925] 1984), which sought to apply the Mises-Wicksell theory of the business cycle to contemporary events.

Building on Mises's *The Theory of Money and Credit* (1912), Hayek refined both the technical understanding of capital coordination and the institutional details of credit policy. Seminal studies in monetary theory and the trade cycle followed. Hayek's first book, *Monetary Theory and the Trade Cycle* ([1929] 1933), analyzed the effects of credit expansion on the capital structure of an economy.

Publication of that book prompted an invitation for Hayek to lecture at the LSE. His lectures there were published in a second book on the "Austrian Theory of the Trade Cycle," *Prices and Production* (1931), which was cited by the Nobel Prize Committee in 1974.

Hayek's 1930–1931 lectures at the LSE were received with such great acclaim that he was called back and appointed Tooke Professor of Economic Science and Statistics. At age 32, Hayek had secured one of the more prestigious appointments in the economics profession. As he has said in an interview with Axel Leijonhufvud, "When you get an appointment as a professor in London at 32, you take it" (Hayek [1978] 1983).

The Mises-Hayek theory of the trade cycle explained the "cluster of errors" that characterizes the cycle. Credit expansion, made possible by the artificial lowering of interest rates, misleads businessmen, who are led to engage in ventures that would not otherwise have appeared profitable. The false signal generated by credit expansion leads to a malcoordination of the production and consumption plans of economic actors. This malcoordination first manifests itself in a "boom," and then, later, in a "bust" as the time pattern of production adjusts to the real pattern of savings and consumption in the economy.

Hayek Versus Keynes

Soon after Hayek's arrival in London, he crossed swords with John Maynard Keynes. The Hayek-Keynes debate was perhaps the most fundamental debate in monetary economics in the early twentieth century. Beginning with his essay, "The End of Laissez-Faire" (1926), Keynes presented his position in the language of pragmatic liberalism. As a result, Keynes was heralded as the "savior of capitalism," rather than being viewed as a critic of the existing order. The Hayek-Keynes debate was of a different nature than Hayek's debate with the market socialists, but ultimately turned on similar issues related to the nature of the price system and the institutional infrastructure within which economic activity takes place.

Hayek believed he had pinpointed the fundamental problems with Keynes's economics—his failure to understand the role that interest rates and the capital structure play in a market economy. Because of Keynes's habit of using aggregate (collective) concepts, he failed to address these issues adequately in *A Treatise on Money* (1930). Hayek pointed out that Keynes's aggregation tended to redirect the analytical focus of the economist away from examining how the industrial structure of the economy emerged from the economic choices of individuals.

Keynes did not take kindly to Hayek's criticism. Hayek had accused Keynes of dropping the capital theory and microeconomic analysis of intertemporal coordination from the Wicksellian system. Those elements in the Wicksellian system were being developed by Mises and Hayek. In essence, Hayek was criticizing Keynes for not incorporating the Mises-Hayek work into his analysis, despite the fact that Keynes's work was written before Mises's *Theory of Money and Credit* had been translated into English, and before Hayek had published *Prices and Production*. Keynes chose to respond at first by attacking Hayek's *Prices and Production*. As Keynes wrote: "The book, as it stands, seems to me to be one of the most frightful muddles I have ever read, with scarcely a sound proposition in it beginning with page 45, and yet it remains a book of some interest, which is likely to leave its mark on the mind of the reader. It is an extraordinary example of how, starting with a mistake, a remorseless logician can end up in bedlam" (1931, 394). Rather than judging the Mises-Hayek theory of industrial fluctuations as one of the first systematic attempts to integrate micro and macro and provide a choice-theoretic foundation for industrial fluctuations and economic coordination more generally, Keynes judged the effort as a muddle. This would remain the professional consensus basically for the next 40 years until the microfoundations and rational expectations revolution in macroeconomics took hold in the 1970s and 1980s.

But Keynes's second intellectual move was equally interesting and proved very effective as well. Keynes claimed that he no longer believed what he had written in *A Treatise on Money*, and turned his attention to writing another book, *The General Theory of Employment, Interest, and Money* (1936), which, in time, became the most influential book on economic policy in the twentieth century. As Mark Blaug remarks in his *Economic Theory in Retrospect* (Blaug 1997, 642), never before had we seen such a quick and complete conversion of the profession to the new paradigm as we saw in the decade after the publication of *The General Theory*. Throughout the USA and Europe, Keynesian thought dominated economic discourse. The entire discipline of economics was transformed as a result, and the discipline that Hayek was trained in—and practiced— seemed to vanish as he was still working out the implications of his own thinking.

Rather than attempting to criticize directly what Keynes presented in his *General Theory*, Hayek turned his analytical attention to refining capital theory. Hayek was convinced that the essential point to convey to Keynes and the rest of the economics profession concerning monetary policy lay in working out the implications of a consistent and coherent capital theory.[3] Thus, Hayek proceeded to set forth his thesis in *The Pure Theory of Capital* ([1941] 2007). However correct his assessment may have been, this book, Hayek's most technical, was his least influential. In the eyes of the public, Keynes had defeated Hayek. Hayek lost standing in the profession and with students.

During this time, Hayek was also involved in another grand debate in economic policy—the socialist calculation debate, triggered by a 1920 article by Mises ([1920] 2012) that stated that socialism was technically impossible because abolishing private property in the means of production would mean no market prices for capital goods. Without prices guiding production decisions, economic planning would be lost amid the sea of economic possibilities. Socialist planning, Mises demonstrated, would not be able to calculate the opportunity cost of alternative investment plans. The Socialist Planner would not know, for example, whether to build railroad tracks out of platinum or steel due to the inability to engage in rational economic calculation. Mises had refined this argument in 1922 in *Socialism: An Economic and Sociological Analysis* ([1922] 1981), the book which had profoundly impressed the young Hayek (and the young Lionel Robbins). Hayek developed Mises's argument further in several articles during the 1930s. In 1935, he collected and edited a series of essays on the problems of socialist economic organization: *Collectivist Economic Planning* (1935), in which Mises's original 1920 article was published in English for the first time. Mises's *Socialism* was also translated and published in English in 1936 due to the efforts of Hayek and Robbins. Hayek would write additional essays critiquing the model of "market socialism," which had been developed by Oskar Lange and Abba Lerner to respond to Mises and Hayek. These essays were later collected in *Individualism and Economic Order* ([1948] 1980). Moreover, Robbins published *Economic Planning and the International Order* in 1937.

Again, the economics profession and the intellectual community in general did not view Hayek's criticism as decisive in the dispute. The socialist calculation debate of the 1930s took place on two levels—as a

---

[3] It is probably important to note that Hayek believed that Keynes's argument in *The General Theory* would not have any lasting impact on the economics profession because it was based on an assumption of abundance rather than scarcity, an assumption that causes "confusion among economists and even the wider public" ([1941] 2007, 341).

technical question of economic theory and as an outgrowth of the progressive, social, cultural, and philosophical approach to modernity. As a proposition of economic theory, following Mises's original challenge in 1920, economists had developed in more detail the perfectly competitive model and refined the general equilibrium concept central to neoclassical economics. The early Austrian economists viewed themselves as squarely in the scientific mainstream of neoclassical economics that was emerging in the late nineteenth and early twentieth centuries. But by the 1930s, it was becoming increasingly clear to Mises, and especially Hayek, that the neoclassical tradition of price determination modeled as a simultaneous system of equations within a perfectly competitive economy had diverged significantly from the Austrian school's understanding of the theory of price formation through the "higgling and bargaining" in the entrepreneurial and competitive market economy. Competition in the model of perfect competition was no longer seen as a rivalrous activity, but instead, as an equilibrium state of affairs with a set of corresponding optimality conditions. To the Austrian economists, in contrast, the competitive market *process* emerges out of the ongoing exchange relations and productive activities that are engaged in by economic participants and the institutions within which these activities take place.[4]

The strategic move made by Oskar Lange and Abba Lerner was in developing the model of market socialism analogous to the Walrasian auctioneer and the tâtonnement process under general competitive equilibrium. Simply stated, market socialism would substitute a Central

---

[4] In a letter to Fritz Machlup dated July 31, 1941, where Hayek is responding to a request by Machlup to comment on the early drafts of *Monopoly and Competition*: "Let me only say I was particularly pleased to see that your developments fit in so well with my methodological views and that in many ways border on views on competition which I hoped myself some time to develop. You more or less imply what I always stress, that competition is a process and not a state, and that if it were ever 'perfect' in the strict sense it would at the same time disappear." Also see Mises's *Notes and Recollections* ([1940] 2013), where he describes the Austrian approach as one focusing on the real-world dynamics of price formation and market coordination in opposition to the equilibrium theorizing of other branches of neoclassical economics. In a letter Mises wrote to Hayek in 1941 after attending the American Economic Association (AEA) meetings, he refers to "our" method of "process analysis." The modern Austrian school (e.g. Kirzner) mantra of methodological individualism, radical subjectivism, and market process analysis was evident from Menger to Mises and was understood as common knowledge among the Viennese students of the tradition. Also see Erwin Dekker, *The Viennese Students of Civilization* (2016) for a discussion of the core ideas in the Austrian tradition, and especially the intellectual community in the 1920s and 1930s.

Planning Board and instruct managers of state-owned firms to follow an optimality rule of P=MC and produce at that level that minimizes average costs as the guide to production. If the essence of either the capitalist or socialist system was captured in the simultaneous equation system of general competitive equilibrium, then the institutional background of private property or collective ownership should not matter for the achievement of optimality in allocation and production decisions. They argued that such a response to Mises (and to Hayek) effectively answered the challenge of economic calculation. Production could in fact be rationalized under socialism. Lange argued that his model had demonstrated that socialist economies in theory could achieve the same optimality results as those achieved in the market, and also that socialist planning would outperform capitalist economies in practice since under socialism, the problems of monopolistic exploitation and the instability of business cycles would be eliminated. In addition, the injustice of the capitalist system would be overcome because distribution would be determined through socialist and democratic deliberation.

Alongside the technical economic theory arguments for market socialism, there was also a general cultural sense that modern science and technology had delivered mankind into such an advanced state of affairs that more rational control over the economy was not only possible, but a moral imperative. Had not modern science given man the ability to control and design society according to moral rules of his own choosing? The planned society envisioned under socialism was supposed to be not only as efficient as capitalism, but also morally superior with its promise of social justice. Moreover, it was considered the wave of the future. Only a reactionary, it was argued, could resist the inevitable tide of history. Not only had Hayek appeared to lose the technical economic debate with Keynes and the Keynesians concerning the causes of business cycles, but his general philosophical perspective was increasingly seen as decidedly out of step with the march of progress.

The experience of the 1930s and 1940s dramatically shaped Hayek's subsequent research program. Why was it that economists trained in the early neoclassical tradition got so offtrack from the fundamental questions of the monetary economy, the capital structure, the price system, and the competitive market process? The discerning reader of Hayek will see in his "Trend of Economic Thinking" (1933) the claim that neoclassical economics provides the proper analytics for studying the problems of economic coordination in a systematic way, yet by the time that same reader is confronting "Economics and Knowledge" (1937), let alone "The Use of Knowledge in Society" (1945), she will see that Hayek is arguing that the preoccupation among neoclassical theorists with the equilibrium conditions is causing confusion rather than illumination.

In order to understand the events of the previous decade, Hayek undertook two important foundational scientific and scholarly moves in the 1940s. He began his "Abuse of Reason" project critical of the underlying philosophical and methodological underpinnings of modern social science, and also took an "institutional turn" in his research to draw attention to the institutional framework within which economic activity takes place. Both new directions are interrelated, and deeply connected to his analytical perspective as a technical economist. As I have argued elsewhere, "the most productive reading of Hayek is one which sees the common thread in his work from psychology to economics to the philosophy of science to political science to law and finally to philosophical anthropology and social theory. The common thread is decisive *epistemic* turn to *comparative institutional analysis*" (Boettke 1999, xv, emphasis in original).

The Road to Serfdom

In response to the debate first with Keynes and then with the market socialists, Hayek continued to refine the argument for economic liberalism. The problems of socialism that he had observed in Nazi Germany and that he saw beginning in Britain led him to write *The Road to Serfdom* (1944). Hayek pointed out that if socialism required the replacement of the market with a central plan, then an institution must be established that would be responsible for formulating this plan. He referred to this institution as the Central Planning Bureau. To implement the plan and to control the flow of resources, the bureau would have to exercise broad discretionary power in economic affairs. Yet, the Central Planning Bureau in a socialist society would have no market prices to serve as guides and no means of knowing which production possibilities were economically feasible. The absence of a pricing system, Hayek said, would prove to be socialism's fatal flaw. Mises's essential criticisms were indeed correct and had to be the starting point of any discussion of the economic problems of socialism.

In *The Road to Serfdom*, Hayek argued that since the Central Planning Bureau could not base decisions on economic criterion, those in positions of power would base decisions on some other basis. The economic logic of the situation would give rise to the organizational logic of socialist planning. Thus, there was good reason to suspect that those who would rise to the top in a socialistic regime would be those who had a comparative advantage in exercising discretionary power and were willing to make unpleasant decisions. And it was inevitable that these powerful men would run the system to their own personal advantage. The economic problem with socialism led directly to the political problem of socialism. The *Road to Serfdom* thus presented to advocates of socialism the political realities inherent in granting a single institution these kinds of powers over economic affairs.[5]

Totalitarianism is not a historical accident that emerges solely because of a poor choice of leaders under a socialist regime. Totalitarianism, Hayek shows, is the *logical* outcome of the institutional order of socialist planning.

Why was it so hard for Hayek to penetrate not only the popular imagination with this message, but more importantly, the intellectual imagination of professional economists who he thought would be his ally in

---

[5] As Keynes famously commented on Hayek's *The Road to Serfdom* in a letter dated June 28, 1944, "In my opinion it is a grand book. ... Morally and philosophically I find myself in agreement with virtually the whole of it: and not only in agreement with it, but in deeply moved agreement." Keynes goes further and states his disagreement, arguing for a "middle way" course, which Hayek found to be inherently unstable: "I come finally to what is really my only serious criticism of the book. You admit here and there that it is a question of knowing where to draw the line. You agree that the line has to be drawn somewhere [between free-enterprise and planning], and that the logical extreme is not possible. But you give us no guidance whatever as to where to draw it. In a sense this is shirking the practical issue. It is true that you and I would probably draw it in different places. I should guess that according to my ideas you greatly underestimate the practicability of the middle course. But as soon as you admit that the extreme is not possible, and that a line has to be drawn, you are, on your own argument, done for since you are trying to persuade us that as soon as one moves an inch in the planned direction you are necessarily launched on the slippery path which will lead you in due course over the precipice" Reprinted in John Maynard Keynes, *Activities 1940–1946. Shaping the Post-War World: Employment and Commodities* (1980, 385).

the battle of ideas against historicism and collectivism? To answer this question, Hayek turned his attention away from technical economics and concentrated on restating the principles of classical liberalism. Hayek had pointed out the need for market prices as conveyors of dispersed economic information. He showed that attempts to replace or control the market lead to a knowledge problem. Hayek also described the totalitarian problem associated with placing discretionary power in the hands of a few. These insights led him to examine the intellectual prejudices that blind men from seeing the problems of government economic planning.

During the 1940s, Hayek published a series of essays in professional journals examining the dominant philosophical trends that prejudiced intellectuals in a way that did not allow them to recognize the systemic problems that economic planners would confront. These essays were later collected and published as *The Counter-Revolution of Science* ([1952b] 1979). *The Counter-Revolution* provides a detailed intellectual history of "rational constructivism" and the problems of "scientism" in the social sciences. It is in this work that Hayek articulates his version of the Scottish Enlightenment project of David Hume and Adam Smith of "using reason to whittle down the claims of Reason." Modern civilization was threatened by the abuse of reason, specifically by rational constructivists trying to consciously design the modern world that had placed mankind in chains of his own making.

In 1950, Hayek moved to the University of Chicago,[6] where he taught until 1962 in the Committee on Social Thought. While there, he wrote *The Constitution of Liberty* (1960). This work represented Hayek's first systemic treatise on classical liberal political economy. Beginning with the work that had resulted in *The Road to Serfdom*, Hayek had wanted to call attention to the framework assumed in economic analysis and high-

---

[6] Though beyond the scope of this book, the circumstances of this decision are worth noting here. Hayek married his first wife, Helen Berta Maria von Fristch, on August 4, 1926, with whom he had two children, Christine Maria Felicitas in 1929 and Laurence Joseph Heinrich in 1934 (Ebenstein 2003, 44). Hayek later recounted the circumstances of the marriage, his subsequent divorce, and remarriage: "I married on the rebound when the girl [Helen Bitterlich] I had loved, a cousin, married somebody else. She is now my present wife. But for 25 years I was married to the girl whom I married on the rebound, who was a very good wife to me, but I wasn't happy in that marriage. She refused to give me a divorce, and finally I enforced it" (Hayek [1978] 1983, 395).

light its importance. Basic economics begins with the assumption of clearly defined and strictly enforced private property rights which forms the basis of mutually beneficial exchange between the parties. Private property and freedom of contract embodied in the rule of law is the assumed background. But it was so far in the background of analysis by the 1930s and 1940s that it was in fact easy for thinkers to forget. And they proceeded as if economic relationships were merely technical optimality conditions and could be determined under a variety of institutional settings.

What Hayek had accomplished in *The Road to Serfdom* was to demonstrate the incompatibility of socialist planning with democracy and the rule of law. What he sought to derive in *The Constitution of Liberty* was a historical explanation for the co-evolution of Western civilization and the Rule of Law, and then to develop an approach to contemporary public policy grounded in the generality norm upon which the Rule of Law is based. It is important to stress that for Hayek, the Rule of Law was not merely rule by laws, but had specific content associated with the generality norm that bound not only the actors within the system, but the governors that were called to provide oversight of the system. Hayek's conception of the "good society" was one that exhibited neither dominion nor discrimination.

In 1962, Hayek moved to Germany, where he had obtained a position at the University of Freiburg. He then increasingly centered his efforts on examining and elaborating the "spontaneous" ordering of economic and social activity. Hayek set about to reconstruct liberal social theory and to provide a vision of peaceful social cooperation and productive specialization among free individuals.

With his three-volume study, *Law, Legislation and Liberty* (1973, 1976, 1979) and his final book, *The Fatal Conceit* (1988), Hayek extended his analysis of society to an examination of the "spontaneous" emergence of legal and moral rules. His political and legal theory emphasized that the rule of law was the necessary foundation for peaceful co-existence. He contrasted the tradition of the common law with that of statute law, that is, legislative decrees. He showed how the common law emerges, case by case, as judges apply to particular cases general rules that are themselves products of cultural evolution. Thus, he explained that embedded within the common law is knowledge gained through a long history of trial and error. This insight led Hayek to the conclusion that law, like the market, is a "spontaneous" order—the result of human action, but not of human design.

Conclusion

F. A. Hayek had a long and productive career. He had to endure the curse of achieving fame at a young age and then having that fame turn to ridicule as the intellectual and political world moved away from his ideas. However, he lived long enough to see his original ideas recognized again. In many ways, all of his intellectual opponents at a methodological, analytical, and dare we say, ideological level were eventually challenged by the tide of events and the penetrating logic of Hayek's analysis. At the time of his death, classical liberalism was once again a vibrant body of thought. The Austrian school of economics has re-emerged as a major school of economic thought, and younger scholars in law, history, economics, politics, and philosophy are pursuing Hayekian themes. And since his death, these trends have in fact grown in momentum. Consider the renewed interest in Hayek's work in monetary theory and the trade cycle in the wake of the global financial crisis of 2008, or the critique of development planning found in works such as William Easterly (2014), or the focus on the institutional infrastructure in the development of the West found in such works as North et al. (2013).

Scholars should be judged not only by the answers they provided to the problems they tackled during their careers, but the questions they motivate others to ask and the new avenues of inquiry their work opens up. Hayek's work continues to serve as the basis for a progressive research program in the social sciences from technical economics to social philosophy. It is this evolution of the Hayekian vision that will occupy the rest of this book. Joseph Schumpeter (1954) described "vision" in the scientific enterprise as a "pre-analytic cognitive act," which is an essential prerequisite to progress in scientific analysis. It is the vision that provides the raw material that the scientist engages in theoretical analysis and empirical investigation. The Hayekian vision is that of the *epistemic* function of alternative *institutional arrangements* and its impact on productive specialization and peaceful social cooperation. In what follows, we will first discuss the early developments of this Hayekian vision with respect to a capital-using and money-using economy and the role of relative prices as guides to production and exchange activity. Hayek's earlier work in monetary theory and the trade cycle will serve as the backdrop, and our focus will be to connect the debates of his day with the discussions of our time in explaining the anatomy of an economic crisis.

Hayek's debate in macroeconomics simultaneously took place with his debate on the problems of economic planning and economic calculation under socialism. What started out for Hayek as a simple exercise in editing of classic economic texts that had settled a dispute a generation before became a preoccupation for the rest of his career.[7] We will show how the Hayekian vision of the price system and the market order emerged from this dispute over market socialism, and that it has broader implications not only about the way we envision the puzzles and paradoxes of planning, but also market theory and the price system.

One of the "main results of most of the discussions of the 1930s," Hayek has written, "was to create an interest and an awareness of the methodological problems of our science which I had not had before" (1963, 61). This led Hayek to take both a philosophical and an institutional turn in the 1940s–1950s in order to address troubling questions raised by the experience in the evolution of economic doctrine in the 1930s. I see my main interpretative contribution as connecting explicitly those two turns in what I have described as Hayek's *epistemological institutionalism* and its continuing relevance for economics, political economy, and social philosophy.

---

[7] In the University of California, Los Angeles (UCLA) oral history interviews, Hayek, in response to a question as to whether he consciously moved from technical economics to social philosophy, responded in the 1930s, "No, it came from my interest in the history of the ideas that had first led economics in the wrong direction. That's what I did in the 'counterrevolution of science' series of articles, which again sprung from my occupation with planning similar things, and it was these which led me to see connections between what happened in economics and what happened in the approach to the other social sciences. So I acquired gradually a philosophy, in the first instance, because I needed it for interpreting economic phenomena that were applicable to other phenomena. It's an approach to social science very much opposed to the scientistic approach of sociology, but I find it appropriate to the specialized disciplines of the social sciences—essentially economics and linguistics, which are very similar in their problems" (Hayek [1978] 1983, 196).

Epilogue: Hayek's Century

Hayek was born in 1899, and died in 1992. These dates matter because they set the *historical context* in which he made his contributions. He was born in *fin de siècle* Vienna, served in WWI, matured during the interwar years witnessing the rise of Bolshevik communism and Nazi fascism, escaped to the democratic West suffering through the Great Depression, experienced the bombing of London during WWII, migrated to the USA in the 1950s, and then back to Germany in the 1960s. In the 1970s, he saw his longtime warnings about the consequences of pursuing Keynesian macroeconomic policy seem to be confirmed with "stagflation." In the 1980s, he witnessed free market policies revive in the UK, the USA, and New Zealand, and the collapse of communist systems of East and Central Europe in 1989.

Hayek was born into a world where people moved around in horse and buggy, and where transatlantic travel shortened from ocean liners (4.5 to 5 days) to airplanes (3.5 for the Concorde to 7 hours for a regular flight from New York to London). He witnessed technological innovations that promised unimaginable improvements in human well-being, but also capable of delivering unimaginable horror and human suffering. The tragic experience of mustard gas in WWI, Nazi concentration camps and the Holocaust during WWII, Soviet Collectivization, the Ukrainian Holdomor, the Soviet Great Purge, the Soviet Gulag, the development and deployment of the atomic bomb and nuclear weapons, Mao's Great Leap Forward were every bit as much of his lived experience as the development of jet air travel, space flight, and the advancements in telecommunications and computing. The Hayek beginning his career could not have imagined appearing on TV to discuss his ideas, let alone that eBook versions of his *Collected Works* which can be read by anyone on their phone would be a possibility.

In a recent book, Karl Sigmund—a professor of mathematics at the University of Vienna—describes the interwar years in Vienna as *Exact Thinking in Demented Times* (2017)—and that title seems appropriate for Hayek's intellectual quest throughout the Hayek Century. Keep in mind that almost every intellectual trend moved in the opposite direction of

Hayek's, yet the empirical reality arguably continued to confirm Hayek's prognosis of the situation from his analysis in the 1920s about the coming market crash to his 1970s warnings about the pretense of knowledge in his Nobel lecture. The alliance between scientism and statism corrupts science and impedes progress in the disciplines of economics and political economy. We have, indeed, as Hayek put it, made a mess of things, as economists as the recent Global Financial Crisis revealed yet once more. And I have not even talked about his analysis of socialism and the intimate connection between economic freedom and political freedom, an argument that played out historically in the Soviet Collectivization, Mao's Great Leap Forward, and Pol Pot's Killing Fields and which for anyone willing to open their eyes to see is being played out today in the sad reality of Venezuela.

The twentieth century no doubt saw an amazing progress as a cursory look at several human development indicators would demonstrate—perhaps the most important of these is the reduction of the number of individuals living in extreme poverty. It is nothing short of miraculous that this has occurred and what it means for the life and well-being of billions. Few today would want to go back to the world of 1899. Yet, there should be little doubt that man-made horrors of WWI, the Great Depression, WWII, and the Cold War will disturb even the rosiest of pictures of the twentieth century. Individuals such as Hayek born at the turn of the twentieth century were witnesses not only to feats of human ingenuity such as the Wright Brothers' first flight in 1903 and Neil Armstrong walk on the moon in 1969, but the development of weapons of mass destruction as was demonstrated in Hiroshima and Nagasaki.

Hayek was born in an age when empire and colonies still reigned, but lived through the birth of democratic nations throughout the world as the Independence movement gained momentum after WWII. And Hayek witnessed not only the Russian Revolution and the spread of Soviet influence across East and Central Europe, including the construction of the Berlin Wall, but the collapse of communism in 1989 and the destruction of the Berlin Wall. The struggle between liberty and power was on display in the most graphic of details throughout his life. Hayek, no less than the other famous German-speaking scientists, philosophers, and others, was forced to live a life as a scholar in exile due to the totalitarianism of Hitler's regime that destroyed their homeland and left their intellectual culture shattered and dispersed.

This was Hayek's century, and it served as the historical background against which he constructed his social philosophical system. The tensions, anomalies, paradoxes, and contradictions of the era certainly did not escape him. As he argued in his Nobel Prize lecture, the technological progress of this era made intellectuals dizzy with the success of the natural sciences, and thus, drew them all like moths to a flame to attempt to imitate that success by following the methods of the natural sciences. But in the sciences of man, Hayek warned, this was a mistake of significant proportions, and turned these intellectuals not only into potential tyrants over their fellow citizens, but into destroyers of civilization. And no discipline got more confused and corrupted by this intellectual error than economics.

That is a heady judgment to make of a discipline, especially when you were just awarded its highest honor of scientific achievement—the Nobel Prize. In his toast at the award ceremony, Hayek elaborated that had he been asked if such a prize should have been created, he would have argued against because it falsely grants a scientific authority to a man (or woman) in the affairs of man that is not only not deserved, but is downright dangerous.[8] We will have occasion to come back to Hayek's Nobel Lecture throughout the discussion, and readers are encouraged to put this book down now and read "The Pretense of Knowledge," but before you do so, remember it is not directed at the attempt to engage in comprehensive central planning that socialism inspired, but at the Keynesian-inspired effort at aggregate demand management. As we will see, "The Fatal Conceit" is a much deeper problem to Hayek than the debate over central economic planning. But for now, setting the historical background should get us thinking—how actually would one engage in "exact thinking during demented times"? One answer was provided by the Vienna Circle, the other was provided by Hayek.

---

[8] See   https://www.nobelprize.org/nobel_prizes/economic-sciences/laureates/1974/hayek-speech.html.

Bibliography

Blaug, Mark. 1997. *Economic Theory in Retrospect*. Cambridge: Cambridge University Press.

Boettke, Peter J., ed. 1999. *The Legacy of Friedrich von Hayek Volume 1: Politics*. Northampton: Edward Elgar.

———. 2018. *A Living Bibliography of Works on Hayek*, April 24. https://ppe.mercatus.org/essays/living-bibliography-works-hayek

Caldwell, Bruce J. 2004. *Hayek's Challenge: An Intellectual Biography of F. A. Hayek*. Chicago: University of Chicago Press.

Dekker, Erwin. 2016. *The Viennese Students of Civilization*. Cambridge: Cambridge University Press.

Easterly, William. 2014. *The Tyranny of Experts: Economists, Dictators, and the Forgotten Rights of the Poor*. New York: Basic Books.

Ebenstein, Alan. 2003. *Hayek's Journey: The Mind of Friedrich Hayek*. London: Palgrave Macmillan.

Hayek, F.A. [1925] 1984. The Monetary Policy of the United States After the Recovery from the 1920 Crisis. In *Money, Capital, and Fluctuations: Early Essays*, ed. Roy McCloughry. Chicago: University of Chicago Press.

———. [1929] 1933. *Monetary Theory and the Trade Cycle*. New York: Harcourt, Brace.

———. 1931. *Prices and Production*. London: Routledge.

———. 1933. The Trend of Economic Thinking. *Economica* 40: 121–137.

———., ed. 1935. *Collectivist Economic Planning*. London: Routledge and Kegan Paul.

———. 1937. Economics and Knowledge. *Economica* 4 (13): 33–54.

———. [1941] 2007. The Pure Theory of Capital. In *The Collected Works of F.A. Hayek Vol. 12*, ed. Lawrence H White. Chicago: University of Chicago Press.

———. 1944. *The Road to Serfdom*. Chicago: University of Chicago Press.

———. 1945. The Use of Knowledge in Society. *The American Economic Review* 35 (4): 519–530.

———. [1948] 1980. *Individualism and Economic Order*. Chicago: University of Chicago Press.

———. 1952a. *The Sensory Order: An Inquiry into the Foundations of Theoretical Psychology*. Chicago: University of Chicago Press.

———. [1952b] 1979. *The Counter-Revolution of Science*. 2nd ed. Indianapolis: Liberty Fund.

———. 1960. *The Constitution of Liberty*. Chicago: University of Chicago Press.

———. 1973. *Law, Legislation and Liberty: A New Statement of the Liberal Principles of Justice and Political Economy, Vol. 1: Rules and Order*. London: Routledge.

———. 1976. *Law, Legislation and Liberty: A New Statement of the Liberal Principles of Justice and Political Economy, Vol. 2: The Mirage of Social Justice*. London: Routledge.

———. [1978] 1983. *Interviewed by Axel Leijonhufvud*. Los Angeles: University of California. https://archive.org/details/nobelprizewinnin00haye.

———. 1978. *New Studies in Philosophy, Politics, Economics and the History of Ideas*. London: University of Chicago Press.

———. 1979. *Law, Legislation and Liberty: A New Statement of the Liberal Principles of Justice and Political Economy, Vol. 3: The Political Order of a Free People*. London: Routledge.

———. 1988. *The Fatal Conceit: The Errors of Socialism*. The Collected Works of F. A. Hayek, ed. W. W. Bartley, III. Chicago: University of Chicago Press.

Howson, Susan. 2011. *Lionel Robbins (Historical Perspectives on Modern Economics)*. Cambridge: Cambridge University Press.

Keynes, John Maynard. 1926. *The End of Laissez-Faire*. London: Hogarth Press.

———. 1930. *A Treatise on Money*. New York: Harcourt, Brace, and Company.

———. 1931. The Pure Theory of Money: A Reply to Dr. Hayek. *Economica* 34: 387–397.

———. 1936. *The General Theory of Employment, Interest, and Money*. London: Palgrave Macmillan.

———. 1980. *Activities 1940–1946: Shaping the Post-War World: Employment and Commodities*. The Collected Writings of John Maynard Keynes, vol. 27, ed. Elizabeth Johnson and Donald Moggridge. Cambridge: Cambridge University Press.

Menger, Carl. [1871] 1953. *Principles of Economics*. Vienna: Braumüller.

Mises, Ludwig von. 1912. *The Theory of Money and Credit*. New Haven: Yale University Press.

———. [1920] 2012. *Economic Calculation in the Socialist Commonwealth*. Auburn: Ludwig von Mises Institute.

———. [1922] 1981. *Socialism: An Economic and Sociological Analysis*. Indianapolis: Liberty Fund.

———. [1940] 2013. *Notes and Recollections*. Indianapolis: Liberty Fund.

North, Douglass C., John Joseph Wallis, and Barry R. Weingast. 2013. *Violence and Social Orders: A Conceptual Framework for Interpreting Recorded and Human History*. New York: Cambridge University Press.

Robbins, Lionel. 1937. *Economic Planning and International Order*. London: Macmillan.

———. 1971. *Autobiography of an Economist*. London: Palgrave Macmillan.

Schumpeter, Joseph. 1954. *History of Economic Analysis*. London: Allen & Unwin Ltd..

Sigmund, Karl. 2017. *Exact Thinking in Demented Times: The Vienna Circle and the Epic Quest for the Foundations of Science*. New York: Basic Books.

Skarbek, David. 2009. F.A. Hayek's Influence on Nobel Prize Winners. *Review of Austrian Economics* 22 (1): 109–112.

3

The Anatomy of an Economic Crisis: Money, Prices, and Economic Order

Introduction

At the very end of his presidency, then President George W. Bush made the following statement about the policy steps he had taken in response to the Global Financial Crisis: "Well, I have obviously made a decision to make sure the economy doesn't collapse. I've abandoned free market principles to save the free market system" (interview with CNN December 16, 2008). Bush was certainly not the first American President to make such a declaration in the wake of severe economic disruption. Consider the following remarks from the newly elected President Franklin D. Roosevelt in his first inaugural address in 1933. Roosevelt began with his famous line, "Let me assert my firm belief that the only thing we have to fear is fear itself—nameless, unreasoning, unjustified terror which paralyzes needed efforts to convert retreat into advance" (Roosevelt [1933] 1938, 11). He then quickly related this statement to tackling the economic situation. Roosevelt denounced the false god of material wealth and the "money changers" and indicted the "rulers of the exchange of mankind's goods" ([1933] 1938, 11–12). He called upon his fellow citizens to adopt "social values more noble than mere monetary profit" (12).

© The Author(s) 2018
Peter J. Boettke, *F. A. Hayek*, Great Thinkers in Economics,
https://doi.org/10.1057/978-1-137-41160-0_3

Roosevelt argued that the economic depression of the 1930s was unlike any other dark situation faced in the past because it was characterized by poverty amid plenty. "Plenty is at our door step," he stated, "but a generous use of it languishes in the very sight of the supply" (11–12). Moreover, Roosevelt criticized the current state of the policy response to this dire situation, stating that "withered leaves of industrial enterprise lie on every side; farmers find no markets for their produce; and the savings of many years in thousands of families are gone. More important, a host of unemployed citizens face the grim problem of existence, and an equally great number toil with little return" (11). The policy problem is that "their efforts have been cast in the pattern of an outworn tradition" (12). Roosevelt continued: "They only know the rules of a generation of self-seekers. They have no vision, and when there is no vision the people perish" (12). Thus, the solution Roosevelt offered was "Government itself." The evils of the "old order" must never be returned to, and with decisive action, strict supervision of banking, credit, and investment must be enforced, and speculation must be banned (13; 11–16).

Roosevelt utilized stronger rhetorical flourish and indicted the free market system in a more systemic way than Bush did. But the basic idea is the same—the free market economy must be abandoned due to the emergency nature of the situation. These criticisms of the free market during times of economic crises are not limited to politicians, but can be heard by various economic thinkers—from Rexford Tugwell in the 1930s to Paul Krugman in the 2000s. Take, for example, Tugwell's declaration during the Great Depression: "The jig is up. The cat is out of the bag. There is no invisible hand. There never was" (as quoted in White 2012, 111). And similarly, Krugman's stance after the financial crisis was to blame the free market for the economic downturn, stating, "Free market fundamentalists have been wrong about everything" (Krugman 2010).

Of course, these declarations fail to raise the important questions concerning the "what and why" of industrial fluctuations. Perhaps the very art of economic controversy was born in the debate over the possibility of a "General Glut" within a market economy, as discussed by Fiona Maclachlan in her article on Malthus and Ricardo (1999). Malthus wanted to challenge Adam Smith's proposition that "every prodigal appears to be a public enemy, and every frugal man a public benefactor."

Malthus did not argue that saving was never beneficial, but he did challenge that saving was necessarily beneficial. His development of the theory of underconsumption was consistent with his general discomfort with what he considered the unhealthy habit of overgeneralization in economics. For political economy to make progress, the statement of general principles must be accompanied by admissions to the complications, limitations, and exceptions. In response, Ricardo reasserted the logical status of the general principles and received support from J. B. Say and James Mill in this regard. Say, in his *Letters to Malthus* (1821), explains in detail how price adjustments would work to ensure that a "general glut" would not appear naturally on the market. In many ways, this has been the terms of the debate about industrial fluctuations for the past 200 years, with John Maynard Keynes picking up the mantle of Malthus[1] in the twentieth century and developing the argument into a new orthodoxy. F. A. Hayek was Keynes's adversary then and now in this dispute.

In fact, in the wake of the Global Financial Crisis and the renewed public policy debates concerning government policy, an economic "rap video" that pitted Keynes against Hayek went quasi-viral. "Fear the Boom and the Bust" has recorded over five million views since 2010, while "Fight of the Century: Round Two" from 2011 has recorded over three million views. In these rap videos—the joint effort of economist Russ Roberts and video producer John Papola—the entire array of issues in dispute are laid out for listeners and the program of spending (Keynes) is pitted against the program of saving and investment (Hayek). At the center of the controversy is the assessment of whether the market economy is self-correcting and generates coordination of economic activity, or whether the market economy is inherently unstable and prone to malcoordination of economic activity.

Malthus versus Ricardo and Say in the nineteenth century gave way to Keynes versus Hayek in the twentieth century. In the 1930s, Keynes and Hayek were recognized as the main alternatives, but after that time,

---

[1] Keynes both praises and acknowledges his debt to Malthus, not only in his *General Theory*, but also in an earlier essay ([1933] 1972) entitled "Thomas Robert Malthus: The First of the Cambridge Economists." Reprinted in *The Collected Writings of John Maynard Keynes*, Vol. 10. London: Macmillan for the Royal Economic Society, 71–103.

they clearly were not.[2] To understand this it is important to realize that Hayek's theory of industrial fluctuations was grounded in price theory, and a classic institutional analysis of the existing money and banking system. Hayek's work, in this regard, is the complete opposite of the aggregate economics of Keynes. As Hayek stated in the UCLA interviews: "I'm quite clear why, from the Austrian point of view, you could never be happy with a macroeconomic approach. It's almost a different view of the world from which you start" ([1978] 1983, 194). And to put a fine point on it, Hayek later stressed: "The whole trade-cycle theory rested on the idea that prices determined the direction of production" ([1978] 1983, 383).

Precisely due to the fact that after Keynes, economics adopted this macroeconomic perspective, Hayek's status as the main alternative to Keynes was lost in the professional and public imagination. If anyone would have been the alternative to Keynesianism during the 1950–2000 period, it would have been Milton Friedman and monetarism, and then Robert Lucas and New Classical macroeconomics. I do not dispute that intellectual history truth, but stress that Friedman ultimately was a criticism within the Keynesian system of aggregate economics. While Lucas sought to reclaim the microeconomic foundations, his own rendition of a price-theoretic theory of the business cycle was almost immediately supplanted by real business cycle, which drew analytical attention away from monetary factors and how monetary policy can distort relative prices, and thus, the coordination of economic plans through time. In short, the non-Hayekian rendering in the dispute insisted that there is no economic problem to be explained, whereas the Keynesians argued there was no solution outside of government activism. As the citation patterns reflect (see Appendix A), Hayekian ideas get a bump in attention during times of severe economic crisis—such as the stagflation of the 1970s, or the Global Financial Crisis of 2008.

---

[2] See John Hick's (1967, 203) description of the intellectual drama: "When the definitive history of economic analysis during the nineteen thirties comes to be written, a leading character in the drama (it was quite a drama) will be Professor Hayek … there was a time when the new theories of Hayek were the principal rival of the new theories of Keynes. Which was right, Keynes or Hayek?"

The Anatomy of the Global Financial Crisis

The economic volatility that has engulfed the world since 2007 is the byproduct of a "perfect storm" in macroeconomic policy failures dating back to at least two decades prior to the crisis. In contrast to a more widely discussed debt-deflation theory of economic depressions, it makes more sense to discuss the debt-*inflation* theory for this particular financial crisis (Boettke and Coyne 2011). This position does not necessarily challenge Irving Fisher's famous theory of how the "debt disease" and the "dollar disease" combine to generate an economic downturn, but it instead emphasizes a different set of channels by which economic volatility is introduced into the system. The argument draws on a tradition that goes back to Adam Smith in economics and public policy. This idea focuses on *public debt* as a trigger for the manipulation of money and credit by the monetary authority, which initiates the pattern of economic behavior that produces the coordination failures revealed during the crisis.

Smith argued that the governmental habit of running deficits that lead to accumulating public debt, which is then addressed by a debasement of the currency, could be described as a "juggling trick." Governments, ancient as well as modern, Smith argued, continually resorted to this juggling trick that eventually had deleterious consequences on the economy. While Fisher's debt-deflation theory of the depression examined the consequences of private indebtedness *during* the downturn, it seems critically important to examine the economic situation *prior* to the downturn. One possible channel to investigate is how the pre-crisis fiscal imbalances result in a monetary expansion which caused distortions in the investment behavior within the economy. If we consider both the distortions prior and the difficulties during the crisis, the Smithean "juggling tricks" and the Fisherean theory of depression can be squared. As Roger Koppl (2014, 33, fn 7) recently explains, "the monetary expansion creates both the 'debt disease' and the 'dollar disease.' It creates a debt disease by injecting false credit into the system. It creates a dollar disease because, in the absence of hyper-inflation, the monetary expansion must eventually slow down relative to expectations, creating a liquidity crisis."

The critical issue for the Hayekian narrative is the distortion of the price signals, and thus the malcoordination of economic activities that must be corrected. What must be explained is the "cluster of errors" that resulted in the "boom" period, and the necessity of the recalculation of economic investment and production activity during the "bust" period. "It's by discovering the function of prices as guiding what people ought to do," Hayek states, "that I finally began to put it in that form." (Hayek [1978] 1983, 383). Hayek thought that macroeconomic thinking obscured the economic problem, and that the key was to study the coordination of economic activity through time guided by changes in relative prices. Prices are not summaries of previous decisions, but guides for future decisions concerning exchange and production. Prices guide production, and prices are necessary inputs into the economic calculations that enable complex coordination of economic activities. The meshing of production plans with consumption demands through time is accomplished by the adjustment of relative prices. The ability of economic decision-makers to utilize the price system is necessary to making rational economic calculations about alternative courses of action in commercial activity.

The analytical parts of the Hayekian narrative take place against the backdrop of the commercial activity of advanced material production. Production is for an uncertain future, and the production activity requires the combination of various heterogeneous capital goods that have multiple-specific uses. We must always remember that the economic problem is the allocation of scare means among competing uses. The time element is never to be forgotten in the Hayekian narrative, and in fact, Hayek's original work in economics was focused on this problem of imputation. Put rather bluntly, the theory of imputation demonstrates how the value of hogs raised on a farm and maintained by the farmer is derived from the value of ham and bacon that the farmer can fetch on the market. If the hogs did not fetch this market price in the future, then the farmer would need to reconsider the investment activity of raising hogs.

Interest rates coordinate intertemporal activity. Investment and productive activity must be engaged in today in order to realize the outputs and return on investment in the future. In this sense, the interest rate is the price for loanable funds. It coordinates the savings of some into the investment funds for others. Movements of this price, just like all relative prices, set in motion processes of adjustment and adaptation.

Finally, in the Hayek narrative, we have the non-neutrality of money, and the consequences of a monopoly monetary authority. Money, by definition, is the medium of exchange, and thus the importance of money is that it is one half of all exchanges in an economy. Money is a joint that connects all economic activity that, in Hayek's narrative, is neither a tight joint (as in the monetarist rendering) nor a broken joint (as in the Keynesian rendering), but a loose joint. It is precisely because it is a loose joint that the manipulation of money and credit can distort the processes of investment and production, but also correct that distortion as economic reality asserts itself against the illusion that was previously created. Thus, we get a "boom" and a "bust" of the business cycle due to the manipulation of money and credit by the monopoly monetary authority. When you put all the constitute parts of the narrative together, the consequences of malcoordination are not trivial, but are significantly costly due to the misallocation of capital goods. Human capital is also misallocated because labor skills are similarly not perfectly homogeneous, but exhibit various degrees of heterogeneity and multiple-specificity. Adjustments are then required that sacrifice both time and wealth.

The Hayek story is a macroeconomic story with a microeconomic explanation. Hayek insisted against Keynes that it was a methodological mistake to begin the analysis in any place other than full employment because it was only by beginning at full employment that one can explain the mechanisms that give rise to unemployment and examine how that social ill can be effectively addressed. Keynes's theory *begins* with an aggregate demand failure, and thus, with unemployment. Idle resources are postulated, not explained. From that vantage point, Keynes was able to explain a path out, but not why the economy was in that position in the first place. In Keynes's work, the economic actors are prone to speculative behavior (read irrational), the price system does not guide their decisions, the link between savings and investment has been broken, and thus nothing within the system itself could produce the feedback required, let alone guide the readjustment of economic plans to make them less erroneous than before. Keynes's puzzle was the problem of poverty amid plenty. Hayek's puzzle was how the price system guides the coordination of economic activity through time in a world of scarcity.

Keynes warned that the dark forces of time and ignorance conspired to engulf private actors in an intractable situation and this resulted in coordination failures due to insufficient aggregate demand. This situation was incapable of self-correction; only the government was in a position to serve as a corrective. And in particular, government spending. Hayek, on the other hand, was focused on how the price system guides individuals through the thick fog caused by time and ignorance so they can achieve the complex coordination of economic activity that constitutes a modern capital-using economy. Keynes postulated an epistemic dilemma for economic actors that could only be solved by actors removed from that context, whereas Hayek sought to articulate how the actors engulfed in this epistemic dilemma found their way out via the institutional configuration of property, prices, and profit-and-loss. If they are repeatedly failing to escape from the dilemma, then the blame in Hayek's story was not on the cognitive limitations of the private actors, but to be found in the institutional environment within which they were operating that prevented the necessary learning. Keynes's theory was one of an epistemic trap; Hayek's theory was one of epistemic institutionalism.

Nevertheless, Keynes won the day among economists and the public policy community. Keynes was able to connect the greatest resentment of capitalism—the idle rich—with the greatest fear of capitalism—mass unemployment—in such a way that captured the *zeitgeist* emerging from the "Gilded Age." This narrative was so powerful that its staying power in the imagination of intellectuals and policy decision-makers has held all these years. The basic Hayek versus Keynes narrative is played out constantly in the newspapers and policy discussion even if one half of that debate is largely forgotten.

For many economists, the financial crisis was caused by "irrational" behavior of various economic actors—including borrowers and bank lenders.[3] While this may be true, it would make sense to ask *why*

---

[3] See, for example, George Akerlof and Robert Shiller (2009) *Animal Spirits: How Human Psychology Drives the Economy and Why it Matters for Global Capitalism.* There is a lot to learn, I would argue, from comparing the argument in this work of Akerlof and Shiller with Keynes's own argument laid

individuals began to act and invest "irrationally." In the Hayekian narrative, individuals began to act this way because the Federal Reserve's manipulation of money and credit (along with other fiscal policies) altered their incentives such that what seemed to be "irrational" behavior was in fact a "rational" response to the incentives they faced.

Employing the "Austrian" monetary theory of industrial fluctuations effectively explains the boom-bust cycle of the 2000s. This analysis is similar to the work by John Taylor on how monetary policy got "off track" during this period and how interest rates were held artificially low, thereby stimulating investment in longer-term projects (Taylor 2009). Boettke and Horwitz (2009) analyze why the distortions were directed in this particular case to the housing sector. They argue that this direction was a consequence of public policies on both the demand and the supply side of the housing market, and in particular with respect to the mortgage market that tended to steer activity toward the housing sector and away from others. The combination of monetary and fiscal policy geared toward the housing sector resulted in a "bust" in the fall of 2008.

According to the Austrian Business Cycle Theory, the manipulation of money and credit by a monopoly supplier of the currency distorts the pattern of exchange and production in an economy. Once those distortions are revealed, a recalculation process ensues that guides a reshuffling of the pattern of exchange and production throughout the economy. Monetary policy is critical in this narrative because in a modern economy, money is one half of all exchanges—goods buy money, and money buys goods, but goods never buy goods. The manipulation of money therefore also manipulates all exchange ratios, or prices, and this distorts the pattern of production. Rational, profit-seeking actors always react to the signals of the market contained in relative prices—this includes the market rate of interest for loanable funds. These profit-seeking actors can be "misled" in their decisions by investing in production plans that are not "justified" by the "real" savings and consumption decisions of others within the economy. In other words, these individuals are reacting to artificially low interest rates, which creates a "bubble" or "boom" in the

---

out in his essay "The End of Laissez Faire" (1926), which challenges the rationality postulate, the role of the price system, and thus ultimately, the "invisible hand" theory.

economy. To sustain this boom, the monetary authority would need to expand the supply of money and credit at highly accelerating rates, and thus, create hyperinflation. Or, if the monetary authority slows the rate of acceleration, this would trigger the "bust" phase—in other words, "bursting" the bubble. The bust phase is the recalculation of economic activity as time reshuffles the capital structure and the labor market to be more aligned with the consumption plans of individuals, thereby correcting the previous artificial boom of the economy.

The manifestation of the "boom" in the housing sector during the 2000s is a consequence of a variety of rules and regulations with regard to home ownership, the origination of mortgages, the role of government-sponsored enterprises, and the evolution of financial instruments that resulted from these changes. The consequence of the bust phase is declining home prices, loss of wealth, unemployment, and economic insecurity. But because this was deemed an economic emergency, policymakers turned to a variety of aggressive policy measures to ease the pain of the bust—these include: fiscal policy (Troubled Asset Relief Program, or TARP); monetary policy (Quantitative Easing and Operation Twist); and regulations of the financial industry (Dodd-Frank).

The effectiveness of these measures is a continuing controversy in the media and in academic circles. For example, a recent survey of economic experts at the Booth School of Business at the University of Chicago asked economists whether or not they believed that the fiscal policies initiated in 2008 were effective at addressing the economic situation of the financial crisis. The economists were asked to rate on a scale of 1–10 the effectiveness of the policy (10 being most effective) and to also rate on a scale of 1–10 the confidence with which they make that judgment (10 being extremely confident in their judgment). The vast majority of experts agreed that the aggressive fiscal policies pursued were effective. These survey results were widely reported in the mainstream media and social media sites, but the reported summary was somewhat misleading. A close examination of the answers shows that most of these "experts" put the effectiveness of fiscal policy in the 6–7 range, and their confidence in the 3–5 range. Another problem with this study was that the "expert" status of those asked was questionable as many of those who answered the survey had never, in fact, studied fiscal policy. However, Alberto Alesina, whose research does focus on fiscal policy and its effectiveness throughout the world, argued that US fiscal policy since 2008 has been ineffective (see Alesina 2012; Alesina and Giavazzi 2013). As Alesina writes, in March 2010, "the unemployment rate was 9.7%, which was way above what the [Obama] administration had predicted it would be without the recovery plan. So, the recovery plan seemed to have no effect. In March 2011, the unemployment rate was 8.8%, which is exactly what it was predicted to be without the recovery plan" (Alesina 2012, 432). The results of Alesina and Ardagna (2010) suggest that tax cuts are more expansionary than spending increases in the cases of a fiscal stimulus. For fiscal adjustments, they argue that spending cuts are much more effective than tax increases in stabilizing the debt and avoiding economic downturns. Yet, his position was *not* the one discussed in the mainstream media or on various social media outlets.

One of the common misunderstandings discussed in the introduction is that an unhampered market is to blame for the 2008 financial crisis. The narrative is that Keynesian economics, which counters the ideas of the free market, has been banned in Washington since the 1980s. But this narrative cannot be sustained under close scrutiny. Since immediately after WWII, the tool kit of aggregate demand management has been the policy rule in Washington. Keynesian ideas captured the imagination of economists and policymakers, Keynesian-inspired institutions of public policy administration were constructed, and Keynesian-directed data collection was institutionalized in both the public and private sectors.

Consider the basic macroeconomic policy intuition that has deep-seated roots in the scientific and policy community for the past 60 years. During a liquidity trap, monetary policy will be as ineffective as "pushing on a string," and thus, fiscal policy will be the preferred remedy. However, during normal times, the Federal Reserve and the Treasury will deploy a mix of monetary and fiscal policy to meet the objective of full employment in the economy. Since the late 1940s, Keynesian policy has ruled economic policy in Washington. The only difference between administrations has been either a liberal Keynesianism policy or a conservative Keynesianism policy. While there was a Monetarist Counter-Revolution, a rise of New Classical Economics, and electoral victories of Ronald Reagan or Margaret Thatcher, the policy arena was still dominated by

Keynesian demand management in macroeconomic policy. In other words, it is true that the intellectual space during the 1970s and 1980s fractured the Keynesian hegemony, but it was only short-lived as a new generation of Keynesian economists quickly found ways to provide "microfoundations" for their analysis on aggregate demand and aggregate supply. Therefore, the policy tools in Washington have continued to be Keynesian in nature.

Thus, it is my contention that many of the economic problems and recessions are caused by distortions of incentives and information mechanisms with Keynesian economic policies. Take for example the celebrated period from 1950 to 1975, where supposedly Western democracies experienced economic growth, low unemployment, and a more equitable distribution of income. But one could also argue that during this period, policymakers were continually engaging in policies that promised short-term relief from economic adjustment, passing the costs of the policies adopted farther off in time. The policies of the 1950s and 1960s begot the stagflation of the 1970s—in the same way the economic recovery with Reagan, and then Clinton in the 1980s and 1990s, respectively, begot the problems we are facing today. If Lawrence Kotlikoff and Scott Burns are accurate in *The Coming Generational Storm* (2005) and *The Clash of Generations* (2012) regarding their analysis of intergenerational accounting, the $211 trillion fiscal gap today is a consequence of decades of profligate fiscal policy brought on by the logic of the promissory politics that went hand in hand with the ascendency of Keynesianism. As Luigi Zingales (2009a) argued in *The Economist*:

> Keynesianism has conquered the hearts and minds of politicians and ordinary people alike because it provides a theoretical justification for irresponsible behaviour. Medical science has established that one or two glasses of wine per day are good for your long-term health, but no doctor would recommend a recovering alcoholic to follow this prescription. Unfortunately, Keynesian economists do exactly this. They tell politicians, who are addicted to spending our money, that government expenditures are good. And they tell consumers, who are affected by severe spending problems, that consuming is good, while saving is bad. In medicine, such behaviour would get you expelled from the medical profession; in economics, it gives you a job in Washington.

In a variety of ways, Zingales's remarks echo those made decades earlier by James Buchanan and Richard Wagner in *Democracy in Deficit* (1977). Buchanan and Wagner (1977, 75) argue that: "A regime of permanent budget deficits, inflation and increasing public sector share of national income—these seem to us to be the consequences of the application of Keynesian precepts in American democracy." Buchanan and Wagner argue that Keynesianism has produced an unstable situation in the economy that can be addressed within this mindset only by further restrictions on freedom of individuals within the market system: "Sober assessment suggests that ... politically, Keynesianism may represent a substantial disease, one that can, over the long run, prove fatal for a functioning democracy" (1977, 57).

In response to challenges to his original statement in *The Economist*, Zingales (2009b) further argues that the Keynesian position is characterized as holding the following. First, monetary policy is relatively ineffective in stabilizing an economy, and completely ineffective at some critical times due to a liquidity trap. Second, through government spending, fiscal policy is not only effective, but also the preferred policy tool to combat economic instability. Third, short-run consequences should outweigh long-run consequences in policymaking, even though this cannot be maintained scientifically by economists. Zingales states, "I disagree, not because I believe that the government should sit on the sideline and do nothing. I disagree because I think that these policies can worsen the problem. As economists we cannot be (let alone should be) Keynesians now. Scientists can believe God created the world, but they cannot believe in it as scientists. In the same way today economists can support Keynesian policies for personal and political reasons, but they cannot support them as economists, because they are in contradiction with most economic principles we believe in (or at least I thought we believed in) as economists." In other words, to follow Keynesian economic policies requires an abandonment of basic economic reasoning. It requires an abandonment of understanding individual decision-making, the role of the price system in coordinating economic affairs through time, the disciplining role of profit/loss accounting, and the "invisible hand" of a self-regulating market economy.

Furthermore, Richard Wagner, in *Deficits, Debt and Democracy* (2012), argues that the current situation of public indebtedness follows from the budgetary process in a democratic system struggling with the tragedy of the fiscal commons. That fiscal commons in public policy was created by changes in the rules associated with public budgeting following WWII. As James Buchanan repeatedly stressed, Keynesian fiscal policies had the consequence of relaxing all the previous informal and formal constraints on Adam Smith's "juggling tricks" of deficits and debts. Where the old-time fiscal religion once sought to stop—or at least highly restrain—the "juggling tricks," the "New Economics" of Keynes embraced the art of "juggling" and sought to train subsequent generations of economists to become master jugglers of policy instruments in order to manage the macroeconomic system. In Buchanan's narrative (e.g. 1987), this is how Keynesian policy becomes Keynesian follies with a deleterious impact on the long-run health of the economy and the polity.

A price-theoretic narrative of the financial crisis provides an alternative approach to the dominating Keynesian narrative, which espouses the idea that the unfolding crisis is merely an example of aggregate demand failure with a liquidity trap, loss of investor confidence, and an unemployment equilibrium. Coordination failures in the Keynesian perspective emerge due not to confusions in the economic decisions signals, but to swings of optimism and pessimism, the breakdown of the link between savings and investment, and the rigidity of the price mechanism. The core Hayekian puzzle of how rational profit maximizing actors can be misled by distortions in the price system is replaced by the economic dilemma set in motion by "animal spirits," corrected only through the discretionary action of policymakers. In the preceding section, we will accept for the sake of argument the theoretical possibilities of Keynesian economic policies and evaluate these policies from a political economy perspective.

Tacit Presuppositions and the Game of Political Economy

For Keynesian solutions to provide an answer to Keynesian problems in the economy, there has to be an alignment with the policymaker and the citizen. Any deviation from this unique environment in the policy space means that Keynesian policies will do little to address social ills. In fact, the deviations could even exacerbate the social ills. As Koppl (2002) has argued, Keynesian policies can produce the Keynesian world they are trying to avoid rather than fix the economic crisis.

Critical to understanding our argument is the explicit recognition of the *tacit presuppositions of political economy* from which the standard analysis in economic policy proceeds. The concept of the "tacit presuppositions of political economy" comes from James Buchanan's analysis of post-communist political economy (Buchanan 1997). Buchanan urged economists to consider the situation of the typical post-communist economic actor, whose only experience with the market has been the "black market" dealings under the communist/socialist regimes in East and Central Europe and the former Soviet Union. That experience with reality was defined as follows: (a) an official shortage economy with a queuing system, (b) since there is no alternative supply network, those who control the goods and services for sale dictate the terms of exchange, and (c) there is little recourse to register consumer complaints either through the market mechanism of buying and abstaining from buying (exit), or appealing to a third party (voice). There was a certain "take it or leave it" aspect to their experience with the market, and it no way mimicked a typical market experience that placed consumer satisfaction at the forefront. If that was the historical experience with the market for these residents, then what should residents expect for future market experiences once the market has been granted a degree of freedom and legitimacy through political change? In other words, if the previous experience with markets reinforced the tacit presupposition that markets are arenas of negative sum games, then the idea that positive sum games will be experienced under the new regime might seem like merely a theoretical fantasy of a new generation of ideological peddlers. One implication of recognizing these tacit presuppositions is that market reformers in East and Central Europe and the former Soviet Union must be more creative and culturally sensitive in their constitutional designs during the transition to capitalism. Otherwise, their changes may undermine the long-term legitimacy of the reform efforts.

Buchanan's point on the tacit presuppositions can also be applied to the Keynesian model, both in its diagnosis of the problem and its offered solution.[4] To simplify, here are the tacit presuppositions in the Keynesian model: (a) Keynesian theory of aggregate demand failure is the *right* explanation of the anatomy of the crisis; (b) Keynesian policy of aggregate demand management through fiscal policy to fix the failure is the *right* policy choice; and (c) the citizens in the economy both trust and passively respond to the policy choices made by the trained experts in economic policy. The rise of Keynesian theory coincided with the transformation of public administration, especially in the USA. As a result, there was also a transformation of what it meant to be an "economic policy maker" and of what was *useful* economic theory for policymakers. When these tacit presuppositions of political economy are aligned with the empirical reality, then Keynesian policies will in fact be the appropriate remedy to the dire economic situation. Full employment will be approximated through the judicious policies of demand management without the threat of inflation or long-lasting fiscal imbalance. It is important to stress that for the vast majority of Keynesian economists, the policy program is initiated by an economic emergency that must be addressed in the short run and not a long-term shift in public policy. In the long run, a successful economy is not plagued by permanent budget deficits, accumulating public debt, and accelerating inflation. Instead, long-run economic growth and development is as much a goal for Keynesian economists as it for classical political economists.[5]

In what follows, an argumentative strategy similar to Glaeser et al. (2001) will be pursued. In an effort to understand the various forms of transition from socialism to capitalism in the 1990s, they developed a model to identify when economic regulation by governments would outperform self-regulation of the market (including self-regulation grounded

[4] See, for example, Buchanan and Wagner (1977, 79–94). In this section, Buchanan and Wagner discuss the "Harvey Road Presuppositions," which are the presumptions in Keynes's models. They argue that Keynes envisioned policies to be implemented by a small, enlightened, and intellectual government—a "benevolent despot." In doing so, Keynes did not consider the potential of governments to be influenced by special interest groups or the formation of coalitions within the government or a host of other considerations that reflect the complexities of real-world politics.

[5] Though Abba Lerner in correspondence with Laurence Moss in the 1970s adamantly rejected that the differences between Keynes and Hayek could be addressed as a difference between short run and long run, he argued instead that Hayek's theory of unemployment and his rejection of macroeconomic thinking did not permit such an easy reconciliation. See Lerner Papers Box 3, letter dated July 31, 1978.

in contract law protected by the courts). The model divided the regulatory apparatus into Judges and Regulators, both of whom could be either competent or incompetent. The authors then examined the different permutations. If the combination were a competent judge with either a competent or incompetent regulator, then the market mechanism of self-regulation and contract law would be superior to agency regulation for economic growth and development. An incompetent judge paired with an incompetent regulator would also yield in favor of self-regulation. However, if the situation were one characterized by an incompetent judge with competent regulator, then state regulation of the economy would be superior. Glaeser et al. (2001) argue that this combination was indeed the situation in post-communism even in the most favorable environments for economic reform, and therefore conclude that economic regulation by government is superior to self-regulation.[6]

Applying this argumentative strategy to analyze the conditions necessary for Keynesian economic policies to "succeed" in the real world, I am essentially asking what practical conditions must be met in order for Keynesian solutions to work. Buchanan and Wagner (1977, 79–94) explain that Keynes himself relied on the "Harvey Road Presuppositions" of an idealized, small, and elite government that could effectively implement policies. But the Harvey Road Presuppositions are not the conditions of real-world politics. Buchanan and Wagner explain (1977, 79–80):

> An idealized set of policy prescriptions may be formulated for a truly benevolent despotism. But this set may be far distant from the ideal prescriptions for the complex "game" of democratic politics, a game that involves the participation of citizens as voters who are simultaneously taxpayers and public-service beneficiaries, the activities of professional politicians whose electoral successes depend on pleasing these voters, the struggles of the sometimes fragile coalitions reflected in organized or unorganized political parties, and, finally, the machinations of bureaucrats who are employed by government but who tend, indirectly, to control the details of government operation.

---

[6] Stringham et al. (2008) respond to this paper by providing contrary evidence and concluding that the optimal policy is actually self-regulation.

Because Keynesian mechanisms rely heavily on the behavior of both citizens and policymakers, I want to first look at the conditions under which citizens are trusting or distrusting of policymakers (and their proposed policies) and whether policymakers are sincere/insincere and capable/incapable. Trusting and distrusting citizenry refers to whether citizens believe the policy proposals. For example, if policymakers announce that there will be a temporary fiscal stimulus, then a trusting citizenry will believe that this fiscal stimulus is in fact temporary and will behave differently from a citizenry who believes government spending will increase indefinitely. With either a trusting or distrusting citizenry, policymakers can be either sincere or insincere with regard to policies benefiting the public. For example, a sincere policymaker would propose fiscal stimulus in order to help the economy from sliding into a deeper recession while an insincere policymaker would propose automobile bailouts in order to gain support and votes from the automobile workers union. Furthermore, capability refers to whether policymakers are in fact knowledgeable and able to properly implement the right policies to "solve" the problems in the economy. Based on these characteristics of citizens and policymakers, we have created four different cases to analyze. In Fig. 3.1, we provide an

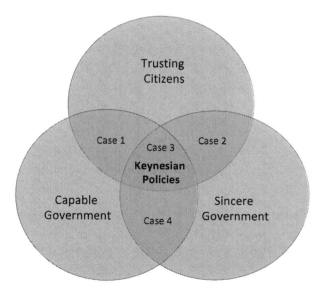

Fig. 3.1 The game of political economy

illustration of the different cases that can arise from the characteristics of citizens and policymakers.

Case 1: Trusting Citizens with a Capable, but Insincere Government
Although citizens may be trusting and the government capable of creating a perfect stimulus package to help the economy out of a recession, insincerity of the government means that policies will reflect not what is in the public interest, but what is in the special interest of politicians. Although proper fiscal stimulus could theoretically work, politicians are interested in maximizing their own self-interest by catering to special interest groups. Therefore, they will implement policies that are beneficial for a small group (special interest) at the expense of the larger group (the public). Policymakers may choose which sectors or industries receive the fiscal stimulus based on lobbying efforts as well as the support the politician can acquire from these special interest groups as future votes. This creates a difficulty for Keynesian solutions to solve macroeconomic problems because policies will not be implemented that remedy problems in the economy. Rather, policies will be implemented that benefit special interest groups under a Keynesian rhetoric to "help" the economy. For example, the classic Keynesian arguments on deficit spending assume that government spending will decrease and will be financed later through budget surpluses. But with insincere politicians, this does not happen because they are benefitting from continuous budget deficits. Thus, insincere governments continue to increase spending because it is not in the self-interest of politicians to cut spending.

Case 2: Trusting Citizens with a Sincere, but Incapable Government
In this scenario, policymakers *are* interested in implementing policies to benefit the public, not in catering to special interest groups. However, even with the best intentions, they are not able to determine the proper fiscal stimulus amount and can cause severe problems in the economy from "overshooting" the optimal fiscal stimulus package. Even with a fiscal stimulus that is too small, there will be problems of continuing to blindly implement stimulus packages that may be far removed from the problem by the time the second stimulus package is approved by Congress. Furthermore, policymakers do not know which sectors to target and which projects to implement. This means that socially valuable resources

in one sector may be diverted to another sector that has little impact on creating a strong Keynesian "multiplier effect." Thus, with an incapable government, Keynesian solutions will not be able to properly address problems in the economy.

Case 3: Trusting Citizens with a Sincere and Capable Government

This case is where Keynesian policies will be able to solve the problems in the economy. With trusting citizens, fiscal stimulus in the form of a tax rebate will mean that citizens will spend without hesitation about paying the money back in the future with taxes. Citizens believe that during economic booms, spending will cut back, and the government will pay back the deficit accrued during the recession by running budget surpluses during the "good times." Furthermore, sincere and capable policymakers means that governments propose only those policies that are beneficial for the public and that they are able to effectively implement the "perfect" stimulus package to help the economy recover from recession.

Case 4: Distrusting Citizens with a Sincere and Capable Government

A distrusting citizenry means that individuals regard fiscal stimulus and bailouts as increasing their future tax burden. Therefore, tax rebates will not translate into consumption spending, but will instead be saved to pay off future tax burdens[7] due to indefinitely greater government spending. If consumers are not spending (or at least not spending as much to have large multiplier effects), then fiscal stimulus in the economy during a recession is ineffective. Furthermore, consumers may distrust that fiscal stimulus packages are temporary, as politicians propose them to be. Even with government bailouts, distrusting citizens will assume that the companies will not pay back the government loans, which means that citizens will be liable to pay back the "gifts" to the companies in the future. In such a case, they will again save today in order to pay higher taxes in the future. Thus, in this scenario, citizens are distrusting that deficit spending now will be compensated in the future with budget surpluses. These considerations impact the behavior of citizens such that they no longer

---

[7] This follows the Ricardian equivalence argument: Consumers are forward-looking and have realistic expectations about the government's budget constraints and their future tax payments when making choices about their current consumption.

continue with their normal consumption patterns, and will in fact cut back on spending, which makes Keynesian recovery policies ineffective.

Thus, only when all three conditions are met will Keynesian aggregate demand management policies be able to remedy problems in economic recessions. These conditions are: a trusting citizenry; a sincere government; and a capable government.[8] If any *one* of the conditions is not satisfied, Keynesian policies will be ineffective and we will be faced with Cases 1, 2, or 4. In other words, in order to demonstrate that we are not in Case 3 in the real world, we only have to show that one of those conditions does not hold in practice.

There is an extensive empirical debate on whether Ricardian equivalence holds in practice.[9] For the purposes of this book, we will not address this debate, but instead, focus on the conditions of sincerity and capability of policymakers. To assume that governments are sincere would be to assume that public choice problems do not plague the political system. However, in the real world, politicians do cater to special interest groups at the expense of the public. The "default" reality is that politicians do care about maximizing their own interest, and thus, supporters of Keynesian economic recovery policies must demonstrate that politicians are free from special interest influence. Furthermore, not only are politicians heavily influenced by special interest groups, but they are also often unable to know exactly how much fiscal stimulus is needed and in which sectors. Take for example the stimulus package implemented after the financial crisis. For years after the first stimulus package, policymakers argued that "it was not enough" and that they needed more trials of the package. Given that there is one "optimal" stimulus package size (or narrow range), the probability that governments will overshoot or undershoot is extremely high. In this case, then, the condition of "capable" government also fails to hold in practice.

---

[8] I am not considering the cases where a distrusting government is coupled with either an insincere or incapable government because that was already ruled out in the previous cases with a trusting citizenry—that the combination of either an insincere or incapable government cannot lead to successful Keynesian policies.

[9] Results testing whether Ricardian Equivalence holds in practice are mixed. Some find that Ricardian Equivalence does hold; see, for example: Barro (1979), Aschauer (1985), Kormendi and Meguire (1990). Others reject Ricardian Equivalence: Feldstein (1982) and Graham (1993).

In short, except for the very rare case where sincere and capable policy-makers align perfectly with trusting citizens, the enthusiasm exhibited by Keynesian economists from Lorie Torshis to Larry Summers as "Doctors to the world" and that "macroeconomics is the medicine" is simply unwarranted. Keynesian solutions to Keynesian identified problems *only hold* in a very limited realm, and the evidentiary burden is on scholars to prove that all three of those conditions hold in the real world. Unless and until it is proven that those conditions hold in the real world, Keynesian solutions cannot be prosed to "work" in solving real-world economic problems. Thus, independent of the assessment of the logical validity of Keynesian models, the practical relevance of Keynesian solutions are limited to a political economy game that is rarely, if ever, descriptive of the reality in which the economy and the polity find themselves. The fact that this was not widely recognized is perhaps due to a result of the tacit presuppositions of political economy that economists and political economists of earlier generations confronted in their training under the influence of twentieth-century philosophy of public administration and public policy, which permeated the intellectual culture in the Western democracies of Europe and the USA.[10]

We also argue that Keynesian economic policies are destabilizing to the economic environment and are counterproductive. This is because, if the three conditions are not met, then Keynesian policies provide no benefit, and thus any positive cost associated with the policies means that these policies cause a net harm. Consider again the fiscal stimulus or the bailouts: the "costs" of the policy range anywhere from distorting the price system to misallocating resources to projects that are counterproductive and wasteful. The other major costs are due to long-term problems of

---

[10] Take, for example, what biographer R. F. Harrod said about Keynes: "We have seen that he [Keynes] was strongly imbued with what I have called the presuppositions of Harvey Road. One of these presuppositions may perhaps be summarized in the idea that the government of Britain was and could continue to be in the hands of an intellectual aristocracy using the method of persuasion" (as quoted in Buchanan and Wagner 1977, 80, Fn. 1). And, on reflecting why it may be the case that Keynes did not see the dilemma between his policies and the problems of democracies, Harrod says: "It may be that the presuppositions of Harvey Road were so much of a second nature to Keynes that he did not give this dilemma the full consideration which it deserves" (as quoted in Buchanan and Wagner 1977, 81). Economists in the twentieth century were heavily influenced by and trained in the Keynesian tradition—thus perhaps reflecting similar "Harvey Road Presuppositions."

future business cycles, persistent deficit spending, and the eventual currency debasement that follows from Keynesian economic policies. Thus, it is not just that Keynesian economic policies are less effective than advertised, but as Zingales suggests, they actually make the situation worse. Keynesian solutions to Keynesian diagnosis are far more fragile than previously thought.

Extraordinary Measures amid an Extraordinary Crisis

The tacit presuppositions of political economy in the democratic West since the end of WWII have made the Keynesian diagnosis and remedy the default policy position. Crises are endogenously created within the economy, but can be exogenously addressed by the trained experts in public policy. The tacit presuppositions by definition cannot be "revealed" during a crisis; otherwise, they would cease to be "tacit." The problem is that Keynesian solutions are proposed and implemented with confidence and without much question. This attitude is reflected in the works on the recent global financial crisis that have been published by key decision-makers—for instance Timothy Geithner's *Stress Test* (2014); Henry Paulson's *On the Brink* (2010); and Ben Bernanke's *The Federal Reserve and the Financial Crisis* (2013). The tacit presuppositions of political economy also underlie the analysis one finds in Daniel Drezner's *The System Worked* (2014), though Drezner's analysis draws attention to the international institutions that regulate the global economy. We are not suggesting that the tacit presuppositions give policymakers a ready-made formula for public policy. Rather that their training has given them a set of recipes in the policy space from which to draw. Therefore, these policymakers believe that these recipes have proven to be effective in the past 60 years of policy experience in the USA.

The works of Geithner, Paulson, and Bernanke all rely on the tacit presuppositions of the policy game we have outlined in the proceeding section. Their policy recommendations are guided under the assumption that all the pieces are aligned in the policy space, which means that (in this instance) a radical Keynesian diagnosis can be followed by an aggressive set of Keynesian policy prescriptions that could stabilize the economy. Geithner's and Paulson's books stress the Armageddon nature of the economic situation and thereby provide justification for the extreme measures that had to be taken, and their unique willingness to take the necessary decisions at the necessary moments to stave off another Great Depression. In both instances, success (and to some extent, heroic victory) is measured by what did not occur, not by what has happened.

The tenor and tone of Bernanke's book is much different. However, at times, he too suggests that every action taken by the Federal Reserve Bank was the correct action for the crisis at the time and that one need not worry about any long-term consequences because they are all: (a) better than the alternative, and (b) will be taken care of as deemed necessary. In short, Bernanke's main message is that the Fed was established to conduct monetary policy in a way that preserved financial stability and the Fed needed to act in this way in order to preserve financial stability during this economic recession. Bernanke's analysis stems from his years of learning the critical lessons of the Fed's past failures. He learned that the Federal Reserve made a number of mistakes (small and large) during the Great Depression, the Great Moderation, and the Great Inflation, and now during the Great Recession, the Federal Reserve needs to use the tools of monetary policy to preserve financial stability and provide the right environment for sustainable long-term economic growth and development.

The "taken for granted" empirical reality in Bernanke's narrative is that the "boom" phase was not due to easy money and credit policies by the Fed during the decade preceding the "bust." Rather, the problem was to be found in private sector vulnerabilities, which resulted in a failure in the non-bank financial sector and, if left unaddressed, would have destroyed the entire investment environment. Bernanke argues that this private sector vulnerability was deeper and more global than is genuinely recognized, and the impact of the counterparty contagion of a collapse in this non-bank investment system would have indeed produced a crisis worse than the Great Depression. Though stated more timidly than in the works of Geithner and Paulson, Bernanke still insists that the right decisions were made at the right time, the evidence being that a complete collapse of the global financial system did not occur.

The problem is that it is near impossible to argue against such a counter-factual thought experiment. It is easier to show the consequences of a policy error once it is committed, rather than to show what might have been had an alternative policy path been pursued. All we can *know* is what we have witnessed—the system did not collapse. We were told it was teetering on collapse, and decisive action that went against long-held ideological beliefs on the sanctity of the market (e.g. Paulson) or the academic literature on rules versus discretionary action (e.g. Bernanke) was taken and responsible for the collapse not happening. But this leaves scholars with two main questions: (1) can the lingering and lackluster recovery perhaps be explained by the lack of alignment in the policy game between the players and the reality of the situation and (2) will the long-run costs associated with the policy steps followed in 2008 be counted into an analysis of whether the correct action was taken?

Political Economy and the Counter-Factual

In hindsight, should we consider the government bailout and other emergency economic measures to have been successful in averting a financial meltdown of the USA? Some economists, including Tyler Cowen, support this position and urge others to take "all things considered" and come to the same conclusion.[11] I would argue that when "all things" really are considered, it is difficult to argue that the bailouts or other forms of emergency economic measures were a good idea. This is because "all things considered" takes into account an empirically grounded and theoretically consistent political economy that looks at both the direct and indirect effect of public policies.

The long-run negative consequences that Cowen admits might cause real problems (perhaps even serious ones) must be accounted for. The endless cycle of deficits, debt, and debasement does not just cause economic disturbances against a long-term growth trend; it has historically

---

[11] See, for example, Cowen's post, "Were the Bailouts a Good Idea?" on *Marginal Revolution,* August 25, 2009.

destroyed the economies of nations. This is why Adam Smith was concerned with these "juggling tricks," why Buchanan and Wagner feared the functioning of a democratic polity as a consequence of the Keynesian hegemony, and why Hayek, in his quest to articulate a monetary policy consistent with the rule of law, argued the following:

> [T]he chief source of the existing inflationary bias is the general belief that deflation, the opposite of inflation, is so much to be feared that in order to keep on the safe side, a persistent error in the direction of inflation is preferable. But, as we do not know how to keep prices completely stable and achieve stability only by correcting any small movement in either direction, the determined effort to avoid deflation at any cost must result in cumulative inflation. (1960, 330)

What seems to be overlooked is the idea that emergency economic measures and shifts in both the traditional roles of the Fed and Treasury unleash this cycle of deficits, debt, and debasement. If emergency economic measures unleash rather than constrain this cycle, then our national economic policies are placed on a path of ruin that may set the US economy back for decades. Furthermore, the problem is also that government activism to cure a crisis is often the cause of a crisis. The argument put forth by Cowen and Drezner in *The System Worked* (2014) rests upon claims that if factually true, would lead readers to arrive at similar conclusions reached by the authors. The argument developed here claims that Cowen and Drezner's argument relies on faulty empirical claims and ignores important economic theoretical perspectives. We have to look at these questions of the anatomy of a crisis and the appropriate public policy responses through a different prism if we want to avoid the governmental treadmill of deficits, debt and debasement, and the economic instability that follows.

1. World of the Second, or Third, or N-th Best

We do not live in an ideal institutional environment. Many of the propositions of basic economics are worked out against the backdrop of an unhampered market economy operating within an institutional setting of property, contract, and consent. But that is not the world within which we exist. Reasoning from the blackboard to the real world is as much an "art" as it is a "science." One way to think about the Hayekian narrative is that in making this intellectual move, the basic economic lessons worked out on the blackboard provide a necessary intellectual discipline in our artistic efforts in political economy. The devil in the analysis will always be found in the institutional details, but we can see the devil precisely because we are guided by the pure logic of choice and the situational logic of social interaction. In other words, while there may be macroeconomic problems, there are only microeconomic explanations and solutions. Whenever in doubt, return to price theory and examine the incentives, information, and innovative features of property, prices and profit/loss, and the consequences of perversion of the incentives, distortions in the information, and redirections of the lure of pure profits, and the blockages to the discipline of loss.

In the world of central banks, policy analysis cannot be pursued as if we were existing in an ideal, free banking system, where decentralized banks respond to market signals and adjust money supply to meet money demand in the most effective way possible. Instead, central bank monetary policy relies on clunky and inefficient mechanisms to try to accomplish this task of matching money supply with money demand. In this central banking world, it is much more difficult to distinguish between "good" deflation and "bad" deflation. "Good" deflation corresponds to declining prices due to productivity increases. "Bad" deflation corresponds to falling prices that can be attributed to mismanagement of money supply relative to money demand (Selgin 1997). However, due to the wide-scale acceptance of Milton Friedman's and Anna Schwartz's explanation of the Great Depression (1963), economists have fought inflation in theory, but feared deflation in practice, to such an extent that any downward market correction has been met by easy monetary policy to prevent "deflation." The Greenspan years of Fed leadership in this interpretation were far from the "perfected practice of a maestro," but instead, created an inflationary practice that produced malinvestment and coordination failures. This is a similar argument to John Taylor's *Getting Off Track* (2009), where he illustrates the consequences of deviations from the Taylor Rule and how easy credit fueled the artificial booms in housing we saw in the 2002–2007 period.

Furthermore, what is often overlooked is the long-run problem associated with continued inflation and its distortion of relative price signals. Though there is an argument to be made to "ease" the pain and suffering with emergency economic measures, it is only wise to alleviate short-term pain and suffering, provided that this does not create even worse pain and suffering down the road. In other words, at what cost are we pursuing short-term relief? If the cost is long-run disaster, then when "all things" are considered, emergency economic policies should not be pursued.

We should find policy rules that do not bend to the constant demand for short-term relief from economic adjustment at the cost of long-term economic growth and development. The recession is the correction, and if we constantly engage in policy steps to mute the signals of readjustment (and sometimes very painful readjustments), then we will not get the needed corrections. If we do not let prices guide the reallocation of capital and labor because the recalculation process is costly in the short run, then we will not find ourselves in a situation where capital and labor is allocated in a manner consistent with the underlying tastes, technology, and resource availability at any point in time. Coordination failures will be endemic to the system, and the gains from social cooperation under the division of labor that allow us to live better together despite our differences will be forgone.

The global financial crisis was not a crisis of confidence, but instead, a crisis of insolvency compounded by regime uncertainty caused by government activism. In other words, we did not have a credit lock-up in the fall of 2008 due to liquidity issues; it occurred due to regime uncertainty brought on by government decisions on who to bail out for their bad decisions. Resources needed to be reallocated and guided by price adjustment to bring production plans into alignment with consumption demands, but bailouts prevent the needed adjustments.

2. Counter-Factual and Post Hoc Ergo Propter Hoc

Markets are amazingly robust and resilient—gains from trade and gains from innovation can offset many problems caused by the government. This means that wealth creation and economic growth can take place even in the face of government obstructions—as Adam Smith ([1776] 1976, 540) argued:

The natural effort of every individual to better his own condition, when suffered to exert itself with freedom and security is so powerful a principle that it is alone, and without any assistance, not only capable of carrying on the society to wealth and prosperity, but of surmounting a hundred impertinent obstructions with which the folly of human laws too often incumbers its operations; though the effect of these obstructions is always more or less either to encroach upon its freedom, or to diminish its security.

In other words, as long as the gains from trade and innovation outweigh the problems caused by government intervention, economic progress will continue. Tomorrow's trough will be higher than today's peak, and thus, betting on the economic future of our future generations continues to make sense. But the problem arises when the harms caused by government intervention, such as restricting trade or blocking innovation, outweigh or restrict the benefits emerging from trade and innovation. If government intervention hampers the benefits of trade and innovation, then tomorrow can in fact be much worse than today.

In weighing the costs and benefits of the comparative policy space in which responses to crises are formed, and the tractability problem caused by the counter-factual, it is important to keep in mind Hayek's discussion of expediency versus principle in *Law, Legislation and Liberty*, Vol. 1 (1973). Expediency tends to defeat principle in political discourse because of the focus on direct and immediate effects—whereas principle tends to focus on indirect and long-run effects. Was it expedient to pursue the bailout? Of course. But was it a policy move that followed a working principle of public policy? Of course not. Once we include those indirect and long-run negative consequences to assess the effectiveness of the bailout on averting disaster, it is not as easy as "of course"—as Cowen, Drezner, Geithner, Paulson, and Bernanke want us to believe.

Conclusion

There can be no doubt that extraordinary measures were taken by the Fed, the Treasury, and Congress in the fall of 2008 in order to address the global financial crisis. The steps taken were extraordinary in magnitude, but they were not unique to the 2008 financial crisis. These steps were derived from the same intellectual toolkit that had been employed in government management of the economic system in the Western democracies since WWII. This time Keynesian remedies by Keynesian policymakers were just accompanied by even greater demands for power to make decisions and control economic activity.

What followed were violations of what could be termed "a rule of law" approach to public policy—the approach sketched out in the writings of F. A. Hayek (1960, 1973), Milton Friedman ([1962] 2002); Friedman and Friedman (1980), and James Buchanan (1962, 1999). These thinkers approached public policy in this way because they did not have the same idealistic "Harvey Road Presuppositions" as Keynes. But the problem is that the Harvey Road Presuppositions are not realistic. We have argued in this chapter that Keynesian solutions remedy the economic problems if we live in a world where there are sincere and capable governments with trusting citizens. But this policy space is rarely, if ever, characteristic of political and economic reality, and thus, the Keynesian policies proposed would fail to work as planned.

Discretionary policymakers outside of that unique cell must have their hands tied and be bound by rules. Failure to effectively bind them will result in further destabilization of long-term economic growth and development. This argument is simply a restatement of a broader concern raised by thinkers such as Hayek, Friedman, and Buchanan. Friedman makes this argument in *Capitalism and Freedom* ([1962] 2002, 50–51) that with respect to a central banking system:

> Any system which gives so much power and so much discretion to a few men that mistakes—excusable or not—can have such far-reaching effects is a bad system. It is a bad system to believers in freedom just because it gives a few men such power without any effective check by the body politic—this is the key political argument against an "independent" central bank. But it is a bad system even to those who set security higher than freedom. Mistakes, excusable or not, cannot be avoided in a system which disperses responsibility yet gives a few men great power, and which thereby makes important policy actions highly dependent on accidents of personality. This is the key technical argument against an "independent" bank. To paraphrase Clemenceau, money is much too serious a matter to be left to the Central Bankers.

Ben Bernanke has repeatedly said that we have learned from Milton Friedman the central lesson of his work on the Great Depression and the failure of the Fed, but he has not acknowledged or internalized Friedman's basic idea on why policymakers need to be bound by rules. Certainly, the extraordinary measures and extraordinary powers afforded him as Fed chairman during the financial crisis suggest otherwise. And once they have been granted, they are there in place.

From a Hayekian perspective, this reflects both the "Fatal Conceit" and the institutional "dynamics" that produces not a robust and resilient political economy, but a fragile and vulnerable one. Taken together, it is why the economics profession has, as Hayek argued in "The Pretence of Knowledge" (1989) made a mess of things. It is time we thought more seriously about the right institutional solutions to institutional problems.

Epilogue: What Would Hayek Do?

In 2008, at around the same time as the Global Financial Crisis was beginning to become part of the public consciousness as the ripple effects of the great recalculation were spreading and disrupting lives, my colleague Lawrence H. White published an important paper in intellectual history in the *Journal of Money, Credit and Banking*. White (2008) sought to clarify and correct some misconceptions about Hayek's views on monetary policy in the wake of a financial crisis. It had long been folklore that Hayek (and Robbins) were *Liquidationists*, a position which basically means an intellectual and policy passivity amid a deflationary death spiral. According to Keynesian economists, and especially public intellectuals influenced by Keynesian economics, the Treasury View (the idea that fiscal policy will be ineffective due to "crowding out" of private investment) combined with the Liquidationist View constituted the economic equivalent of the Flat Earth Society, and Hayek was one of its leading proponents. And if this view is given credence in the policy space, the argument continues, the consequences will be disastrous for a modern financial economy. But it was not just Keynesians that perpetuated this intellectual folklore. Milton Friedman was actually one of the strongest voices stressing this reading of Hayek. And not only did Friedman argue that Hayek and Robbins were wrong, but he argued that their views were unfortunately influential in the UK and the USA in the 1930s. As Friedman stated in a 1998 interview with Gene Epstein for *Barron's*: "I think the Austrian business-cycle theory has done the world a great deal of harm. If you go back to the 1930s, which is a key point, here you had the Austrians sitting in London, Hayek and Lionel Robbins, and saying you just have to let the bottom drop out of the world. You've just got to let it cure itself. You can't do anything about it. You will only make it worse. … I think by encouraging that kind of do-nothing policy both in Britain and the United States, they did harm."[12]

White correctly challenges Friedman. White demonstrates that Hayek's position was not "to let the depression runs its course," but one that sought to stabilize nominal income. No doubt, Hayek thought that the previous credit-induced boom required correction, and thus the recalculation of investment and production, and thus the price system must be allowed to freely adjust to effectively guide this process. But there was no virtue in Hayek's system to "secondary" deflation. To put this flippantly, the Austrians, such as Mises and Hayek, long argued that if you run over someone with your car, you do not fix that problem by putting the car in reverse. So, monetary policy during crises must achieve a fine balance between meeting the excess demand for money balances, and yet, not distorting the price system further by reinflating a new boom.

So, while Hayek did argue against "cheap-money" and public policies that would obstruct the process of adjustment, he did not advocate intellectual and policy passivity in the wake of deflationary spiral. If we simply follow the approach I am laying out for this book, the question that ultimately vexed Hayek was how the central bankers would come to know how to achieve this balancing act. Would the institutional environment of a government monopoly over the money supply provide the right epistemic institutional arrangement for decision-makers to learn how best to manage that task?

As with other examples provided throughout this book, Hayek's ideas continually evolved throughout his career. Hayek ([1924] 1999,

---

[12] See https://www.barrons.com/articles/SB903738915698011000.

Ch. 1; 1937) began his monetary research focusing on improving the technical aspects of monetary policy, including refining index data. For instance, Hayek ([1925] 1999, 115) writes that the "most urgent goal is to find the right indicator for determining at which precise moment credit restrictions should be put into effect." Largely, to Hayek, successful monetary policy could be achieved with adequate technical refinement and improved measurement techniques. While central banks might have growing pains in developing monetary policy, Hayek held they could succeed with the help of economists. While he acknowledged public choice concerns, Hayek, in his early years, fell short of incorporating them into his monetary research, outright rejecting the practicality of free banking (Hayek 1937, 77). Hayek ([1944] 2007, 72) wrote, "There were many obvious tasks, such as our handling of the monetary system ... where there could be no doubt that the governments possessed enormous powers for good and evil; and there was every reason to expect that, with a better understanding of the problems, we should some day be able to use these powers successfully."

Hayek, in a 1945 radio interview, suggested that no sensible person held that the government should not control the monetary structure (White 1999, 763). Hayek (1960, 324) argued that the spontaneous forces of the market would be unable to supply a reliable means of exchange: "It is important to be clear at the outset that this is not only politically impracticable today but would probably be undesirable if it were possible." In a footnote, Hayek (1960, 520) explained he was convinced a central bank was necessary, though he doubted it was desirable or necessary for government to have a monopoly on note issue.

Hayek (1960, 325) referred to money as a "loose joint" that could interfere with the entire self-adjustment process of the market, which rendered a central bank necessary. He supported this position with three justifications. First, disruptions in the supply of money are far more harmful to the economy than disruptions regarding other commodities. Changes in the supply of money cause ripples that gradually extend throughout the economy, altering relative prices and thereby undermining their epistemic function. Thus, Hayek argued that a monetary authority was necessary for monetary and economic stability.

Second, Hayek felt a central bank was necessary to restrict or ease credit when the spontaneous fluctuations of the market oversupplied or undersupplied it. Hayek believed this was a function that market forces could not carry out, but that monetary authorities, with enough research and experience, could.

Third, Hayek believed that although the high level of government expenditure was undesirable and it would be desirable to divorce monetary institutions as much as possible from financing fiscal policy, if government expenditures were to be high relative to national income, monetary policy needed to be coordinated with the financing of fiscal policies.

Hayek (1976a, 14) showed disillusionment with the ability of the government to manage monetary affairs with the publication in 1976 of *Choice in Currency*, an essay based off a speech he had delivered at the Geneva Gold and Monetary Conference: "I do not want to question that a very intelligent and wholly independent national or international monetary authority might do better than an international gold standard, or any other sort of automatic system. But I see not the slightest hope that any government, or any institution subject to political pressure, will ever be able to act in such a manner."

Hayek (1976a, 16) went on: "Money is certainly too dangerous an instrument to leave to the fortuitous expediency of politicians—or, it seems, economists." Hayek was beginning to realize that monetary institutions could not be designed without a proper accounting of robust political economy. Hayek (1976b) followed up this lecture in depth with *The Denationalisation of Money*. In it, Hayek expressed frustration that the government's monopoly on currency invariably leads to inflation, economic instability, undisciplined fiscal profligacy, and economic nationalism. Radically departing from his previous views, Hayek explored the theoretical possibility and political feasibility of eliminating the government's monopoly on note issue.

Hayek now held that in a contemporary democracy there are always some special-interest groups clamoring for inflationary measures to benefit themselves in the short term. Politicians, thinking not about the long-run consequences of their policies but about their next election, pursue inflationary policies, even if those policies are at odds with the general interest. These policies, along with their concomitant artificially low interest rates, lead to overinvestment. In addition, Hayek saw that government control of money supported Keynesian policies and caused a vast increase in the size of government relative to national income.

Allowing competition in currency, Hayek (1976b, 100) now argued, is the only way to eliminate these problems:

> We have always had bad money because private enterprise was not permitted to give us a better one. In a world governed by the pressure of organized interests, the important truth to keep in mind is that we cannot count on intelligence or understanding but only on sheer self-interest to give us the institutions we need. Blessed indeed will be the day when it will no longer be from the benevolence of the government that we expect good money but from the regard of the banks for their own interest.[13]

Hayek (1978) next released a second edition of *The Denationalisation of Money* that expanded upon his original arguments. Most conspicuous is the expansion of his "Monetary policy neither desirable nor possible" chapter, which now included a subchapter "The abolition of central banks," in which Hayek argued that elimination of the government's monopoly on money would require the elimination of the central bank as well as interest rate policy. Just like any other price in the market, Hayek now argued, interest rates should be allowed to develop in an unfettered market. A central bank could never match the free market's ability to adjust the interest rate continuously to the dispersed and rapidly changing factors influencing the supply of and demand for money. However, as Hayek acknowledged, even under this type of monetary regime, the government would still have some influence over interest rates through debt-financed fiscal policies; the government would just no longer have the ability to keep interest rates artificially low to support government debt. Hayek ([1981] 1999) ultimately turned his monetary research to investigating the operation of free market competition in currency.

---

[13] It is important to note that competition in currency, as Hayek understood it, differs in important ways from what modern scholars refer to as "free banking" (Selgin 2014; White 1999).

As a young researcher, Hayek had argued not only that a central bank was necessary but also desirable. Toward the end of his career, Hayek argued to the contrary that money can and should be provided through market mechanisms rather than by politically influenced and imperfectly informed monetary authorities. His earlier case had depended upon generous assumptions about the motivations and cognitive abilities of monetary authorities. When Hayek later more thoroughly thought through the epistemic institutionalism of monetary policy, and the political economy of monetary regimes, he came to the conclusion that the only robust monetary regime was the free market. As he summed up his position in an interview with Axel Leijonhufvud:

> I have come to the conclusion that it is not sufficient to deprive government of other arbitrary powers, but we can never hope to preserve a free economic order unless you take from government the monopoly of issuing money. So, this forces one back to rethink a good deal about monetary theory and I'm at the moment trying to get back to ... the question: is the stabilization of money compatible with its functions? ... I became aware that there is no chance of effectively limiting the power of government over the economy except by depriving it (of a monopoly), plus the insight that in the present political order it is impossible for government to conduct a sensible monetary policy.[14]

I view Hayek's constant learning throughout his career as one of the most attractive features of his work. He was never satisfied that he provided *the* answer, but was concerned with always probing and always exploring. He was not afraid of asking questions that might not have definitive answers, and maintained throughout his career that such an attitude was far superior to one that provided answers that could not be questioned. It is the quest in lifelong learning by an economist, political economist, and social philosopher that makes Hayek's career worth studying, and Hayekian ideas worth exploring for their evolutionary potential.

---

[14] See http://hayek.ufm.edu/index.php?title=Axel_Leijonhufvud_Part_II. See also Jordan, Jerry L. (2014). "Hayek on Sensible Monetary Policy." https://www.aier.org/article/sound-money-project/hayek-sensible-monetary-policy.

Bibliography

Akerlof, George, and Robert Shiller. 2009. *Animal Spirits: How Human Psychology Drives the Economy and Why It Matters for Global Capitalism.* Princeton: Princeton University Press.

Alesina, Alberto. 2012. Fiscal Policy after the Great Recession. *Atlantic Economic Journal* 40 (4): 429–435.

Alesina, Alberto, and Silvia Ardagna. 2010. Large Changes in Fiscal Policy: Taxes Versus Spending. *Tax Policy and the Economy* 24 (1): 35–68.

Alesina, Alberto, and Francesco Giavazzi, eds. 2013. *Financial Policy after the Financial Crisis.* Chicago: University of Chicago Press.

Aschauer, David. 1985. Fiscal Policy and Aggregate Demand. *American Economic Review* 75 (1): 117–127.

Barro, Robert J. 1979. On the Determination of the Public Debt. *Journal of Political Economy* 87 (5): 940–971.

Bernanke, Ben. 2013. *The Federal Reserve and the Financial Crisis.* Princeton: Princeton University Press.

Boettke, Peter J., and Chris Coyne. 2011. The Debt-Inflation Cycle and the Global Financial Crisis. *Global Policy* 2 (2): 184–189.

Boettke, Peter J., and Steven Horwitz. 2009. *The House that Uncle Sam Built: The Untold Story of the Great Recession of 2008.* Irvington-on-Hudson: Foundation for Economic Education.

Buchanan, James M. 1962. Predictability: The Criterion for a Monetary Constitution. In *Search of a Monetary Constitution*, ed. Leland B. Yeager, 155–183. Cambridge, MA: Harvard University Press.

———. 1987. Keynesian Follies. In *The Legacy of Keynes*, ed. D. Reese, 130–145. New York: Harper and Row.

———. 1997. *Post-Socialist Political Economy.* Cheltanham: Edward Elgar Publishing.

———. 1999. *The Collected Works of James M. Buchanan. Vol. 1, The Logical Foundations of Constitutional Liberty.* Indianapolis: Liberty Fund.

Buchanan, James M., and Richard E. Wagner. 1977. *Democracy in Deficit: The Political Legacy of Lord Keynes.* New York: Academic Press.

Bush, George W. 2010. State of the Union with Candy Crowley. *CNN Transcripts.* Retrieved: http://www.cnn.com/TRANSCRIPTS/1011/14/sotu.02.html

Cowen, Tyler. 2009. Were the Bailouts a Good Idea? *Marginal Revolution*, August 25.

Drezner, Daniel. 2014. *The System Worked: How the World Stopped Another Great Depression*. Oxford: Oxford University Press.

Feldstein, Martin. 1982. Government Deficits and Aggregate Demand. *Journal of Monetary Economics* 9 (1): 1–20.

Friedman, Milton. [1962] 2002. *Capitalism and Freedom*. Chicago: University of Chicago Press.

Friedman, Milton, and Rose Friedman. 1980. *Free to Choose: A Personal Statement*. New York: Harcourt.

Friedman, Milton, and Anna Jacobson Schwartz. 1963. *A Monetary History of the United States 1867–1960*. Princeton: Princeton University Press.

Geithner, Timothy. 2014. *Stress Test: Reflections on Financial Crises*. New York: Crown Publishers.

Glaeser, Edward, Simon Johnson, and Andrei Shleifer. 2001. Coase vs. the Coasians. *Quarterly Journal of Economics* 116 (3): 853–899.

Graham, Fred C. 1993. Fiscal Policy and Aggregate Demand: Comment. *American Economic Review* 83 (3): 659–666.

Hayek, F.A. [1924] 1999. A Survey of Recent American Writing: Stabilization Problems in Gold Exchange Standard Countries. In Good Money, Part I: *The Collected Works of F. A. Hayek,* ed. Stephen Kresge. Indianapolis: Liberty Fund Inc.

———. [1925] 1999. Monetary Policy in the United States after the Recovery from the Crisis of 1920. In Good Money, Part I: *The Collected Works of F. A. Hayek,* ed. Stephen Kresge. Indianapolis: Liberty Fund Inc.

———. 1937. *Monetary Nationalism and International Stability*. London: Longman, Green.

———. [1944] 2007. *The Road to Serfdom*. Ed. Bruce Caldwell. Chicago: The University of Chicago Press.

———. 1960. *The Constitution of Liberty*. Chicago: University of Chicago Press.

———. 1973. *Law, Legislation, and Liberty, Vol.1: Rules and Order*. Chicago: University of Chicago Press.

———. 1976a. *Choice in Currency*. London: Institute for Economic Affairs.

———. 1976b. *Denationalisation of Money*. Great Britain: The Institute of Economic Affairs.

———. 1978. *Denationalisation of Money: The Argument Refined*. London: The Institute of Economic Affairs.

———. [1978] 1983. *Interviewed by Axel Leijonhufvud*. Los Angeles: University of California. https://archive.org/details/nobelprizewinnin00haye

———. [1981] 1999. The Future Unit of Value. In *Good Money Part II: The Collected Works of F. A. Hayek*, ed. Stephen Kresge, 238–252. Indianapolis: Liberty Fund Inc.

———. 1989. The Pretence of Knowledge. *American Economic Review* 79 (6): 3–7.

Hicks, John R. 1967. *Critical Essays in Monetary Theory*. Oxford: Clarendon Press.

Keynes, John M. [1926] 2010. The End of Laissez-Faire. In *Essays in Persuasion*, 272–294. London: Palgrave Macmillan.

———. [1933] 1972. Thomas Robert Malthus: The First of the Cambridge Economists. In *The Collected Writings of John Maynard Keynes*, vol. 10, 71–103. London: Macmillan for the Royal Economic Society.

Koppl, Roger. 2002. *Big Players and the Economic Theory of Expectations*. London: Palgrave Macmillan.

———. 2014. *From Crisis to Confidence: Macroeconomics after the Crash*. London: Institute for Economic Affairs.

Kormendi, Roger C., and Philip Meguire. 1990. Government Debt, Government Spending, and Private Sector Behavior: Reply and Update. *American Economic Review* 80 (3): 604–617.

Kotlikoff, Laurence, and Scott Burns. 2005. *The Coming Generational Storm*. Cambridge, MA: MIT Press.

———. 2012. *The Clash of Generations: Saving Ourselves, Our Kids and Our Economy*. Cambridge, MA: MIT Press.

Krugman, Paul. 2010. When Zombies Win. *New York Times*, December 19. Retrieved: http://www.nytimes.com/2010/12/20/opinion/20krugman.html

Maclachlan, Fiona C. 1999. The Ricardo-Malthus Debate on Underconsumption: A Case Study in Economic Conversation. *History of Political Economy* 31 (3): 563–574.

Paulson, Henry M. 2010. *On the Brink: Inside the Race to Stop the Collapse of the Global Financial System*. New York: Hachette Book Group.

Roosevelt, Franklin D. [1933] 1938. Inaugural Address, March 4, 1933. In *The Public Papers of Franklin D. Roosevelt, Volume Two: The Year of Crisis*, ed. Samuel Rosenman, 11–16. New York: Random House.

Say, Jean Baptiste. 1821. *Letters to Mr. Malthus*. London: Sherwood, Neely, and Jones.

Selgin, George. 1997. *Less than Zero: The Case for a Falling Price Level in a Growing Economy*. London: The Institute of Economic Affairs.

Selgin, George A. 2014. Operation Twist-the-Truth: How the Federal Reserve Misrepresents Its History and Performance. *Cato Journal* 34 (2): 229–263.

Smith, Adam. [1776] 1976. *An Inquiry into the Nature and the Causes of the Wealth of Nations.* Chicago: University of Chicago Press.

Stringham, Edward P., Peter J. Boettke, and J.R. Clark. 2008. Are Regulations the Answer for Emerging Stock Markets? Evidence from the Czech Republic and Poland. *The Quarterly Review of Economics and Finance* 48 (3, August): 541–566.

Taylor, John B. 2009. *Getting Off Track: How Government Actions and Interventions Caused, Prolonged, and Worsened the Financial Crisis.* Stanford: Hoover Institute Press.

Wagner, Richard E. 2012. *Deficits, Debt, and Democracy: Wrestling with Tragedy on the Fiscal Commons.* Northampton: Edward Elgar.

White, Lawrence H. 1999. Why Didn't Hayek Favor Laissez Faire in Banking? *History of Political Economy* 31 (4): 753–769.

———. 2008. Did Hayek and Robbins Deepen the Great Depression? *Journal of Money, Credit and Banking* 40 (4): 751–768.

———. 2012. *Clash of Economic Ideas: The Great Policy Debates and Experiments of the Last Hundred Years.* Cambridge, MA: Cambridge University Press.

Zingales, Luigi. 2009a. Economist Debates: Keynesian Principles. *The Economist*, March 10. Retrieved: http://www.economist.com/debate/days/view/276

———. 2009b. Economist Debates: Keynesian Principles. *The Economist*, March 13. Retrieved: http://www.economist.com/debate/days/view/281

4

Hayek on Market Theory and the Price System

Introduction

Perhaps the principal contribution for which Hayek is most widely known is his insight that the central economic problem of society concerns the use of dispersed knowledge under alternative institutional arrangements—especially as presented in his 1945 article, "The Use of Knowledge in Society."[1] During the second half of the twentieth century, mainstream economists would continue to cite Hayek—and his 1945 article in particular—as an important influence on their work, especially *information economics*. This makes Hayek an especially interesting figure in the history of economic thought for another less obvious, but related, reason. For economists and scholars who have studied Hayek's work seriously, there is a persistent sense that Hayek is cited but not understood by many of the mainstream formalist economists who so often claim to have

---

[1] See Appendix B, where Hayek's "Use of Knowledge in Society" paper is listed among the 20 most influential papers published in the *American Economic Review* in its first 100 years. Also note that according to Google Scholar at the time of this writing, that article has over 15,000 citations. To put this in perspective, Paul Samuelson's "Pure Theory of Public Expenditure" garners slightly over 9000, Milton Friedman's "The Role of Monetary Policy" has just over 8000, Kenneth Arrow's "The Economic Implications of Learning by Doing" almost 14,000, but Ronald Coase's "The Problem of Social Cost" has over 32,000 citations.

© The Author(s) 2018
Peter J. Boettke, *F. A. Hayek*, Great Thinkers in Economics,
https://doi.org/10.1057/978-1-137-41160-0_4

grappled with Hayek's ideas. Indeed, it is the apparent failure of mainstream economics to appropriate the insights of Hayek on economics and knowledge into its formalist technical apparatus, despite repeated claims to the contrary, that is most problematic and has proved a detriment in advancing our scientific understanding of the role that prices play in the market process.

A fundamental theme in Hayek's thought, I have argued, is the "coordination problem"—the problem of how "the spontaneous interaction of a number of people, each possessing only bits of knowledge, brings about a state of affairs…which could be brought about by deliberate direction only by somebody who possessed the combined knowledge of all those individuals" (Hayek [1937] 1948, 50–1). The roots of this theme can be seen in Hayek's arguments in the socialist calculation debate during the 1930s, while the difficulties he perceived in effectively winning that debate provided him with an additional impetus to develop his thoughts with greater clarity and force (see Caldwell 1988, 1997; Boettke 1997). Hayek's most important, concise, and articulate expressions of his major insights from working on these problems are undoubtedly "Economics and Knowledge" ([1937] 1948) and "The Use of Knowledge in Society" ([1945] 1948). Though Hayek's thought continued to evolve over the course of his sprawling intellectual career, these particular essays serve as useful foils for examining why Hayek's economics has resisted formalism so strongly, and thus far evaded (successful) appropriation by mainstream economics.

Information economics is the most prominent example of how modern economic theorists have typically interpreted Hayek's ideas and attempted to translate them into a form that could be easily digested and incorporated by mainstream economics. As an input into the development of the information economics in the 1960s and 1970s, Hayek ([1945] 1948) became seen as the most concise statement of Hayek's ideas about economics and information. Information economists have interpreted Hayek (1945) as arguing that information is initially dispersed as incomplete bits across the various members of society, but the central economic problem facing society was how to design mechanisms for the optimal aggregation, communication, and use of that dispersed information. Understood this way, the price system in a free market economy is an efficient, low-cost mechanism for achieving the optimal solution to that problem (Hurwicz 1969; Grossman and Stiglitz 1976; Myerson 2009). From here, information economists sought to examine the "Hayek hypothesis" in a more rigorous fashion than Hayek himself had done, and constructed models that purported to formalize the essential aspects of Hayek's argument. Using formal models as the analytical benchmark, the information economists produced numerous articles alleging to refute "Hayek's hypothesis" of the informational efficiency of the price system, and later challenged nearly all claims of the superior welfare properties of free markets, including the very notion of an "invisible hand" (Stiglitz 2000, 2002).[2]

Ignoring these normative considerations, there are serious reasons to doubt these formal theorists have even adequately grasped the central ideas of Hayek's economics to begin with, let alone refuted his specific analytical and empirical claims. First, as numerous economists have pointed out over the years, Hayek presented his theories through "informal" arguments that favored verbal—over mathematical—logic, which was not unusual for professional economists of the time. As economics became an increasingly mathematical discipline in the mid-twentieth century, verbal theorizing was seen as loose, non-rigorous, and at best simply considered an input into rigorous, theorizing. That there would arise errors in "translating" verbal arguments into formal theory is perhaps inevitable. But we must acknowledge that there are aspects of Hayek that cannot be adequately formalized, and perhaps Hayek's crucial insights would be lost in this translation effort.[3] My colleague Richard

---

[2] Contrast this with Vernon Smith's own examination of the "Hayek hypothesis" with the aid of his market experiments over the course of decades. As Smith (2007, xvi) argued: "Experiments constituted a substitute for the missing dynamic process analysis that had not been part of the standard equilibrium tool kit, a kit that had focused only on what might be the equilibrium shadow cast ahead by any such process." And, as he argued more recently, the strict requirements in the *information space* demanded in most mechanism design models are met repeatedly in an emergent manner in the economic science labs in these market experiments by undergraduate students simply engaged in trading behavior (see Smith 2015). Critical to our discussion, Smith's experiments illustrate a critical Hayekian point that the optimality conditions of the market are not derived from assumptions upon which the analysis proceeds but as by-products from the analysis of the process of market transactions.

[3] What is said about Hayek's ideas not being able to be formalized can equally be said of Keynes's *General Theory*. As Antony Thirlwall (2015, 203) argues, "many economists never read Keynes in the original but only textbook versions, so they never know the subtleties that cannot be mathema-

Wagner (2016, 11–15) distinguishes between demonstrative reasoning and plausible reasoning in political economy, and Hayek's approach would most definitely fit his depiction of plausible reasoning—but so would most of the critical thinkers in the history of our discipline from Adam Smith to Hayek. Hayek had an understanding of the market process that could be considered an "appreciative" theory in line with Nelson and Winter's (1982) categorization of theoretical economics. The value of Hayek's appreciative theory, as opposed to the formal theory of textbook economics, is that it captures the dynamism of the market process and ultimately brings *meaning* and *intelligibility* to social phenomena, which formalism cannot match or replicate.

However, the span of Hayek's theoretical insights reaches much broader and deeper than the fraction of his published work, which might be fairly classified as "appreciative" theory. Hence, a significant causal factor in the failure of formal theorists to appropriate Hayek is the widespread tendency among mainstream economists to treat Hayek as *just* an "appreciative," informal theorist (see Caldwell 1997; Stiglitz 2000, 1444, 1446; Myerson 2009). Rather than being completely unaware of, or unconcerned with, the technical apparatus of formalist economics, Hayek thought deeply about the methodological and epistemological foundations of economic theory, especially formal equilibrium-based theory, which is apparent even in his work from the 1930s while he was still seen as an influential and active economist.

In highlighting several specific methodological and epistemological problems (Hayek 1937), we argue that Hayek predicted many of the challenges of formal economic theory—especially, information economics, game theory, and equilibrium-based analysis more generally—that would only be grappled with decades after his initial arguments (see Samuelson 2004; Foss 2000; Vaughn 1999). Thus, the failure is not that Hayek's informal theory proved too "fuzzy" (Caldwell 1997, 1857–8, 1877) to be formalized, but that formal theory was (is?) fundamentally incapable of capturing Hayek's economics due to the technical limitations inherent to formalism itself, which Hayek accurately described.

---

tised (the Harvard economist, Gregory Mankiw, once said that he lost interest in Keynesian economics when he realised he couldn't put it into maths!)"

Hayek on Economics and Knowledge, and Appreciative Theory

Before we can demonstrate that mainstream economics has persistently failed to appropriate the ideas of Hayek, it will be helpful to restate what those ideas were.[4] We intend primarily to construct a concise statement of Hayek's ideas on economics and knowledge—that is, a *Hayekian framework*—that encapsulates his central insights and enables us to examine why such a framework has evaded the formalism of mainstream economics.

In "Economics and Knowledge," Hayek ([1937] 1948) articulated a number of ideas that would become major themes in his economic thought, as well as his broader social theory. He argued that economic analysis has empirical relevance and conveys understanding about the real world only insofar as it contains explicit assumptions or propositions about how knowledge is acquired, communicated, and used by individuals within the model. In doing so, Hayek discussed the limits of formal equilibrium analysis and criticized the preoccupation with equilibrium analysis for distracting economists from the fundamental problems of economics. At the core of Hayek's criticism was the issue of the role of assumptions and propositions about *knowledge* in formal economic theory, especially as applied to equilibrium analysis. We will not make much progress, Hayek argued, if in our analysis, we continually "fall in effect back on the assumption that everybody knows everything and so evade the solution to the problem" ([1937] 1948, 51). We must, instead of assuming, explain how, and by what process, economic actors will acquire the necessary knowledge to coordinate their plans with one another to realize the mutual benefits of social cooperation under the division of labor.

---

[4] As there already exist a number of apt intellectual histories on the development of Hayek's economic thought, including on the "epistemic turn" in his work, we will not be directly concerned with this side of scholarship. Caldwell (1988) examines the history of the intellectual "transformation" of Hayek from technical economist to a wide-ranging social theorist concerned with political theory, law, and sociology, among other subjects. Boettke et al. (2010) treat the "epistemic turn" in Hayek's thought from the perspective of his involvement with the socialist calculation debate. Boettke (2002) discusses the "epistemic turn" within Austrian economics more generally, and identifies this emphasis on the epistemic-cognitive aspects of the market process as the defining characteristic of the modern Austrian school.

As has been emphasized, in the narrative being constructed here, Hayek was concerned with the epistemic properties of alternative institutional arrangements. He did not, as we saw in our discussion of the socialist calculation debate, deny the incentive properties of institutions. But his emphasis was on how actors within the process are going to learn what they need to learn and when they need to learn it so they can adjust their plans to those of others who are also continually learning and in such a manner that the coordination of economic activities through time is achieved. Equilibrium analysis did much to cloud, rather than clarify, this *epistemic institutionalist* conceptual task.

To address this problem, Hayek set about examining the concept of *equilibrium* and reframing it on more consistently subjectivist footing in terms of the *subjective* knowledge or "data" held by individual actors, the plans and actions based upon this data, and the *objective facts* external to the individual. In fact, as Hayek emphasized, all claims about *equilibrium* necessarily entail claims about the *knowledge* of those individuals' plans and actions—namely, that the individuals have correct foresight or expectations about the objective facts relevant to their situation. For Hayek, then, equilibrium refers to the mutual compatibility of plans between individuals and their external circumstances through time, such that the *subjective data* corresponds with external, *objective facts* ([1937] 1948, 44–5). In other words, "equilibrium" in a Hayekian sense can be thought of as intertemporal plan coordination, where individuals are able to successfully achieve their ends while dovetailing their plans and actions with those of others (also on this point, see Vaughn 1999).

Though often critical of the equilibrium construct, Hayek nevertheless considered the apparent *tendency toward equilibrium* of the market process as the foundation for—and most important problem of—economic theorizing. The proposition that such a tendency exists basically means "that, under certain conditions, the knowledge and intentions of the different members of society are supposed to come more and more into agreement" or, "that the expectations of the people and particularly of the entrepreneurs will become more and more correct" ([1937] 1948, 44–5, 51). Indeed, from here, we can much more clearly follow Hayek's thought when he states that it is "only by this assertion that such a tendency exists that economics ceases to be an exercise in pure logic and becomes an empirical science" (Hayek [1937] 1948, 44).

This point is significant for understanding Hayek's argument that the "really central problem of economics as a social science" is the *coordination problem* that arises from the problem of the *division of knowledge* (Hayek [1937] 1948, 50). That is, the problem of "how the spontaneous interaction of a number of people, each possessing only bits of knowledge, brings about a state of affairs in which prices correspond to costs, etc., and which could be brought about by deliberate direction only by somebody who possessed the combined knowledge of all those individuals" (Hayek [1937] 1948, 50–1). Or, as he would later describe, "it is a problem of the utilization of knowledge which is not given to anyone in its totality" (Hayek [1945] 1948, 78). As a substantive matter, the coordination problem entails the empirical proposition that there indeed exists a tendency toward equilibrium or coordination within the market economy, which, as we have seen, necessarily implies additional propositions about the knowledge of market actors becoming more "correct" ([1937] 1948, 44–5, 51). The analytical challenge then becomes examining and articulating "(a) the *conditions* under which this tendency is supposed to exist and (b) the nature of the *process* by which individual knowledge is changed" ([1937] 1948, 45, emphasis original).

Formal equilibrium analysis, however, did not directly address the problem of "how the 'data' of the different individuals on which they base their plans are adjusted to the objective facts of their environment (which includes the actions of the other people)" (Hayek [1946a, b] 1948, 93). Rather, it "starts from the assumption that people's *knowledge* corresponds with the objective *facts* of the situation, [and] systematically leaves out what is our main task to explain" (Hayek [1945] 1948, 91, emphasis original). Hayek traced the source of this confusion, in part, to the uncritical equivocation of formal economic theory, or the "Pure Logic of Choice," with equilibrium.

Insofar as the Pure Logic of Choice describes an isolated individual, who prefers more utility rather than less, taking their *subjective knowledge* as its relevant "data," it follows tautologically that their actions and plans are necessarily in equilibrium: individuals acting independently will "maximize" their utility. However, in moving from the individual equilibrium of an isolated actor to societal equilibrium of multiple persons interacting with each other, the meaning of equilibrium—and the nature of the "data" to which it refers—is fundamentally transformed. The data which is assumed to be given to individuals in formal equilibrium analysis corresponds directly to the objective facts, which leads to equilibrium by definition ([1937] 1948, 36–9). But even more fundamentally, Hayek argued, neither the Pure Logic of Choice nor formal equilibrium analysis alone can illuminate the causal relationship between the subjective knowledge of the individual and their experience of the external, objective facts ([1937] 1948, 44–8). This means that pure economic theory, especially equilibrium analysis, is incapable of shedding light on the *process* by which the subjective knowledge is sufficiently adjusted so as to bring about intertemporal plan coordination.

In order to do just that, it becomes necessary to introduce into economic analysis additional propositions, or subsidiary hypotheses, about knowledge, such as how it is acquired and communicated, how learning occurs, what kind of knowledge is "relevant," and how much of it must individuals possess for equilibrium. Hayek expressed very clearly his dissatisfaction with how it had "become customary among economists to stress only the need of knowledge of prices"—which is notable in light of later formalist treatments of Hayek ([1937] 1948, 51). In contrast to this myopia, Hayek argued that "price expectations and even the knowledge of current prices are only a very small section of the problem of knowledge as I see it. The wider aspect of the problem of knowledge with which I am concerned is the knowledge of the basic fact of how the different commodities can be obtained and used, and under what conditions they are actually obtained and used" ([1937] 1948, 51). In other words, for there to arise a tendency toward equilibrium (or coordination), individuals must possess some additional knowledge about the underlying "things" being exchanged, in order for the prices of those "things" to actually reflect the alternative uses to which they might be put.

In a sense, "Economics and Knowledge" plays a pivotal role in setting the stage for an alternative "Hayekian" framework for economic analysis. First, Hayek reframed the central question of economics as the *coordination problem* (and *knowledge problem*). Next, he demonstrated that the standard tool of pure economic theory—formal equilibrium analysis—is inadequate for addressing this problem. Lastly, he outlined specific analytical and substantive elements of the problem that economic analysis would have to address, and suggested a few ideas for how to proceed to analyze the problem.

Thus, we can see "The Use of Knowledge in Society" ([1945] 1948) as an elaboration of these themes, where Hayek proposes a few possible solutions and hypotheses in response to the questions and problems he first posed in "Economics and Knowledge," and which he continued to explore in further work, including "The Meaning of Competition" ([1946b] 1948) and "Competition as a Discovery Procedure" ([1968] 2002). However, in contrast to "Economics and Knowledge," which largely focused on methodological and epistemological issues of positive economics, "The Use of Knowledge in Society" was directly concerned with the policy debate over the feasibility (and desirability) of central planning. Despite this difference, "The Use of Knowledge in Society" is an essentially positive economic argument based on comparative institutional analysis of central planning relative to the market process, and as such, contains clear analytical propositions and empirical hypotheses. Hayek famously argued that the knowledge that is relevant to the solution to the economic problem is never given to a single mind, but is widely dispersed throughout society as bits of incomplete, subjective knowledge, much of it tacit in nature and only pertaining to the particular time and place ([1945] 1948). In light of the relevant knowledge being widely dispersed, incomplete, subjective, and of a particular time and place by nature, there are then a few further problems which must be addressed: how much knowledge must each individual possess such that equilibrium (coordination)—or a tendency toward it—is possible, and what the role is for institutions in the coordination problem? (Hayek [1937] 1948, 50–5).

In response to the theoretical and empirical problems he had previously discussed, Hayek constructed and proposed what was essentially an institutional solution. Most notably, Hayek argued that the price system acts as a "mechanism for communicating information" about the relative scarcities of resources, and is crucial in a world of dispersed, imperfect knowledge for solving the "problem of how to secure the best use of resources known to any of the members of society, for ends whose relative importance only these individuals know" ([1945] 1948, 78, 86). Therefore, "in a system in which the knowledge of the relevant facts is dispersed among many people, prices can act to co-ordinate the separate actions of different people in the same way as subjective values help the individual to co-ordinate the parts of his plan" ([1945] 1948, 85).

Within the *institutional context* of a market economy, individuals are free to pursue their desired ends while the price system extends additional information as they need to spontaneously dovetail their plans and actions with those of others (Hayek [1945] 1948, 79). In particular, where price *changes* lead individuals to spontaneously adjust their plans in the right *direction*, it is notable, then, that Hayek sees the value of prices as encouraging actors to make the proper *qualitative* changes to their plans (84–6). However, the most important characteristic of the price system, Hayek explained, "is the economy of knowledge with which it operates, or how little the individual participants need to know in order to be able to take the right action" (86). That is, prices enable individuals to act *as if they possessed more knowledge than a single mind could grasp without the use of the price system*—in this sense, prices serve as "knowledge surrogates" (emphasis added, Thomsen 1992, 41, 43–5).

As we have seen, Hayek argued that knowledge of prices alone is not sufficient for market participants to spontaneously coordinate their plans. They must also have some knowledge of the objective facts about the "things," such as their uses or substitutes. The need for knowledge of the facts about "things," other than their relative scarcities, necessitates an additional mechanism for acquiring and communicating knowledge, besides the price system (alone) which principally conveys information about scarcity. Therefore, Hayek proposed that competition could be considered as a procedure for *discovering* these facts of a broader nature—such as knowledge of what goods and services consumers demand, the lowest cost production technologies, and the conditions of supply and demand for a market more generally—which the theory of competitive equilibrium assumes are data ([1946b] 1948, 95–6; [1968] 2002). That there exists the possibility of a *discovery* of facts, to which individuals were previously *unaware*, implies the existence of sheer (or "radical") ignorance and genuine uncertainty, which is a highly significant element of Hayek's economic thought and marks an important departure from mainstream economics. Indeed, because of these strict epistemic limits on the knowledge that any particular individual can possess, it is only through trial and error experimentation within the competitive market process that alternative courses of action can be meaningfully evaluated as "success" or "failure" ([1946b] 1948, 100; [1968] 2000). Hence, Hayek wrote that the "solution of the economic problem of society is in this respect always a voyage of exploration into the unknown, an attempt to discover new ways of doing things better than they have been done before" ([1946b] 1948, 101).

In some sense, we might even see competition as the fundamental epistemic process that Hayek posits as a solution to the coordination problem. Indeed, Hayek appears to suggest competition is perhaps the most important element of the solution to the problem of adjusting the subjective knowledge of individuals to the objective facts: "Competition is essentially a process of the formation of opinion: by spreading information, it creates that unity and coherence of the economic system which we presuppose when we think of it as one market... It is thus a process which involves a continuous change in the data and whose significance must therefore be completely missed by any theory which treats these data as constant" ([1946b] 1948, 106). But it must be emphasized that competition is an *institutionally-contingent* social process that requires the support of private property rights and a functioning price system to enable profit-loss calculation, as well as a broader structure of liberal institutions, limited government, and rule of law, which foster innovation and experimentation.

Finally, it is important to note that Hayek *did not* claim that the market process or the price system were "optimal" or "perfect" in any sense, especially relative to the idealized optimality properties of formal welfare economics. The market process may never reach a point on the surface of the Pareto frontier, or even equilibrium. Likewise, the price system too is likely never "perfect" in an informational or allocative sense compared to the efficiency properties of the "social planner solution" derived from a set of simultaneous equations. Yet, Hayek argued that all of this is largely irrelevant to any problems of real-world economic phenomena—the standard cannot be a situation unattainable by any known or logical means. Rather, real-world competition and market processes can only be evaluated relative to the outcome (or patterned order) that would realistically emerge without free competition (Hayek [1946b] 1948, 100).

Nevertheless, through this line of economic analysis, Hayek concluded that the unhampered market process, compared to its relevant alternatives, is the institutional framework most likely to ever approach such ideals (Hayek [1968] 2002).

The Complacency of His Neoclassical Peers of the 1940s

The 1930s have been described by G. L. S. Shackle and others as the "years of high theory" (1967). In retrospect, the entire interwar years in Europe was a period of creativity in economic theory, and not just with respect to the Keynesian revolution, but also the development of imperfect competition (Robinson), monopolistic competition (Chamberlin), the continued refinement of the Walrasian model of general competitive equilibrium, and welfare economics.[5] Yet Hayek, in the context of describing how prices continually adapt and guide adjustments by market participants, uses the term "marvel" to depict the functioning of the price system ([1945] 1948, 87). In fact, he says he chose the word deliberately to "shock the reader" out of their complacency. Remember, this article was written for the *American Economic Review*, and his readers were his professional scientific peers. He was not trying to explain the functioning of prices to a popular audience. Hayek was trying to *remind* professional scientific economists what their discipline taught.

In the early 1930s, Hayek firmly believed that a modern trained economist would understand market theory and the price system, and the role of private property and the freedom of contract in allocating resources efficiently and incentivizing innovation and growth through profit opportunities. In short, the trained neoclassical economist would know and appreciate the functioning of the market economy just as their classical political economy predecessors, but with more technical sophistication. The burden of the argument, in other words, would be on those

---

[5] The development of General Competitive Equilibrium and the Fundamental Welfare Theorems would be more pronounced in the late 1940–1960 period, but the roots were laid during this earlier period and the nascent versions of these developments can already been seen in both the Walrasian and Marshallian models of the 1920s and 1930s.

who wanted to suspend or suppress the market system to justify their arguments for planning or interventionism. The public may have been ignorant of the functioning of the price system, but professionally trained economists were not.

So how surprised Hayek must have been when, in the 1930s, the most sophisticated arguments for planning and interventionism came not from critics of neoclassical economics as they had previously in the hands of German Historicists and American Institutionalists, but from the best and the brightest within neoclassical literature—many of whom were Hayek's own students and colleagues at the LSE. In retrospect, many commentators assert that classical and neoclassical economists were never as "market fundamentalist" as Hayek and others may have thought. Concerns with inefficiency, instability, and injustice in an economic system are indeed old and a common theme throughout the eighteenth, nineteenth and into the twentieth centuries. At the time period we are discussing, the USA and the UK were suffering through the Great Depression, and the threats of right-wing and left-wing authoritarianism were becoming widely recognized by those in Western democratic countries. But still, was Hayek so wrong in his assessment that his professional peers needed to be shocked out of their complacency about the role of prices and the functioning of the market process?

I do not think so. Based on an examination of some passages from Marshall's *Principles,* it appears that Hayek was actually right about what was understood as common knowledge among trained economists of that earlier neoclassical period. If this declaration is true, then so is the declaration that the transformation of methodological and analytical nature of economic theorizing during the 1930s and 1940s resulted in knowledge lost. When Hayek first responded to the market socialists about the price system and the problem of economic calculation under central planning, he pointed out that "it has never been denied by anybody, except socialists, that these formal principles *ought* to apply to a socialist society, and the question raised by Mises and others was not whether they ought to apply but whether they could in practice be applied in the absence of a market" ([1940] 1948, 183, emphasis original). This is a critical point, because the price system works by constantly adjusting to changing circumstances so individuals can realize productive specialization and peaceful social cooperation. If the price system does its work to the end, the optimality conditions that follow from all gains from trade being exhausted and all least cost technologies being discovered would result. The optimality conditions of the competitive market: $P = MC$, min AC, the equi-marginal principle, and so on, *all* are by-products of the entrepreneurial market process, and *not* assumptions to be made prior to analysis. These optimality conditions emerge within the market process and are realized only after all the economic forces have done their work. They do not characterize the situation while economic forces are *at work*.

.As Hayek pointed out in "The Use of Knowledge in Society," the problems that economic theory must address "arise always and only in consequence of change" ([1945] 1948, 82). If our tools of reasoning preclude our studying the processes of adaptation and adjustment to changing circumstances, then it is our tools that are failing us. "Any approach, such as that of much of mathematical economics with its simultaneous equations, which in effect starts from the assumption that people's *knowledge* corresponds with the objective *facts* of the situation, systematically leaves out what is our main task to explain" (emphasis original [1945] 1948, 91). That task that must be explained, Hayek had stressed, was the continuous process by which the dispersed knowledge of time and place in the minds of diverse participants is communicated and acquired by other participants so they can coordinate their plans with one another and realize the gains from trade and innovation. Economic theory from the classics to the neoclassicals taught the basic lesson about the functional significance of property, prices and profit/loss in alerting, cajoling, and disciplining participants in the market. As Hayek put it in "Individualism: True and False," the chief concern of these writers was "to find a set of institutions by which man could be induced by his own choice and from motives which determined his ordinary conduct, to contribute as much as possible to the need of all others; and their discovery was that the system of private property did provide such inducements to a much greater extent than had yet been understood" ([1946a 1948], 12–13).

Though this last quote was mainly directed at summarizing the project of Adam Smith and his contemporaries, it can also be seen in the teaching of *all* the classical economists and early neoclassical economics from Smith to Alfred Marshall. Marshall was the dominating figure in British economic thought and teaching from the 1890s to the 1930s. His direct students held over half of all the chaired professorships in economics in the UK and the students of his students filled almost every teaching post throughout the UK. His teaching spread through the USA through the work of Jacob Viner and Frank Knight as well, and his textbook was used almost until the mid-twentieth century. I am working from the eighth edition, and I have not checked earlier editions for consistency, but the quotes are extremely telling for the point Hayek was making.

On the first page of Book V (Marshall [1890] 1920, 269), which is a discussion of those principles of price theory that Hayek mentioned above, we are told that while the equilibrium position provides the "theoretical backbone," the general relations of demand and supply are "connected with the adjustment of price." In the subsequent pages, we will learn from Marshall about the logic of the law of one price, as well as the principle of substitution which in turn leads to the equi-marginal principle. But we also learn that "It is *not* indeed necessary for our argument that any dealers should have a thorough knowledge of the circumstances of the market (emphasis added, 278). The adaptations and adjustments on the market guided by relative prices do not require any concept of perfect knowledge. These adaptations and adjustments bring" into play forces "that steer the market process in the same way that" if a stone hanging by a string is displaced from its equilibrium position, the force of gravity will at once tend to bring it back to its equilibrium position. "But," Marshall continues, "in real life such oscillations are seldom as rhythmical as those of a stone hanging freely from a string; the comparison would be more exact if the string were supposed to hand in the troubled waters of a mill-race, whose stream was at one time allowed to flow freely, and at another partially cut off. Nor are these complexities sufficient to illustrate all the disturbances with which the economist and the merchant alike are forced to concern themselves" (288).

Consider the plight of businessmen in their commercial ventures, according to Marshall, "who bears the penalty of any error in his judgment; and who, if his judgment is approved by events, benefits the community as well as himself. Let him be considering whether to erect dwelling houses, or warehouses, or factories, or shops" (297). He must estimate the costs and he must anticipate what price he may be able to charge. "He brings this estimate of cost into relation with the estimate of the price he is likely to get for any given building together with its site. If he can find no case in which the demand price exceeds his outlays by enough to yield him a good profit, with some margin against risks, he may remain idle" (298).

Indeed, it is "the alert business man" (ibid.) that must deploy his judgment to push investments in this or that direction. Marshall stresses, just as Mises and Hayek did, that he must engage in rational economic calculation. There must be a mechanism in place that can sort between the array of technologically feasible production projects for those that are economically viable. And Marshall tells us, the alert business man "never assumes that roundabout methods will be remunerative in the long run. But, he is always on the look out for roundabout methods that promise to be more effective in proportion to their cost than direct methods; and he adopts the best of them, if it lies within his means" (299).

Marshall, just like the Austrian economists, was concerned with the coordination of economic activities through time, and thus, the market processes that guide investment, production, exchange, and consumption decisions. Both sides are, as Marshall says, "calculating" to discover, to learn, to strive for the least cost and most beneficial path to achieve their ends. It is a *process* of continuous adaptation and adjustment to changing circumstances and how this process works is through the movement of prices. Economic forces *at work* are studied by looking at price adjustments that are made on both sides of the market, and how those adjustments bring about the balancing of supply and demand and the tendency toward equilibrium. As my colleague Richard Wagner likes to say, equilibrium propositions are in the background, but the processes of adjustment are in the foreground of analysis among classical political economists and early neoclassical economists. In the 1930s, this intellectual orientation began to switch, and those educated after this shift find it often impossible to capture this earlier dynamic adjustment economics and what it means for scientific inquiry.[6]

---

[6] Compare Gary Becker's discussion in *Economic Theory* with Hayek's discussion in "The Use of Knowledge in Society" and the learning in the market that Hayek describes, and how the constant adjustment to changing circumstances is aided by the very fact that we can rely on "B stepping in at once when A fails to deliver" ([1945] 1948, 83). Becker, as well, argues that: "The stabilizing

Hayek was caught by surprise in the 1930s and 1940s as neoclassical arguments were deployed not to explain the operation of the economic system, but to redesign it, and even to comprehensively plan it. His subsequent efforts can be seen, as I have been arguing, as attempts to get economics back on track by recapturing the Smithian political economy project and translating the Austrian School's technical refinement of the classical system. Knowledge was definitely lost, and it had to be regained. None of the insights Hayek had about the coordination of economic activities through time guided by the price system relied on perfectly rational actors with full and complete information interacting in zero transaction cost environments. The adjustments in the market, he was quick to add, are never "perfect," but they are ongoing. As Hayek stressed, the model of general competitive equilibrium made economists "blind to the true function of the price mechanism and led us to apply rather misleading standards in judging its efficiency" ([1945] 1948, 87). It is the intellectual complacency brought on by this blindness that Hayek sought to shock his peers out of in his discussion of the "marvel" of the market. He did not succeed in accomplishing that goal, as the post-WWII developments of mainstream microeconomics did not move in a Hayekian direction even while they thought they were wrestling with the Hayek hypothesis concerning dispersed information and decentralization.

Mainstream Interpretations of Hayek

Although Hayek himself had basically left technical economics by mid-century, his ideas about knowledge and information in economic analysis continued to permeate mainstream economics, with citations to Hayek appearing in a number of highly regarded and influential articles and

---

force is the negative slope of the demand curve and the positive slope of the supply curve because they imply that demand exceeds supply below the equilibrium price, and supply exceeds demand above it. A market can overcome this force and become unstable only if lags are introduced that require demanders or suppliers continually to make erroneous decisions." Disequilibrium prices set in motion, Becker argues, a continuous process of adjustment and adaption of economic behavior guided by price movement. And, he assures his readers, "if producers didn't learn, speculators would, for profits would be made by buying and storing the goods when prices were low and selling in the next period when they were high" ([1971] 2008, 92–93).

books. In fact, Hayek's work had a foundational role in the development of the *economics of information* as well as *mechanism design theory*, both of which are commonly considered to be among the most important advances in formal economic theory of the postwar period—for which several of the major contributors to these areas have been awarded Nobel Prizes. The notion that Hayek is cited but not read, or at least not understood, is better understood, then, if we examine how the leading economists in these areas have interpreted Hayek's views on the price system and information, as well as his contributions to the socialist calculation debate—which are, undoubtedly, the ideas for which Hayek is most widely cited. Hence, we trace the development of mechanism design theory and the economics of information, framed by these interpretations, and the belief that mainstream economists have grasped and adequately formalized Hayek's economic insights.

Tjalling Koopmans was a pioneer in the economics of mechanism design, building much of the mathematical foundations for the formal analysis of economic organizations. Interestingly, Koopmans (1977) states that this research agenda was partly inspired by the socialist calculation debate, and the consensus, as he saw it, that the allocation of resources would be efficient under both hypothetical perfect competition and perfect centralization. Unfortunately, the debate had stagnated, according to Koopmans, due to the informal nature of the theoretical arguments, which prevented the participants from reaching definite conclusions or postulating rigorous solutions to the problems at hand. Hence, Koopmans constructed a "*pre*-institutional theory of the allocation of resources"—in which an optimal resource allocation is derived from a set of given environmental and informational constraints, independent from any institutional arrangements—to serve as a formal mathematical framework for the design, analysis, and evaluation of alternative economic mechanisms (Koopmans 1951, 1977, 264–5). In addition, Koopmans offered one of the first mathematical models purporting to formalize, at least partially, the proposition that the price system communicates information to actors, allowing efficient informational decentralization under certain conditions. However, he largely focused on describing the equilibrium conditions of such an informationally decentralized system, while leaving the formal modeling of market processes to others (Koopmans and Beckmann 1957, 60).

Following Koopmans's work on the theory of mechanism design were Thomas Marschak (1959, 1969) and Leonid Hurwicz (1969, 1973), who both examined individual decision-making under different organizational structures, or more precisely, the problem of deriving optimal decision rules such that the decentralized actions of individuals will tend to maximize the objective function of the organization (1959).[7] In addition, they both recognized that one of the central problems of economic analysis is explaining how information is communicated and acquired. Marschak attempted to tackle the issue raised by Koopmans of the need to analyze the mechanisms operating within dynamic adjustment processes in response to changing circumstances, and provided a formal model of such an informational process (1959, 1969). Within this "process" framework, an economy is composed of multiple "agents" and moves through a number of steps as its "process" unfolds. Each agent has their own vector of states containing bits of information, which change at each step as agents "observe" new signals, and then update their own information and send new signals according to a defined function (Marschak 1969, 525–6).

Hurwicz (1969, 1973) continued to refine the theory of mechanism design, in terms of formal rigor, through several technical innovations. Perhaps most important, Hurwicz developed a more rigorous, formal definition of informational decentralization—explicitly citing Hayek's influence on his thinking—which would serve as both constraint and benchmark for the formal analysis of alternative mechanisms and allocation processes. In order to qualify as informationally decentralized, as per Hurwicz's definition, the proposed process or mechanism must "restrict communication to commodity-dimensional messages and also postulate that the only information available to any economic unit concerning the other units is derived from such communication; i.e., except for what can be inferred from such communication, every unit is assumed to be in total ignorance of other units' technologies, preferences, and resource holdings" (1969, 516). In addition to this stringent formal definition of informational

---

[7] In fact, Marschak (1959, 400) argued that this was the central problem of the socialist calculation debate—i.e. designing incentive-compatible rules—and that the Mises-Hayek criticism was simply that market socialism could not properly incentivize the managers of the firms to act as would be required of the efficient economic outcome.

decentralization, Hurwicz proposed other conditions for evaluating the *efficiency* or *optimality* of a mechanism, the most important, for our purposes, being that a process is *non-wasteful*—scarce resources must not be misallocated to a less than optimal use, in light of perfect complete information of the *environment*, and the pre-institutional optimal resource allocation (Hurwicz 1973, 18).

At the same time as these economists were constructing a relatively new technical apparatus for the theory of mechanism design, another group of economists was steadily developing the *economics of information* using fairly standard tools of Marshallian price theory. In "The Economics of Information," George Stigler (1961) developed an economic theory of optimizing *search* behavior in markets under conditions of ignorance, which was seen as an important step toward reconciling the Chicago School's equilibrium-always assumption with the economic realities of a world of constant change and uncertainty. Stigler argued that in a world of uncertainty and ignorance, information is a valuable *resource* for which rational actors will actively *search*—or expend resources to collect—in order to reduce their level of ignorance, continuing until their marginal benefit from reduced ignorance equals the marginal cost of further search. Therefore, Stigler argued, since there are costs to reducing ignorance— namely, the cost of search—the *optimal* level of ignorance is greater than zero, and that, perhaps remarkably, the forces of market competition tend to bring about that level of optimal ignorance. Indeed, Stigler, along with numerous other economists, demonstrated that many "imperfections" and "market failures" could even be re-evaluated as efficient in light of positive information costs, and also provided other insights, including an economic explanation for the social benefits of advertising, reputation and brand names, and various "middlemen" such as department stores (Hirshleifer 1973).

Thus, Stigler (1961) had a pioneering role in moving from what Jack Hirshleifer (1973, 31–2) described as the *passive* economics of uncertainty, where actors merely *react* to incoming signals by adjusting their decisions, to the *active* economics of information, in which individuals act purposively to collect, disseminate, and produce information. Hirshleifer was another pioneer of the *active* economics of information, whose economic analysis often emphasized the dynamic, entrepreneurial nature of the market process, which is especially notable against the historical backdrop of orthodox neoclassical theory (Hirshleifer 1971; also see Hirshleifer 1973).

In order to formalize their models and theories, however, it was necessary for Stigler, Hirshleifer, and other information economists to adopt certain definitions, or perspectives, of a number of important concepts (including information, uncertainty, and ignorance) so as to allow mathematical treatment and tractability. *Information*, therefore, had become treated as an *objective* resource or commodity that can be exchanged, produced, and, in some sense, *exists* independently of the minds in which it is held—there had even been efforts to quantify information in terms of "bits" by applying communications theory (Thomsen 1992, 22–3; Hirshleifer 1973, 33). But on an even more fundamental level, the economics of information ejected *subjectivism* from its analysis, such that the value or *relevance* of a particular bit of information can be automatically and unambiguously recognized by an economic agent without the need for interpretation or entrepreneurial "alertness" (Kirzner 1973; Hirshleifer 1973, 32–3; also Lavoie 1985, 52–65).[8]

Uncertainty, likewise, was systematically treated so as to reduce the intractable "genuine" uncertainty associated with Frank Knight, in which probability distributions are incalculable for a certain class of phenomena, to a form in which actors can simply assign "subjective" probability distributions to every possible state of the world, so as to increase the ease of mathematical modeling (Hirshleifer and Riley 1979, 1378). This interpretation of uncertainty had profound implications for another concept of central importance for Hayek's economic thought—that of *ignorance*. The only kind of ignorance that exists in the world described by the economics of information is *rational* ignorance, as described earlier (Boettke 1997, 28). Yet, this approach implies "that to make such decisions correctly—as must be the case in equilibrium—agents must know beforehand, among other things, what they are ignorant of and the costs and benefits of the knowledge they could acquire; that is, *they must know what it is they do not know*" (emphasis added, Thomsen 1992, 23; also, see

---

[8] On this point, it is notable that Israel Kirzner (1973, 66) specifically refers to Stigler (1961) as a "treatment of the *non*entrepreneurial aspects of knowledge in the market."

Evans and Friedman 2011). In other words, and as we discuss in more detail later, there is no room for *radical* ignorance, or *unawareness*, within formal economic theory—that is, it is not possible to formally model a situation in which an actor *does not know they do not know* something (Samuelson 2004).

By the 1970s and 1980s, the *new information economics* emerged from the work of yet another group of economists—notably including Joseph Stiglitz, Sanford Grossman, and George Akerlof. This subfield absorbed and extended several of the core features from both the economics of information and mechanism design theory. Like their predecessors, the *new information economists* examined the effects of different informational and incentive constraints on a variety of economic and organizational problems. They also strove to develop a more general, yet mathematically rigorous, framework for comparative economic analysis based upon formal equilibrium theorizing (see Stiglitz 2000, 1455–6; Sah and Stiglitz 1985; also see Myerson 2009). Perhaps unsurprisingly, then, Hayek was given special attention within the new information economics, particularly in the work of Grossman (1976) and Grossman and Stiglitz (1976, 1980), whose interpretation, and subsequent formalization, of Hayek is arguably one of the most important influences for how mainstream economics understands Hayek.

In the Grossman-Stiglitz framework, Hayek ([1945] 1948) is interpreted as having argued that: (1) economically relevant information is initially dispersed across society as incomplete bits privately held by individual agents; (2) the primary function of the price system is to communicate to agents the information necessary to achieve an efficient allocation of resources; (3) the competitive mechanism aggregates all private market information into an equilibrium price vector, which summarizes and conveys all such information to every agent in the market; (4) the *equilibrium price* is the *only* bit of information that agents need to know in order to reach the market equilibrium satisfying the standard theorems of welfare economics; and thus, (5) the equilibrium price is a *sufficient statistic* for efficient market outcomes in an informationally decentralized system (Grossman 1976; Grossman and Stiglitz 1976, 1980). It was this interpretation that Grossman and Stiglitz set out to translate into a formal equilibrium model, which would then allow them to rigorously analyze Hayek's supposedly loose, informal arguments.

According to the Grossman-Stiglitz model, an economy is modeled where multiple agents buy and sell two commodities: one standard good and one risky good with an uncertain value. Each agent, however, is given a bit of private information about the value of the risky good, and in making bids and offers for the good, their private information is aggregated by the price, such that in equilibrium, all private information is revealed. In a world of costless information, all relevant information is *aggregated* by the market price *in equilibrium*, and the agents reach an efficient outcome through decentralized actions. On the other hand, if information is *costly*, then agents must choose between observing the market price at zero cost, from which they might then infer market information, or expend resources *searching* for market information, which will then be instantaneously reflected in the price. The problem, as Grossman and Stiglitz highlight, is that the market can never reach equilibrium in a world of costly information where the price system *perfectly summarizes* private information. At the *equilibrium price,* there is no incentive to collect additional information and all agents rely on price as a *sufficient statistic*, but then the price does not reflect all available information and so the market is not in equilibrium. Only when the price system is an *imperfect* mechanism for aggregating information—that is, when the price system contains a degree of *noise*—is it possible for there to be an *imperfect information equilibrium.* Therefore, Grossman and Stiglitz concluded, the notion that the price system is an efficient mechanism for communicating dispersed, private information is false. Hence, whether the competitive market system is informationally decentralized and economically efficient, or even outperforms central planning is also questionable (Grossman 1976; Grossman and Stiglitz 1976, 1980).

Mainstream economists then began to develop a highly formalized approach to comparative economic systems analysis, combining the formal modeling techniques from mechanism design and information economics (Myerson 2009; Sah and Stiglitz 1985). This new approach to comparative economics would therefore emphasize the operation of alternative economic mechanisms under varying informational constraints, with room to consider the strategic behavior of agents in circumstances of imperfect, asymmetric information. In line with this approach, Sah and Stiglitz (1985, 1986) analyze the "architecture," or an economic organization's ability to gather, communicate information, how decisions are made, and the "aggregate" results of these individual choices in different organizational structures. Comparing structures of alternative economic organizations, such as firms in markets, and bureaus in government, Sah and Stiglitz argue that we should expect to see greater occurrence of Type-II errors in markets relative to bureaus and a greater occurrence of Type-I errors in bureaus relative to markets. Entrepreneurs, who are residual claimants of potential profit opportunities in the market process, are more likely to select a larger proportion of available production projects compared to their bureaucratic counterparts acting as managers of state-owned firms. As a result, Stiglitz and Sah felt that the acceptance of unprofitable projects (i.e. Type-II errors) will be relatively greater among entrepreneurs than to bureaucrats, who are more likely to reject profitable projects (i.e. Type-I errors).

This welfare comparison, however true when comparing both outcomes to a situation where all relevant information is given (i.e. perfectly competitive equilibrium), neglects to point out that *in a state of existing disequilibrium*, any decision to accept an unprofitable project (i.e. Type-II error) also implies the rejection of a profitable project (i.e. Type-I error), since resources have alternative uses. Therefore, our concern, from a Hayekian standpoint, is not to appraise the efficiency of the market in terms of an equilibrium state of affairs, which is unachievable, but rather with the efficiency with which Type-I and Type-II errors are discovered and removed through the competitive market process, in accordance with underlying consumer demands. A Type-II error, communicated in the form of a loss to an entrepreneur, *also* communicates the existence of a Type-I error, the correction of which represents a profit opportunity for the entrepreneur who realizes this. The lure of profit, and the discipline of loss, therefore, not only disciplines erring entrepreneurs from making Type-II errors, but in the process of doing so, also signals a future opportunity to correct Type-I errors. Precluded from capturing monetary profits and losses in their decision-making, the bureaucrat will lack the same incentives and knowledge to correct the existence of Type-I errors. The erring entrepreneur is alerted to their error and prodded in the adjustment in a manner that that bumbling bureaucrat is not. And as Hayek pointed out, "the method which under given conditions is the cheapest is a thing which has to be discovered, and to be discovered anew, sometimes almost from day to day, by the entrepreneur, and that, in spite of the strong inducement, *it is by no means regularly the established entrepreneur, the man in charge of the existing plant, who will discover what is the best method.* The force which in a competitive society brings about the reduction of price to the lowest cost at which the quantity salable at that cost can be produced is *the opportunity for anybody who knows a cheaper method to come in at his own risk and to attract customers by underbidding the other producers."* (1948, 196, emphasis added) This competitive filter is simply not in operation in bureaucratic deliberations and non-market investment and production decisions.

To illustrate this point, let us take the testing of pharmaceutical products by the Food and Drug Administration (FDA) as an example. The FDA is responsible for preventing the introduction of new drugs without adequate testing. In an imperfect market process, erring entrepreneurs will indeed introduce drugs that have previously unknown side effects that are harmful to consumers. This is an example of a Type-II error. In a market economy defined by well-defined property rights under the rule of law, such entrepreneurs will be held liable for such an error in the form of lawsuits, monetary losses, and loss of reputation. Built into the institutional context of the market process is not only the incentive to eliminate such a Type-II error, but also the simultaneous creation of knowledge of a previously unnoticed profit opportunity in the form of a previously unnoticed Type-I error, such as the creation of a drug without side effects. For the bureaucrats responsible for eliminating such Type-II errors, however well-motivated and well-intentioned they may be, the information and incentives available in the "architecture" of a bureaucracy will generate a different outcome. The FDA may be responsible for preventing the introduction of new drugs without adequate testing, or eliminating Type-II errors. However, in doing so, what is preventing them from making unintended Type-I errors? How do the bureaucrats perceive the private costs and benefits in their decision-making, as compared to entrepreneurs in the marketplace? In their decision-making, decision-makers in the FDA face two costs: the cost of additional testing will be the lives lost and the suffering not relieved because the drug is not available while it is being tested. Another cost are the lives lost due to the premature introduction of drugs. How will these costs be communicated to decision-makers in the FDA? Let us suppose the FDA approves a drug that turns out to have disastrous side effects. How is this information communicated to the bureaucrat compared to an entrepreneur in the market place? Like the entrepreneur, whose "bad" decision is directly communicated in the form of monetary losses by consumers, this cost will be communicated to the decision-maker, either in the form of demotion or perhaps job loss in response to public outrage communicated through the press. However, the costs of gathering the information necessary to condemn FDA officials for lives lost or suffering endured while testing a drug that eventually proves to be highly successful is high, creating a tendency toward Type-I errors. Therefore, precluded from monetary profits derived from bringing a safe drug to the market, the FDA decision-maker will tend to expend more resources than optimal in testing the drug in order to avoid the cost of a Type-II error, or of accepting an unsafe drug. In doing so, the private benefits of avoiding the acceptance of an unsafe drug (i.e. committing a Type-II error) cannot be made without simultaneously withholding safe drugs from the market (i.e. committing a Type-I error). The difference in outcomes between erring entrepreneurs and bumbling bureaucrats is not based on different motivations, but upon different incentives and information generated by the architecture of alternative economic organizations.

Sappington and Stiglitz (1987) apply the tools of comparative systems analysis developed in Sah and Stiglitz (1985) to privatization, examining the costs and benefits from private versus public production of goods in situations with potential principal-agent problems, and suggest a privatization welfare theorem. Myerson (2009) even returns to the socialist calculation debate, among several other problems of institutional analysis, analyzing several key issues with the formal tools of information economics and mechanism design. Despite this renewed emphasis on both incentive and information problems in comparative economics, including the socialist calculation debate, there seems to be little inherent difference between these two problems; indeed, both can be essentially reduced to incentive problems (see Myerson 2009). Thus, as a result of the efforts described earlier, mainstream economists constructed an apparatus that attempts to grapple with Hayek's ideas on the knowledge problem faced by economic planners, but effectively side-step the issue at the heart of the matter—the discovery of error, and the correction of error through adaptation and adjustment. One of the main reasons the fundamental Hayekian problem is never addressed is because by theoretical construction, these models overestimate the role that equilibrium prices play in Hayek's rendering of the competitive entrepreneurial market process, and they underestimate (to the point of almost completely ignoring) the role that disequilibrium prices play in the Austrian conception of the ongoing *learning* through the market process. Today's inefficiencies are tomorrow's profits for those who recognize the misallocation of resources and seize upon the opportunity to make the required adjustments to eliminate the current wasteful utilization of resources. As Kirzner ([1963] 2011, 327–328, emphasis in original) sums the point up: "Prices and the opportunities for profits that they may present play a *dual* role in the market process whereby resource misallocation is corrected. First, a price discrepancy *exposes* an existing misallocation of resources. The perception of an opportunity for profit is thus a discovery of such misallocation. ... *Second*, a price discrepancy *promotes* corrective action." As he concludes: "The price system not only announces the existence of incorrect employments of resources and makes it worthwhile to correct them; it makes it worthwhile to *ferret out* such cases that may exist."

There are several notable features of the "mainstream Hayekian" perspective that emerged.[9] First, the socialist calculation debate was interpreted to have been fundamentally about the comparative analysis of central planning versus a decentralized market economy in terms of *allocative efficiency*, the *incentive compatibility* between the central planners and managers, and *information costs*, that is, costs of collecting, aggregating, and utilizing decentralized bits of information. Unfortunately, however, the debate was "informal" and therefore incapable of offering rigorous conclusions or insights (Hurwicz 1969, 514–5; Marschak 1959, 399–401; Myerson 2009, 60–2; Oniki 1974, 529–34, 540–1; Stiglitz 2000, 1446, 1448). Second, information and knowledge were conflated

---

[9]To be sure, there is no single mainstream interpretation of Hayek, and differences in perspectives remain. The following, therefore, are not intended to represent *all* mainstream views of Hayek, but instead to reflect what are some of the more prominent features that are commonly shared in these views.

and treated as identical to objective, albeit decentralized and/or imperfect, information or "data" (Boettke 2002). This objective information is itself self-interpreting in a strong sense, requiring little or no creativity, insight, or perspicuity on the part of the actor in order for them to *know* its significance.

Furthermore, the formal apparatus assumes the underlying data to be the same under all institutional arrangements, and that agents have perfect information of their own parameters: production functions, endowments, preferences. The agents behave like automatons, following explicit formal rules that define how they learn, acquire, and communicate information, which operates in an essentially deterministic mechanical fashion with no subjectivism or interpretation. Where agents' own incentives and information matter, they are assumed to behave according to given utility functions and information constraints in a similarly mechanistic manner (Koopmans 1951; Marschak 1969, 525–6; Hurwicz 1969, 514–5; 1973, 16–7; Oniki 1974). This approach is basically able to reduce all problems arising from imperfect, costly, and/or asymmetric information to a few basic categories, such as adverse selection and moral hazard problems. Finally, one of the principal achievements of this formal theory is the argument that even small deviations from perfect information, or the conditions of the fundamental welfare theorems, can dramatically undermine market efficiency (Greenwald and Stiglitz 1986; Myerson 2009; Stiglitz 2000, 2002).

Why the Mainstream Failed to Appropriate Hayek

In discussing the interpretation, influence, and appropriation of Hayek's thinking on economic theory—especially his insights about knowledge and economics—within mainstream economics, I hope it is obvious that there *are* indeed significant differences between the Hayekian framework and the mainstream's appropriation. Which, even if we accept as true, still leaves unanswered the question: why did mainstream economics fail to appropriate F.A. Hayek? Hence, this section offers an explanation for this failure, bringing together the various elements described earlier.

First, and perhaps most obvious, the failure to formalize Hayek may be due to limits of the exercise of rational reconstruction in the intellectual history of economics in general. Of course, this explanation is admittedly vague; in some sense, to clarify would take us too far afield for our present purposes.[10] Still, the mainstream economics literature is filled with cases where Hayek is explicitly linked to a set of claims, while the actual work of Hayek's being cited appears not to even mention that idea, or even directly contradicts it. For example, Hayek is frequently treated as: (a) focusing solely (or at least primarily) on knowledge regarding prices, or price expectations, and (b) arguing that such knowledge is a sufficient condition for attaining market equilibrium. This is the prices as sufficient statistic claim that is often attributed to Hayek. These views about Hayek are showcased in the papers by Grossman and Stiglitz (1976, 1980) purporting to formalize Hayek's claims about the informational efficiency of the price system. For instance, after quoting Hayek (1945) on the "economy of knowledge with which [the price system] operates," Grossman immediately follows with the statement:

> In an economy with complete markets, the price system does act in such a way that individuals, *observing only prices*, and acting in self interest, generate allocations which are efficient. However, such economies need not be stable because prices are revealing so much information that incentives for the collection of information are removed. ... *It is not enough for traders to observe only prices.* (Grossman 1976, 585, emphasis added)

Hence, it is strongly implied, Hayek argued, that knowledge *of prices* is the only knowledge necessary for the operation of the market economy. But as we have demonstrated here, Hayek was explicit that the economically relevant knowledge is of a much broader character than simply knowledge of prices, such as knowing the alternative uses or substitutes for a commodity, as well as knowledge of the particular time and place (Hayek [1937] 1948, 51; [1945] 1948). Further, Hayek sees the price system as a necessary but not sufficient condition for promoting (tendency toward) equilibrium, or rather, that it is only a portion of the fuller

---

[10] Though, perhaps, to get a sense of the issues involved, see my essay "Why Read the Classics in Economics?" http://www.econlib.org/library/Features/feature2.html, originally published in 2000.

explanation. The price system is indeed essential to attaining equilibrium (or movement toward it), but must be coupled with additional knowledge which allows individuals to adapt their plans to new courses of action in light of price changes, and shift their behavior accordingly. And, we must always remember that to Hayek, the price system was embedded in an institutional framework that provides not only the incentive structure but the learning environment that ensures error detection and correction. Israel Kirzner ([1963] 2011, 326) captured this essential Hayekian point when he stated: "An appraisal of the efficacy of the market process therefore involves an appraisal of the way the market process disseminates these missing links of information necessary for the discovery of superior opportunities for the allocation of resources."

That Hayek was concerned with much more than simply the knowledge of prices can be seen even in Hayek's ([1945] 1948) example of the market for tin. Here, a negative supply shock leads to an increase in the price of tin, causing actors to economize on the now scarcer tin, thus leading individuals to adjust their plans and actions in the *direction* of an efficient allocation of resources. Formal economists have tended to emphasize this story as an intuitive explanation of the principles of general equilibrium theory—namely, that relative prices reflect the relative scarcities of goods and enable the spontaneous coordination of the plans and actions of self-interested actors. But the price increase is only one part of the story and *alone* merely implies, at most, that individuals can now afford less tin. The narrative which Hayek provides, however, is replete with descriptions of individuals not only about economizing on the more expensive tin, but also about adapting their plans and actions by shifting to substitutes for tin, adopting new sources of supply, and modifying production methods, all of which necessarily rely upon the actors' additional knowledge of alternative production techniques, supplies, and substitutes for tin.

While Hayek could be labeled an *appreciative theorist*, it remains vitally important to stress that appreciative theory, as explained in Nelson and Winter (1982, 45ff), can be a valuable component of economic understanding in and of itself. Thus, Hayek's intuitive exposition of economic forces at work is a significant intellectual achievement, in part because it gives *meaning* to the proposition that there exist systematic coordinating tendencies within the market process. In offering this perspective, Hayek is fulfilling one of the core didactic duties of the professional economist—that of strengthening our understanding of the principles of spontaneous order through the market process.

However, it may be that the appreciative element of Hayek's economic thought is another explanatory factor in the mainstream's failed appropriation of Hayek. Mainstream economics has tended to treat appreciative theory—or natural language theorizing, more generally—simply as an informal, intuitive input into formal theory. But appreciative theorizing is not necessarily a step toward formalization, nor should it be. Hayek was an incisive and brilliant economist whose economic thought contains numerous insights into the meaning of the market process that formalism is incapable of capturing with the same level of nuance and detail as informal, naturalistic theorizing. These insights include the significance of change, innovation, and creativity for the vitality of the market order, which Hayek perceptively explored in "The Meaning of Competition" ([1946b] 1948) and "Competition as a Discovery Procedure" ([1968] 2002), among other writings. Even the most important of Hayek's theoretical ideas have evaded translation to formal theory, and attempts to formalize them have necessarily lost or distorted Hayek's original insights into the nature of market process and social order.

I believe that too many contemporary economists have thought of Hayek as *just* an appreciative, informal theorist, and that this is an important source of their failure to grasp Hayek's ideas (see Caldwell 1997, 1857–8, 1886). It is true that Hayek likely was not interested in formalizing his theory through mathematical models per se, but instead was more concerned with identifying the epistemological limits of formal economic modeling as a means to understanding empirical reality. To this end, I would argue that Hayek was prescient in his methodological and epistemological critiques, foreseeing a number of critical problems that formal theorists would only begin to grapple with decades after his arguments. Indeed, Hayek's criticism continues to resonate with much economic theory, and the methodological problems he perceived can be identified in the most advanced formal techniques even to this day. Thus, the problem is not that Hayek's informal theory proved too "fuzzy" to be translated to formal theory, but that formal theory is fundamentally incapable of capturing Hayek's economics due to the inherent technical limitations of formalism itself, which Hayek presciently described. In a sense then, Hayek "out-formalized" much of formal, technical economics. As he often said, his criticism was never meant to be a blanket criticism of formal theorizing, but a criticism of what he thought was the wrong type of formal theorizing.[11]

As discussed earlier, Hayek offered a deeply perceptive critique of the equilibrium construct in formal economics. One of the major problems that Hayek highlighted was that the preoccupation with equilibrium analysis in economic theory had resulted in diminished attention given to the *processes* that lead to coordination (Hayek [1937] 1948; [1945] 1948, 91; see also Kaldor 1985). Since this time, economists of the modern Austrian School and heterodox approaches have continued to criticize formal neoclassical economics for its myopic focus on static equilibrium states, while refining both their criticisms and alternative theoretical frameworks. Even several prominent neoclassical economists have admitted that significant gaps and problems in the standard theory remain to be resolved, including how the theory deals with dynamic processes and change (see Arrow 1974, as well as Stiglitz 2002). For example, Stiglitz (2002, 486–7) writes: "Finally, I have become convinced that the dynamics of change may not be well described by equilibrium models that have long been at the center of economic analysis. … Dynamics may be better described by evolutionary processes and models, than by equilibrium processes."[12] Of course, modern Austrian, Institutionalist, and evolutionary economists might view such statements as belated apologia rather than genuine rethinking of scientific methods.[13]

---

[11] Hayek, for example, was attracted to the literature in general systems theory and then with further developments of the early work in complex adaptive systems analysis. See, e.g., Vriend (2002) and also more recently Axtell (2016).

[12] Arrow (1974, 4) identifies similar issues with neoclassical theory, namely, that it lacks an adequate model of dynamic adjustment processes and disequilibrium changes. Still, he argues that neoclassical (and Keynesian) economic theory is valuable on instrumentalist grounds, especially as a tool of prediction and control.

[13] Indeed, in other writings Stiglitz appears to remain staunchly committed to equilibrium analysis, even for the purposes of critically examining general equilibrium theory, arguing that "only with the construction of equilibrium models can one fully confront the inadequacies of the Arrow-Debreu model and its core theorems on existence, optimality, and decentralization" (Stiglitz 2000, 1456).

Yet, Hayek raised another fundamental challenge to equilibrium analysis that remains unresolved by mainstream formalism, and arguably less explored than problems relating to dynamic processes by alternative schools—that is, the epistemic nature of equilibrium, and the implications for understanding the coordination problem. As Hayek ([1937] 1948) explained, equilibrium is a coherent concept, and capable of having meaningful content, only insofar as it is defined in terms of the subjective knowledge of individual actors. Further, the central problem of economics, and indeed of the social sciences, is the coordination problem arising from the nature of the division of knowledge and labor in society (Hayek [1937] 1948, 50–1). Therefore, a fundamental analytical problem for economic theory is to explain the mechanisms and processes whereby the subjective data to the individual actors converges, such that they hold mutually compatible beliefs and expectations about the plans and actions of others and the objective facts of the world, and are able to successfully dovetail their plans and actions.

It might be argued that certain epistemic assumptions (such as perfect information or rational expectations), which essentially guarantee smoothly operating, "frictionless" markets, are instrumentally valuable for the purposes of constructing determinate, tractable models, and can be dropped or modified as needed. However, as economists adopted formal models built upon these epistemic assumptions (explicitly or implicitly) as a central tool for the analysis of informational problems, they began to discover hidden issues deeper than simply mathematical intractability.[14] In their efforts to rigorously explain the mechanisms driving economic outcomes, economists discarded the myriad "imperfections" of reality in order to construct clean, precise models of those operating forces. What they had not realized is the significance—indeed, the necessity—of those "imperfections" for the existence and operation of real-world market processes (see Richardson 1959 for an excellent discussion of this point).[15] It is not simply that formalist economic theory

---

[14] Stiglitz (2000, 1470–1) makes a similar point, though he arguably arrives at that conclusion via a somewhat different path than the one which we pursue.

[15] Hence we arrive at an example of one of the logical dilemmas of the common knowledge assumption. If a large number of producers simultaneously notice a profit opportunity, where this opportunity is common knowledge and costly to pursue, then it is unclear to the individual producer

is "unrealistic" because it abstracts away from the frictions and imperfections that appear obvious to casual observers. It is that, by assuming away these "imperfections," formalist economics renders itself incapable of explaining many of the phenomena that economists purportedly try to understand. This notably includes institutions such as money, contracts, the firm, and even the price system, which lose their significance and meaning in the deterministic world of perfect, complete information and rational expectations, free from genuine uncertainty and sheer ignorance (Hayek [1937] 1948, 55; Richardson 1959; see also Boettke 1997). For economists, the methodological problem therefore becomes how to theorize about the tendency of the market process toward coordination in terms of the limited, subjective knowledge of individual actors, without disregarding institutions from the "epistemic toolkit" that actors utilize in order to plan and act in a world of genuine uncertainty and ignorance.

It is important to emphasize, therefore, the "definite statements about how knowledge is acquired and communicated" ([1937] 1948, 33). What Hayek proposed are not simply assumptions about how hypothetical rational agents would perform mental calculations, form expectations, or update in light of new information. Indeed, Hayek not infrequently appears largely uninterested in examining, theoretically or empirically, such "psychological" elements of economics (cf. Hayek [1937] 1948, 55). Rather, the *processes* that are most significant in the Hayekian framework for understanding the coordination problem are *social* and *institutional* by nature, *not* atomistic or "psychological." It is almost irrelevant to the Hayekian theory whether or not individuals are modeled as perfect-Bayesians or employ heuristics and intuitive rules-of-thumb when making decisions.[16]

---

whether it will be profitable to pursue that opportunity without additional knowledge about the plans of their competitors; "[a] profit opportunity which is known by and available to everybody is available to nobody in particular" (Richardson 1959, 233–4).

[16] In light of the persistent defects of the formal models of knowledge, for example, lack of subjectivism, one might even follow Ludwig Lachmann in arguing that such formal exercises are in fact irrelevant for a much broader range of problems beyond just those of direct concern to the Hayekian framework: "A method of dynamic analysis which fails to allow for variable expectations due to subjective interpretation seems bound to degenerate into a series of economically irrelevant mathematical exercises" (Lachmann 1978, 15).

What matters is the institutional context within which individuals form expectations, make plans, and act to achieve their goals (see Hayek [1946a, b] 1948, 95). Thus, the Hayekian framework is less concerned with how *individuals* learn per se, than with understanding learning in terms of the *social processes* that *emerge* from the interactions of purposive actors. The interesting problem to the Hayekian, then, is how do emergent social orders and patterns "learn," in some sense, from the dispersed bits of subjective knowledge held by numerous individuals. The competitive market process embodies greater knowledge than any single mind could possess because its institutional structure enables individuals to utilize their own subjective knowledge in pursuing their goals, and contains endogenous mechanisms that encourage the entrepreneurial discovery and spontaneous correction of economic errors.

Conclusion

That Hayek's insights into the epistemic-institutional nature of the market process were neither grasped nor adopted by mainstream economics is well illustrated by the contrasting implications each draws from their ostensibly similar concerns with the economics of imperfect knowledge and information. For example, in a most recent article, Bowles et al. (2017) interpret that Hayek's public policy conclusions do not necessarily follow from his understanding of price theory. They argue that, though, Hayek's argument have a continuing relevance today, Hayek's theory of the prices as a communication mechanism "creates incentives to extract information from signals in ways that can be destabilizing" (2017, 217). Indeed, as Hayek argued, price adjustments in the market process are never perfect, but the conclusion that Bowles, Kirman, and Sethi make still follows from an equilibrium view of prices as sufficient statistics to an allocation problem, not a disequilibrium of prices as guides to production, the latter of which was Hayek's understanding of market prices. To quote G. Warren Nutter (1968), prices without property are a grand illusion. From a Hayekian perspective, a destabilized market today creates tomorrow's entrepreneurial profit opportunity to stabilize the market. The institutional prerequisite for this process of error detection, however, is private property, which concentrates benefits and costs on individual decision-making. Such an emphasis on this institutional prerequisite for learning and error correction was missed not only by neoclassical market socialists of the 1930s, but also among neoclassical market failure theorists today.

According to the Fundamental Theorems of Welfare Economics, the "ideal" picture of the market economy is one where society is on the Pareto frontier, defined by a situation where all resources are allocated to their most highly valued uses such that the marginal rates of substitution are equalized across all the alternative ends to which resources might be put. In this view, the first-best market economy, which is theoretically indistinguishable from an idealized market socialist society, achieves an equilibrium allocation of resources that is technically and economically efficient, where no resources are "wasted." For mainstream economics, markets *fail* in situations far from satisfying the assumptions and conditions that formal theory finds necessary for the existence and stability of competitive equilibrium—for example, when there are information asymmetries and incomplete futures markets (cf. Stiglitz 2000, 2002).

If an omniscient economist took a snapshot of the world at any particular moment in time, they could undoubtedly identify myriad unexploited Pareto improvements, economic errors, and misallocated resources. However, the neoclassical theory of competitive general equilibrium is an entirely irrelevant benchmark for evaluating the performance of real-world market processes, since the informational assumptions at its core are epistemologically flawed and logically incoherent. Instead of the perfectly competitive model as the benchmark for evaluating the real-world economic performance of market competition, Hayek ([1946b] 1948, 100) argues for comparative institutional analysis which recognizes the constraints imposed by reality.

In a world of imperfect knowledge, it is not possible to have entrepreneurial success and economic progress without error and failure. However, this is not simply due to principal-agent problems or incentive-compatibility issues arising from the costs of monitoring agent behavior, enforcing contracts, or collecting information as is sometimes treated in formalist economic theory. For example, Sah and Stiglitz (1985, 1986) model alternative organizational structures—ranging from decentralized to central planning-type organization—and analyze their performance at evaluating and selecting from potential projects, which are either "good" or "bad," finding that the decentralized "market" organization accepts more "good" projects than the central-planning-type, but also fails to reject more "bad" projects as well. In the Hayekian framework, there is little sense in which an observing economist can even classify a potential plan or project as *ex ante* "good" or "bad." Only *ex post* evaluation is possible, based upon profit-loss calculations which require a functioning price system. Furthermore, even then, the "bad" projects are not simply a regrettable but necessary "cost of doing business," so to speak. Even where a project or investment is a proven failure and suffers losses, it does not automatically follow that this *individual* entrepreneurial failure represents genuine social waste or deadweight loss. Failure is necessary because it *reveals* what success is, and what is welfare-enhancing, and where entrepreneurship is most needed to reallocate resources and adjust plans. In this spirit, Ludwig Lachmann (1978, 18) writes:

> The ability to turn failure into success and to benefit from the discomfiture of others is the crucial test of true entrepreneurship. A progressive economy is not an economy in which no capital is ever lost, but an economy which can afford to lose capital because the productive opportunities revealed by the loss are vigorously exploited.

To the Hayekian framework, the competitive market process is socially beneficial—even where rivalrous behaviors lead to things that neoclassical economists have often viewed in a critical light, like duplication of effort or advertising—because it is only through the competitive process that entrepreneurs, consumers, and producers can *discover* what is most welfare-enhancing for society.

Hayek noted on various occasions that the preoccupation with formal equilibrium theory had led to the neglect of institutions in economic analysis ([1937] 1948, 55; [1945] 1948; [1946b] 1948; [1968] 2002). In an equilibrium state, where actors' knowledge and expectations are aligned, many institutions are essentially redundant, pointless, or otherwise relegated to much more limited roles than our everyday experience of economic reality would ever suggest—such as money, contract enforcement, courts, firms, and even the price system (Hayek [1937] 1948, 55; Richardson 1959; Malmgren 1961; Radner 1968; Hirshleifer and Riley 1979, 1411–4; see also Boettke 1997). But in situations of dispersed knowledge, imperfect foresight, and radical ignorance—that is, anything that remotely resembles reality—institutions are essential elements of the solution to the problem of social and economic coordination. The failure to appropriate and formalize the economic thought of F.A. Hayek within mainstream economics can therefore be seen as resulting from the persistent failure of the would-be-appropriators to heed Hayek's own critical challenge to the foundations of formal economic theory.

In "Economics and Knowledge," Hayek wrote: "My criticism of the recent tendencies to make economic theory more and more formal is not that they have gone too far but that they have not yet been carried far enough to complete the isolation of this branch of logic and to restore to its rightful place the investigation of causal processes" ([1937] 1948, 35). Despite Hayek having written that statement more than 75 years ago, and in light of the ideas and arguments presented earlier, it seems that Hayekians still have a long way to go in pursuing this methodological and analytical mission.

Bibliography

Akerlof, George, and Robert Shiller. 2009. *Animal Spirits: How Human Psychology Drives the Economy and Why It Matters for Global Capitalism.* Princeton: Princeton University Press.

Arrow, Kenneth J. 1974. Limited Knowledge and Economic Analysis. *American Economic Review* 64 (1): 1–10.

Axtell, Robert. 2016. Hayek Enriched by Complexity Enriched by Hayek. In *Revisiting Hayek's Political Economy*, ed. Peter J. Boettke and Virgil Henry Storr, 63–121. Bingley: Emerald Publishing Group.

Becker, Gary. [1971] 2008. *Economic Theory.* Piscataway: Transaction Publishers.

Boettke, Peter J. 1997. Where Did Economics Go Wrong? Modern Economics as a Flight from Reality. *Critical Review* 11 (1): 11–64.

———. 2000. Why Read the Classics in Economics? *Library of Economics and Liberty*, February 24.

———. 2002. Information and Knowledge: Austrian Economics in Search of Its Uniqueness. *Review of Austrian Economics* 15 (4): 263–274.

Boettke, Peter J., Emily C. Schaeffer, and Nicholas A. Snow. 2010. The Context of Context: The Evolution of Hayek's Epistemic Turn in Economics and Politics. *Advances in Austrian Economics* 14: 69–86.

Bowles, Samuel, Alan Kirman, and Rajiv Sethi. 2017. Retrospectives: Friedrich Hayek and the Market Algorithm. *Journal of Economic Perspectives* 31 (3): 215–230.

Caldwell, Bruce J. 1988. Hayek's Transformation. *History of Political Economy* 20 (4): 513–541.

———. 1997. Hayek and Socialism. *Journal of Economic Literature* 35 (4): 1856–1890.

Evans, Anthony J., and Jeffrey Friedman. 2011. 'Search' vs. 'Browse': A Theory of Error Grounded in Radical (Not Rational) Ignorance. *Critical Review* 23 (1–2): 73–104.

Foss, Nicolai. 2000. Austrian Economics and Game Theory: A Stocktaking and an Evaluation. *Review of Austrian Economics* 13 (1): 41–58.

Greenwald, Bruce C., and Joseph E. Stiglitz. 1986. Externalities in Economies with Imperfect Information and Incomplete Markets. *The Quarterly Journal of Economics* 101 (2): 229–264.

Grossman, Sanford J. 1976. On the Efficiency of Competitive Stock Markets Where Trades Have Diverse Information. *The Journal of Finance* 31 (2): 573–585.

Grossman, Sanford J., and Joseph E. Stiglitz. 1976. Information and Competitive Price Systems. *American Economic Review* 66 (2): 246–253.

———. 1980. On the Impossibility of Informationally Efficient Markets. *American Economic Review* 70 (3): 393–408.

Hayek, F.A. [1937] 1948. Economics and Knowledge. In *Individualism and Economic Order*, 33–56. Chicago: University of Chicago Press, Chapter 2.

———. [1940] 1948. Socialist Calculation III: The Competitive 'Solution'. In *Individualism and Economic Order*, 181–208. Chicago: University of Chicago Press, Chapter 9.

———. [1945] 1948. The Use of Knowledge in Society. In *Individualism and Economic Order*, 77–91. Chicago: University of Chicago Press, Chapter 4.

———. [1946a] 1948. Individualism: True and False. In I*ndividualism and Economic Order*, 1–32. Chicago: University of Chicago Press, Chapter 1.

———. [1946b] 1948. The Meaning of Competition. In *Individualism and Economic Order*, 92–106. Chicago: University of Chicago Press, Chapter 5.

―――. [1968] 2002. Competition as a Discovery Procedure. *The Quarterly Journal of Austrian Economics* 5 (3): 9–23.

Hirshleifer, Jack. 1971. The Private and Social Value of Information and the Reward to Inventive Activity. *American Economic Review* 61 (4): 561–574.

―――. 1973. Where Are We in the Theory of Information? *American Economic Review* 63 (2): 31–39.

Hirshleifer, Jack, and John G. Riley. 1979. The Analytics of Uncertainty and Information–An Expository Survey. *Journal of Economic Literature* 17 (4): 1375–1421.

Hurwicz, Leonid. 1969. On the Concept and Possibility of Informational Decentralization. *American Economic Review* 59 (2): 513–524.

―――. 1973. The Design of Mechanisms for Resource Allocation. *American Economic Review* 63 (2): 1–30.

Kaldor, Nicholas. 1985. *Economics Without Equilibrium*. Armonk: M.E. Sharpe.

Kirzner, Israel M. [1963] 2011. *Market Theory and the Price System*. Indianapolis: Liberty Fund.

―――. 1973. *Competition & Entrepreneurship*. Chicago: University of Chicago Press.

Koopmans, Tjalling C. 1951. Efficient Allocation of Resources. *Econometrica* 19 (4): 455–465.

―――. 1977. Concepts of Optimality and Their Uses. *American Economic Review* 67 (3): 261–274.

Koopmans, Tjalling C., and Martin Beckmann. 1957. Assignment Problems and the Location of Economic Activities. *Econometrica* 25 (1): 53–76.

Lachmann, Ludwig M. 1978. *Capital and Its Structure*. Kansas City: Sheed, Andrews and McMeel, Inc.

Lavoie, Don. 1985. *National Economic Planning: What Is Left?* Cambridge, MA: Ballinger.

Malmgren, H.B. 1961. Information, Expectations, and the Theory of the Firm. *The Quarterly Journal of Economics* 75 (3): 399–421.

Marschak, Thomas. 1959. Centralization and Decentralization in Economic Organizations. *Econometrica* 27 (3): 399–430.

―――. 1969. On the Comparison of Centralized and Decentralized Economies. *American Economic Review* 59 (2): 525–532.

Marshall, Alfred. [1890] 1920. *Principles of Economics*. 8th ed. London: Macmillan.

Myerson, Roger B. 2009. Fundamental Theory of Institutions: A Lecture in Honor of Leo Hurwicz. *Review of Economic Design* 13 (1): 59–75.

Nelson, Richard, and Sidney Winter. 1982. *An Evolutionary Theory of Economic Change*. Cambridge: Harvard University Press.

Nutter, G. Warren. 1968. Markets Without Property: A Grand Illusion. In *Money, the Market, and the State: Economic Essays in Honor of James Muir Waller*. Athens: University of Georgia Press.

Oniki, Hajime. 1974. The Cost of Communication in Economic Organization. *The Quarterly Journal of Economics* 88 (4): 529–550.

Radner, Roy. 1968. Competitive Equilibrium Under Uncertainty. *Econometrica* 36 (1): 31–58.

Richardson, G.B. 1959. Equilibrium, Expectations and Information. *The Economic Journal* 69 (274): 223–237.

Sah, Raaj Kumar, and Joseph E. Stiglitz. 1985. Human Fallibility and Economic Organization. *American Economic Review* 75 (2): 292–297.

———. 1986. The Architecture of Economic Systems: Hierarchies and Polyarchies. *American Economic Review* 76 (4): 716–727.

Samuelson, Larry. 2004. Modeling Knowledge in Economic Analysis. *Journal of Economic Literature* 42 (2): 367–403.

Sappington, David E.M., and Joseph E. Stiglitz. 1987. Privatization, Information and Incentives. *Journal of Policy Analysis and Management* 6 (4): 567–582.

Shackle, G.L.S. 1967. *The Years of High Theory*. London: Cambridge University Press.

Smith, Vernon. 2007. *Rationality in Economics: Constructivist and Ecological Forms*. Cambridge: Cambridge University Press.

———. 2015. Discovery Processes, Science, and 'Knowledge-How:' Competition as a Discovery Procedure in the Laboratory. *The Review of Austrian Economics* 28 (3): 237–245.

Stigler, George J. 1961. The Economics of Information. *Journal of Political Economy* 69 (3): 213–225.

Stiglitz, Joseph E. 2000. The Contributions of the Economics of Information to Twentieth Century Economics. *The Quarterly Journal of Economics* 115 (4): 1441–1478.

———. 2002. Information and the Change in the Paradigm in Economics. *American Economic Review* 92 (3): 460–501.

Thirlwall, Antony. 2015. Keynes, Economic Development and the Developing Countries. In *Essays on Keynesian and Kaldorian Economics*, 149–177. London: Palgrave Macmillan.

Thomsen, Esteban F. 1992. *Prices and Knowledge: A Market Process Perspective*. London/New York: Routledge.

Vaughn, Karen I. 1999. Hayek's Implicit Economics: Rules and the Problem of Order. *Review of Austrian Economics* 11 (1–2): 129–144.

Vriend, Nicholas J. 2002. Was Hayek an Ace? *Southern Economic Journal* 68 (4): 811–840.

Wagner, Richard. 2016. *Politics as a Peculiar Business*. Northampton: Edward Elgar Publishing.

5

Hayek and Market Socialism

Introduction

F. A. Hayek is perhaps best known for his opposition to socialism. His most famous work is undoubtedly *The Road to Serfdom* (1944) and the last work he published, *The Fatal Conceit* (1988), was actually conceived of in the context of attempting to arrange a worldwide debate between advocates of socialism and advocates of capitalism. His founding of the Mont Pelerin Society in 1947 was an attempt to align the opponents of socialism in the intellectual, political, and business worlds so they could form an effective intellectual bulwark against the rising tide of socialism in the democratic West. He directed his argument against the "hot" socialism of Marxism as well as the "cold" socialism of the social democratic welfare state in the post-WWII era.[1]

The fact that Hayek was a critic of government command and control over the economy is well known among scholars and intellectuals. Socialism lacked incentives and presented the central planning authority

---

[1] The terms "hot" and "cold" socialism are introduced in Hayek (1960).

© The Author(s) 2018
Peter J. Boettke, *F. A. Hayek*, Great Thinkers in Economics,
https://doi.org/10.1057/978-1-137-41160-0_5

with too complicated a task. As a result, socialism was too bureaucratic and cumbersome to operate in an economically efficient manner. Moreover, it is also known that Hayek postulated that the very worst elements within government will tend to take advantage of the situation to rise to power, and thus socialism would not only suffer from a "knowledge problem" but also from an "abuse of power problem."[2] Thus, Hayek's political economy can be summarized by three conjectures:

1. Markets work by mobilizing the dispersed knowledge in society through the price system.
2. Socialism does not work as well as capitalism because without the price system, it cannot mobilize the dispersed knowledge in society.
3. Socialism is dangerous to democracy and liberty because economic planning must by necessity concentrate power in the hands of a few, and those with a comparative advantage in exercising that power will rise to the top of the planning bureaucracy.

These "Hayek conjectures" are understood to have emerged in his long battle with socialist economists and intellectuals, and are often invoked as comprising the free market case against government planning of the economy. While they capture, in a superficial way, Hayek's position, the careful student of Hayek is often frustrated with discussions that treat Hayek as an ideological icon as opposed to an economist and political economist. In other words, these conjectures are the by-product of a network of scientific propositions that Hayek established during his career as an economist and political philosopher and cannot be read as mere statements of ideological opinion. It is this network of scientific propositions, concerning the nature and extent of the economic and political problems that must be addressed for any society to achieve

---

[2] Lavoie (1985) is perhaps the most comprehensive discussion (beside Hayek's) of how "planning does not accidentally deteriorate into the militarization of the economy; it is the militarization of economy ... The theory of planning was, from its inception, modeled after feudal and militaristic organizations. Elements of the Left tried to transform it into a radical program, to fit into a progressive revolutionary vision. But it doesn't fit. Attempts to implement this theory invariably reveal its true nature. The practice of planning is nothing but the militarization of the economy" (230).

advanced social cooperation under a division of labor, which underlies these "Hayek conjectures" about the policy world.[3]

Mises's Challenge of Economic Calculation Under Socialism

Hayek inherited his research program from his mentor, Ludwig von Mises. While Hayek was not technically Mises's student at the University of Vienna, as a newly minted doctor of jurisprudence with a concentration in economics, he came under Mises's influence at the Vienna Chamber of Commerce. Hayek worked with Mises on questions of business forecasting and what came to be known as the "Austrian theory of the trade cycle." Critical aspects of that theory were: (1) a picture of the capital structure in an economy as consisting of heterogeneous capital good combinations that had to be maintained or reshuffled in more productive and advantageous combinations; (2) a vision of the production process as one engaged in over time, thus generating a need for a mechanism for the intertemporal coordination of production plans to meet consumer demands; and (3) the notion that increases in the money supply work through the economy not in an instantaneous adjustment of prices, but through relative price adjustments.

Each of these elements of the theory of the trade cycle occupied researchers in the first decades of the twentieth century.[4] For example, in analyzing the production process through time, the concept of the imputation of the value of producer goods from the consumer goods they produce was developed, and the role of interest rates in coordinating production plans was highlighted. Entrepreneurs rely on price signals to guide them in their production process so that they are allocating scarce

---

[3] The other economic arguments invoked in building that case would include the incentive effect of private property rights, the unintended consequences of government intervention in the economy, the wasteful rent-seeking behavior of interest groups in democratic decision making, and the failure of discretionary monetary and fiscal policy to stabilize the economic environment. The major contributors in the twentieth century to this literature, in addition to Hayek, would be Ludwig von Mises, Milton Friedman, James Buchanan, and Gordon Tullock.

[4] See, for example, Kaldor, Nicholas (1932). "The Economic Situation of Austria," *Harvard Business Review* 11(10): 23–34.

capital resources in the most valuable direction and employing the least costly technologies. The capital structure does not automatically replenish itself, but instead requires the careful calculations of economic actors to determine which production projects are the most profitable ones to pursue. If the price signals are confusing, then decisions concerning the maintenance and allocation of capital will be mistaken from the point of view of economic value maximization.

The monetary theory of the trade cycle developed by Mises and Hayek in the 1920s put all the pieces together from the work of Austrian and Swedish neoclassical economists, and contrasted that vision of the capital-using economy with the more mechanistic understanding of a monetary economy associated with economists in the USA and UK and the chaotic vision of economic life associated with the critics of capitalism.

Mises's economic and sociological analysis of socialism ([1920] 1935, [1922] 1981) is based on the subjective theory of value as applied in the context of a capital-using economy. In fact, Mises went so far as to claim: "To understand the problem of economic calculation it was necessary to recognize the true nature of the exchange relations expressed in the prices of the market. The existence of this important problem could be revealed only by the methods of the modern subjective theory of value" ([1922] 1981, 186).

Mises provided a comprehensive critique of socialist schemes of all varieties. In his writings, one can find a critique based on the perverse incentives of collective ownership, the cumbersomeness of bureaucracy, and the inability to simulate entrepreneurial innovation outside the context of a market economy and the lure of profit and the penalties of loss. But the critical point Mises raised was that collective ownership in the means of production would render rational economic calculation impossible.[5] Without private property in the means of production, there would

[5] The emphasis Mises put on economic calculation in his critique of socialist blueprints is a result of two considerations. First, at the time of his original challenge, it was considered illegitimate to invoke incentive-based arguments against socialism because advocates of socialism had assumed that man's nature would be transformed by the move to socialist production. The avarice of a market society would give way to a new spirit of cooperation. Second, for the sake of argument, Mises granted this utopian assumption, but pointed out that even if socialist economic planners were motivated to accomplish the task rationally, without the ability to engage in monetary calculation, they would not know how to complete the task. There would be no metric with which to measure

be no market for the means of production. Without a market for the means of production, there would be no market prices for the means of production. Without market prices (reflecting the relative scarcities of capital goods), economic planners would not be able rationally to calculate the most economically efficient investment path. Without the ability to engage in rational economic calculation, "all production by lengthy and roundabout processes would be so many steps in the dark" ([1922] 1981, 101). No individual or group of individuals could discriminate between the numerous possibilities of methods of production to determine which ones are the most cost-effective without recourse to monetary prices. "In societies based on the division of labor, the distribution of property rights effects a kind of mental division of labor, without which neither economy nor systemic production would be possible"([1922] 1981, 101). Monetary prices and profit and loss accounting are indispensable guides in the business of economic administration. "Without such assistance, in the bewildering chaos of alternative materials and processes the human mind would be at a complete loss. Whenever we had to decide between different processes or different centres of production, we would be entirely at sea" ([1922] 1981, 102). In its attempt to overcome the anarchy of production, socialism substitutes planned chaos. As Mises puts it:

> To suppose that a socialist community could substitute calculations in kind for calculations in terms of money is an illusion. In a community that does not practice exchange, calculation in kind can never cover more than consumption goods. They break down completely where goods of higher order are concerned. Once society abandons free pricing of production goods rational production becomes impossible. Every step that leads away from private ownership of the means of production and the use of money is a step away from rational economic activity. ([1922] 1981, 102)

Mises's critique was greeted with resistance. In the German language, a heated debate ensued in the 1920s and included such figures as Karl

---

the result of activity. Here, Mises makes an important point about the intimate connection between the calculation argument and the incentive argument. "We cannot act economically," he wrote, "if we are not in a position to understand economizing" ([1920] 1935, 120).

Polanyi and Eduard Heimann and Austro-Marxists such as Otto Neurath. In the English language, contributors to the debate include Fred Taylor (1929), Frank Knight (1936), Oskar Lange (1936, 1937), and Abba Lerner (1934, 1935, 1936). Amid the discussion, the Western capitalist economies were embroiled in the Great Depression while the socialist Soviet system transformed a peasant country into an industrial economy in one generation. The events of the 1930s supposedly proved capitalism to be not only unjust, but unstable. Socialist planning, on the other hand, provided the Soviet Union with the material base to fight the fascist threat that arose in Germany in the 1930s and 1940s.

It is in this intellectual and analytical context that Hayek started to develop his own presentation of the issues which Mises had raised. The reading of Hayek that I want to stress is one that sees him as groping for answers in an intellectual context that did not make sense to him. While he was convinced of the power of Mises's argument against socialism, he understood that many others were not convinced. This led him to search for reasons why others did not see the power of Mises's arguments, and for alternative ways to express Mises's insights so that perhaps they would be more persuasive. In the process, Hayek would, over the coming decades, refine and extend Mises's foundational work on the methodology of the human sciences, the analytical method of economics, and the social philosophy of liberalism.

The Surprising Emergence of Neoclassical Socialism

In 1931, Hayek visited the LSE and gave a series of lectures that were later published as *Prices and Production* ([1931] 1967). Hayek subsequently joined the faculty at the LSE, assuming the Tooke Professorship in Economic Science and Statistics. He and Robbins established the curriculum and considered it part of their mission to introduce the ideas developed by neoclassical economists in continental Europe to English-speaking audiences.

In "The Trend of Economic Thinking" (1933), Hayek argued that economics was born in the intellectual exercise of critically engaging utopian schemes, that the liberal economists are no less concerned with the disadvantaged in society than are their intellectual opponents on the left, and that economics has vastly improved as a consequence of the marginal revolution and the development of neoclassical theory. Ironically, Hayek contended that neoclassical economics had repaired the problems in the classical system identified in the historicist critique, but that the general intellectual world largely ignored these positive developments in the body of economic thought. Instead, the intellectual and policy class proceeded as if the historicist critique held sway over contemporary economic theorizing. As a result, various utopian schemes that would be refuted by careful economic analysis retained a popular support which was far in excess of the merits of the schemes. "Refusing to believe in general laws," Hayek argued, "the Historical School had the special attraction that its method was constitutionally unable to refute even the wildest of Utopias, and was, therefore, not likely to bring disappointment associated with theoretical analysis"(1933, 125).

The 1930s were a decade of great success for Hayek. He emerged as the major theoretical rival to John Maynard Keynes within the English community of economists. From his intellectual home at the LSE, Hayek, together with Robbins, effectively challenged the "Oxbridge" hegemony in economic research and teaching. Talented students and junior faculty were attracted to the LSE and included such superstars as Ronald Coase, Abba Lerner, John Hicks, Nicholas Kaldor, Ludwig Lachmann, and G. L. S. Shackle. In the early-to-mid-1930s, students and faculty were attracted to Hayek's monetary theory of the trade cycle and the government-induced credit expansion explanation for the boom-bust associated with the Great Depression. However, by the end of the decade, the Keynesian dominance was beginning to take hold even at the LSE. Hayek was blindsided by the defection of his students and junior colleagues to the Keynesian argument. But despite his disbelief in the staying power of Keynes's economics of abundance, he could understand that Keynes had written a tract for the times and that serious people could get caught up in the policy concerns of the day.

What Hayek could not fathom was the development of schemes for socialism that utilized the very price theory that he had taught. Socialism and neoclassical economics, in Hayek's frame of reference, were incompatible. He certainly understood that marginal economics was utilized by Fabians at the LSE, but Hayek thought that the English economists had not fully understood the implications of the subjective theory of value and the marginal conditions of equilibrium. The work of Barone, Pareto, and Wieser had established early on that socialism and capitalism faced a formal similarity with respect to the marginal conditions if they wanted to allocate scarce resources efficiently. Formal similarity, though, does not mean that the mechanism and probability of attainment are identical between the different social systems.

In the belief that socialism, if it was to achieve its claimed outcomes of advanced material production, must satisfy the formal conditions of economic efficiency stipulated by marginalist principles, Frederick Taylor, Frank Knight, H. D. Dickinson (1933), and Abba Lerner began developing an argument that used modern neoclassical economics to ensure the efficiency of socialist economic planning. Using the same line of neoclassical reasoning, Oskar Lange was able to formulate his critique of Mises.

In deploying the formal similarity argument, Lange provided the following blueprint. First, allow a market for consumer goods and labor allocation. Second, put the productive sector into state hands but provide strict production guidelines to firms. Namely, inform managers that they must price their output equal to marginal costs, and produce that level of output that minimizes average costs. Adjustments can be made on a trial and error basis, using inventory as the signal. The production guidelines will ensure that the full opportunity cost of production will be taken into account and that all least-cost technologies will be employed. In short, these production guidelines will ensure that productive efficiency is achieved even in a setting of state ownership of the means of production.

Lange went even further in his argument for socialism. Not only is socialism, by mimicking the efficiency conditions of capitalism, able theoretically to achieve the same level of efficient production as the market, but it would actually outperform capitalism by purging society of monopoly and business cycles that plague real-world capitalism. Moreover, since the means of production would rest in the hands of authorities, market socialism would also be able to pursue egalitarian distributions in a manner unobtainable with private ownership. In the hands of Lange (and Lerner), neoclassical theory was to become a powerful tool of social control. Modern economic theory, which Mises and Hayek had thought so convincingly established their argument, was now used to show that they were wrong.

What was most ironic about the response leveled against Mises by the market socialists was the claim that Mises's argument had been based upon a rejection neoclassical economic theory! As Lange argued:

> It has been maintained, indeed, by Marx and by the historical school (in so far as the latter recognised any economic laws at all), that all economic laws have only historico-relative validity. But it is most surprising to find this institutionalist view supported by a prominent member of the Austrian school, which did so much to emphasise the universal validity of the fundamental principles of economic theory. Thus Professor Mises' denial of the possibility of economic calculation in a socialist system must be rejected. (Lange 1936, 55)

Therefore, Lange goes further to state that the Mises's denial of the possibility of economic calculation in a socialist economy implies of a denial of rational choice, which is "plainly institutionalist" (Lange 1936, 55, fn.2).

Our point here is not to emphasize the details of Lange's response to Mises. Rather, it is to illustrate two broader points about the evolution of economic methodology that had taken place by the mid-twentieth century. First, any discussion of institutions, which had been a part of the shared understanding of economic science among early neoclassicals, became regarded as a rejection of the universal validity of rational choice across time and place. Second, any discussions of the incentives in a market economy also were defined outside the scope of neoclassical theory because for economists, discussions of incentives became analogous to an analysis of motivations, which was regarded as the realm of psychology and sociology, not that of economics (Boettke and Piano forthcoming). For example, Abba Lerner criticized a fellow market socialist, Evan F. M. Durbin, for having addressed the possibility of incentive incompatibilities under capitalism. As Lerner wrote:

In this comparison we must take the theoretical system in both cases i.e., leaving apart such *sociological questions as incentive*, etc. In general Mr. Durbin refuses to discuss these matters in the article considered and he is well justified in refusing to accept in the context of the problem of economic accounting such criticisms of socialism as depend upon these considerations. He is, however, guilty of a similar sin in the opposite direction when he declares it to be a disadvantage of capitalistic production that the managers of joint-stock companies will reinvest their quasi-rents in their own enterprise, even if the yield is greater elsewhere, because by so doing they safeguard their own jobs… *This is not an accounting but a personal or sociological problem which may well be even more serious in some forms of socialist economy.* (emphasis added, Lerner 1937, 267, fn. 1)

To summarize, by the 1940s, both the utilization and rejection of mainstream neoclassical economic theory by its defenders and critics, respectively, became based upon an analysis of the formal conditions of competitive equilibrium. It is for this reason that Hayek (and Mises) had to rethink and rearticulate their understanding of the neoclassical economics. In doing so, however, "Mises and Hayek were not simply reiterating the main features of their earlier shared economic principles (which these new developments were replacing). What Mises and Hayek were doing (in their respective contributions during the 1937–48 decade) was to attain a deeper insight and more articulated understanding of what they had believed to be *the shared, settled principles of all 'modern' schools of economics*" (emphasis added, Kirzner 2017, 864–865).

Market Socialism and Market Processes

Lange's argument presented a formidable challenge for believers in the productive superiority of capitalism, a challenge that Hayek would devote the better part of the 1940s to attempting to meet.[6] Hayek's response to Lange's model for market socialism came in the form of a multipronged argument. First, Hayek argued that the models proposed by Lange and

---

[6] Hayek's essays are collected in Hayek ([1948] 1980). See Caldwell (1997) for a discussion of the development of Hayek's thought that was brought on by his debate over socialism.

others reflected a preoccupation with equilibrium. The models possessed no ability to discuss the necessary adaptations to changing conditions required in real economic life. The imputation of value of capital goods from consumer goods represented a classic case in point. Schumpeter (1942, 175) had argued that once consumer goods were valued in the market (as they would be in Lange's model), a market for producer goods was unnecessary because we could impute the value of the corresponding capital goods *ipso facto*.

This "solution" was of course accurate in the model of general equilibrium where there is a pre-reconciliation of plans (i.e. no false trades). Hayek's concern, however (like Mises's) was not with the model of general equilibrium, but with how imputation actually takes place within the market process so that production plans come to be coordinated with consumer demands through time. This is not a trivial procedure and requires various market signals to guide entrepreneurs in their decision process on the use of capital good combinations in production projects. In a fundamental sense, Hayek was arguing that Mises's calculation argument could not be addressed by assuming it away. Of course, if we focus our analytical attention on the properties of a world in which all plans have already been fully coordinated (general competitive equilibrium), then the process by which that coordination came about in the first place will not be highlighted since the process will have already been worked out by assumption. "The statement that, if people know everything, they are in equilibrium is true simply because that is how we define equilibrium," Hayek writes. "The assumption of a perfect market in this sense is just another way of saying that equilibrium exists but does not get us any nearer an explanation of when and how such a state will come about. It is clear that, if we want to make the assertion that, under certain conditions, people will approach that state, we must explain by what process they will acquire the necessary knowledge" ([1937] 1948, 46).

This was Hayek's central point. Absent certain institutions and practices, the process that brings about the coordination of plans would not take place. Some alternative process would have to be relied upon for decision-making concerning resources, and that process would by necessity be one that could not rely on the guides of private property incentives, relative price signals, and profit/loss accounting since the socialist project had explicitly abolished them. In other words, the *ipso facto* proposition of competitive equilibrium was irrelevant for the world outside of that state of equilibrium. The fact that leading neoclassical economists (such as Knight and Schumpeter) had not recognized this elementary point demonstrated the havoc that a preoccupation with the state of equilibrium can have on economic science.

In Hayek's view, the problem with concentrating on a state of affairs as opposed to the process was not limited to its assumption of that which must be argued for, but also included the direction of attention away from how changing circumstances require adaptations on the part of participants. Equilibrium, by definition, is a state of affairs in which no agent within the system has any incentive to change. If all the data were frozen, then indeed the logic of the situation would lead individuals to a state of rest where all plans were coordinated and resources were used in the most efficient manner currently known.

The Lange/Lerner conditions would hold—prices would be set to marginal cost (and thus the full opportunity cost of production would be reflected in the price) and production would be at the minimum point on the firm's average cost curve (and thus the least-cost technologies would be employed). But what, Hayek asked, do these conditions tell us about a world where the data are not frozen? What happens when tastes and technologies change?

Marginal conditions, he noted, do not provide any guide to action; they are instead outcomes of a process of learning within a competitive situation. In a tautological sense, competition exists in all social settings, and thus individuals find that in order to do the best that they can, given the situation, they will stumble toward equating marginal costs and marginal benefits. This is true at the individual level, no matter what system we are talking about. But this says nothing about the first optimality rule proposed in the Lange/Lerner model—that of setting price equal to marginal cost—nor does it address the second optimality rule of the model—that of producing at the level which minimizes average costs. Both rules are definitions of an end point in a certain competitive process, but are not guiding rules for actors caught within that process. Prices are not given to us from above. Rather, entrepreneurs must discover anew each day what the best price to offer is, what the least-cost methods of production are, and how to best satisfy consumer tastes.

Effective allocation of resources requires that there is a correspondence between the underlying conditions of tastes, technology, and resource endowments, and the induced variables of prices and profit and loss accounting. In perfect competition, the underlying variables and the induced variables are in perfect alignment, and thus there are no coordination problems. Traditions in economic scholarship that reject the self-regulation proposition tend to deny that there is any correspondence between the underlying conditions and the induced variables in the market.

Hayek, in contrast to both of these alternatives, sought to explain the lag between the underlying and the induced. Economics for him is a science of tendency and direction, not one of exact determination. Changes in the underlying conditions set in motion accommodating adjustments that are reflected in the induced variables on the market. The induced variables lag behind, but are continually pulled toward the underlying conditions.[7]

The detour on equilibration versus equilibrium in the core of economic theory was important because of the turn the debate took after Lange's paper and the transformation of basic language in economics. Hayek tended to emphasize the dynamic aspects of competition more than Lange did. Market efficiency is adaptive to Hayek, but to Lange and the neoclassicists, it is a question of static efficiency. Similarly, to Hayek, prices not only represent exchange ratios, but also serve a crucial role in economizing on information, utilizing knowledge, and critical learning.

Hayek's fundamental critique of Lange's contribution was that economists ought not to assume what they must in fact demonstrate for their argument to hold. Informational assumptions were particularly problematic in this regard. As Hayek developed his argument, he, for the most part, steered clear of motivational issues and claimed that individuals (both privately and as planners) would have the best of intentions. However, while assuming moral perfection, he refused to assume

---

[7] Kirzner (1992) provides perhaps the most thorough discussion of this vision of the market process.

intellectual perfection. This was quite understandable. If one assumes both moral and intellectual perfection, then what possible objection could anyone raise to any social system of production? In line with our discussion earlier about equilibration versus equilibrium, Hayek argues that perfect knowledge is a defining characteristic of equilibrium, but cannot be an assumption within the process of equilibration. The question instead is: how do individuals come to learn that which is necessary for them to have in order to coordinate their plans with others?

Consider the following lengthy passage from his response to the market socialists in "Socialist Calculation: The Competitive 'Solution'" (1940, 139):

> For the purposes of the argument it may be granted that [socialist managers] will be as capable and as anxious to produce cheaply as the average capitalist entrepreneur. The problem arises because one of the most important forces which in a truly competitive economy brings about the reduction of costs to the minimum discoverable will be absent, namely, price competition. In the discussion of this sort of problem, as in the discussion of so much of economic theory at the present time, the question is frequently treated as if the cost curves were objectively given facts. What is forgotten is that the method which under given conditions is the cheapest is a thing that has to be discovered, and to be discovered anew, sometimes almost from day to day, by the entrepreneur, and that, in spite of the strong inducement, it is by no means regularly the established entrepreneur, the man in charge of the existing plant, who will discover what is the best method. The force which in a competitive society brings about the reduction of price to the lowest cost at which the quantity salable at that cost can be produced is the opportunity for anybody who knows a cheaper method to come in at his own risk and to attract customers by underbidding the other producers. But, if prices are fixed by the authority, this method is excluded.

In "Economics and Knowledge"([1937] 1948) and "The Use of Knowledge in Society"(1945), Hayek develops the argument that the way in which economic agents come to learn represents the crucial empirical element of economics, and that price signals represent the key institutional guidepost for learning within the market process. Traditional neoclassical theory taught that prices were incentive devices—which indeed they are. But Hayek pointed out that prices also serve an informational role, which is, unfortunately, often overlooked. Prices serve this role by economizing on the amount of information that market participants must process and by translating the subjective trade-offs that other participants make into "objective" information that others can use in formulating and carrying out their plans.

As the debate progressed, Hayek emphasized different aspects of the argument developed in these two classic articles and came to place particular emphasis on the contextual nature of the knowledge that is utilized within the market process. Knowledge, he pointed out, does not exist disembodied from the context of its discovery and use. Economic participants base their actions on concrete knowledge of particular times and places. This local knowledge that market participants utilize in orienting their actions is simply not abstract and objective, and thus is incapable of being used by planners outside that context to plan the large-scale organization of society.

Hayek's reasons for holding that planning cannot work are not limited to the problem that the information required for the task of coordinating the plans of a multitude of individuals is too vast to organize effectively. The knowledge utilized within the market by entrepreneurs does not exist outside that local context, and thus cannot even be organized in principle. It is not that planners would face a complex computational task; it is that they face an impossible task, because the knowledge required is not accessible to them, no matter what technological developments may come along to ease the computational burden.

Hayek and the Political Economy of Liberalism and Socialism

The classical economists' argument for liberalism demonstrated its robustness in the face of a world of less-than-benevolent individuals. It is easy to show that liberalism will work well when all individuals are assumed to be perfectly benevolent. But how does it deal with more realistic assumptions? The classical economists sought to show that even in a society populated by completely self-interested individuals, the market would ensure that the desires of men would be satisfied. Smith's famous invisible hand postulate illustrated how, under conditions of respect for property, contract, and consent, each person pursuing his or her own interests will lead to the promotion of society's interests as a whole. His most famous quote from the *Wealth of Nations* summarizes this point nicely: "It is not from the benevolence of the butcher, the brewer, or the baker, that we expect our dinner, but from their regard to their own interest. We address ourselves, not to their humanity, but to their self-love" (Smith [1776] 1976, 18).

Even in the case of knavish men, Smith demonstrated that economic liberalism enabled peaceful social cooperation that leads to increases in productivity. Indeed, he pointed out that liberalism could not only deal with a world of selfish individuals, but actually harnessed man's self-interested motivation for the benefit of everyone. Under liberalism, selfish and rapacious man is "led by an invisible hand to promote an end which was no part of his intention"—the interest of society (Smith [1776] 1976, 477). It was within this framework that the classical economists formulated their argument for liberalism. As Hayek stated it:

> [T]he main point about which there can be little doubt is that Smith's chief concern was not so much with what man might occasionally achieve when he was at his best but that he should have as little opportunity to do harm when he was at his worst. It would scarcely be too much to claim that the main merit of the individualism which he and his contemporaries advocated is that it is a system under which bad men can do least harm. It is a social system which does not depend for its functioning on our finding good men for running it, or on all men becoming better than they now are, but which makes use of men in all their given variety and complexity, sometimes good and sometimes bad, sometimes intelligent and more often stupid. ([1946] 1948, 11–12)

David Hume's "On the Independency of Parliament" makes it clear that like Smith, he too is interested in developing a case for liberalism that satisfies the hard case rather than the easy one. "In constraining any system of government and fixing the several checks and controls of the constitution," Hume argued, "every man ought to be supposed a knave and to have no other end, in all his actions, than private interest" ([1777] 1985, 42). In this way, Hume, like Smith, demonstrated how liberalism intended to construct a robust political and economic system.

Hayek restated this argument for the robustness of liberalism in *The Constitution of Liberty* (1960) and later in *Law, Legislation, and Liberty* (1973, 1976, 1979), where he developed the idea of the importance of particular institutions as the backdrop against which erring and ignorant agents can learn to adapt their behavior so as to coordinate their activities with those of others. According to Hayek, the institutions of private property, contract, and consent, embedded in a system of general rules that protect these institutions, are crucial not only to mobilizing incentives, but also in ensuring that economic actors are able to utilize their individual knowledge of time and place in making decisions in such a way that their plans may be realized. These institutions Hayek cites are precisely the institutions of liberalism—private property and freedom of contract protected under a rule of law. And through them, Hayek shows us, liberalism is able effectively to deal with actor ignorance. In fact, Hayek went as far as to state the case for liberalism on the grounds of our ignorance:

> If there were omniscient men, if we could know not only all that affects the attainment of our present wishes but also our future wants and desires, there would be little case for liberty. And, in turn, liberty of the individual would, of course, make complete foresight impossible. Liberty is essential in order to leave room for the unforeseeable and unpredictable; we want it because we have learned to expect from it the opportunity of realizing many of our aims. It is because every individual knows so little and, in particular, because we rarely know which of us knows best that we trust the independent and competitive efforts of many to induce the emergence of what we shall want when we see it. (1960, 29)

Conclusion

Hayek's research program in political economy emerged in his career-long struggle with arguments advocating socialist economic planning as a corrective to the economic woes of laissez-faire capitalism. Hayek started his career under the guidance of Wieser as a technical economist, but the issues he worked on were related to the core questions of the intertemporal coordination of production plans with consumption demands. In essence, his research path from the beginning dealt with the essence of the economic arguments concerning capitalism and socialism.

Once he moved beyond the technical question of the imputation of value for capital goods, Hayek focused on questions related to the effects of monetary disturbances on the coordination of plans. Alongside Mises, Hayek was able to develop the monetary theory of the trade cycle and offer the most coherent non-Keynesian explanation for the Great Depression. Hayek rose in scientific stature quickly, but soon found himself embroiled in debate, with Keynes on the one side, and market socialists on the other.

In response to these two criticisms of economic liberalism, Hayek would find himself over the next decades searching for answers, in the catallactic (or exchange) tradition of economic theorizing as opposed to the maximizing and equilibrium tradition; in the methodological critique of scientism as opposed to the near-universal acceptance of methodological monism; and in the institutional analysis of liberalism as opposed to the institutionally antiseptic theory of post-WWII neoclassical economics. The debates that Hayek initiated on methodology and policy continue still.[8] In this regard, Hayek's work remains part of our "extended present," as Kenneth Boulding (1971) would have put it in discussing the continuing relevance of an economic figure long dead. The plausibility of the "Hayek conjectures" with which we started this essay is a function of the plausibility of the network of scientific propositions he weaved in support of them, in economics, political economy, and social philosophy. And, as he argued in the 2nd volume of *Law, Legislation and Liberty*: "Morals, to be viable, must satisfy certain requirements, requirements which we may not be able to specify but may only be able to find out by trial and error. What is required is not merely consistency, or

---

[8] On the current status of the debate over markets and socialism, see volume 9 of Boettke (2000), which is a collection of the main contemporary papers on the subject. On the continuing debates over the implications of Hayek's economics and political economy for contemporary scholarship, see Caldwell (2004).

compatibility of the rules as well as the acts demanded by them. A system of morals also must produce a functioning order, capable of maintaining the apparatus of civilization which it presupposes" (1976, 98).

Unfortunately, this point was obscured in the debate over socialism among economists and political economists. Our moral intuitions, which have evolved from our small group past, are simply at odds with the moral demands of the Great Society. Liberalism is a doctrine that emerged to help cultivate the morality required to realize productive specialization and peaceful social cooperation in the extended order. The failure of socialism was not due to the corruption of morality by man, but to a moral system that cannot work to deliver liberty, prosperity, and peace. Hayek demonstrated from the more or less technical economic problems found in *Collective Economic Planning* (1935) to the more or less philosophical and anthropological problems found in *The Fatal Conceit* (1988) that socialism was little more than a false promise and that efforts to realize socialism in practice resulted in a loss of economic and political freedom, and a decline in human well-being. Socialism, in short, is not a morality fit for human flourishing.

Bibliography

Boettke, Peter J. 2000. *Socialism and the Market, Vol. 9: The Current Status of the Debate*. London: Routledge.

Boettke, Peter J., and Ennio Piano. Forthcoming. The Hayek Drama at the LSE. In *The History of Economics at the London School of Economics*, ed. Robert Cord. New York: Palgrave Macmillan.

Boulding, Kenneth E. 1971. After Samuelson, Who Needs Adam Smith? *History of Political Economy* 3 (2): 225–237.

Caldwell, Bruce J. 1997. Hayek and Socialism. *Journal of Economic Literature* 35 (4): 1856–1890.

———. 2004. *Hayek's Challenge: An Intellectual Biography of F. A. Hayek*. Chicago: University of Chicago Press.

Dickinson, H.D. 1933. Price Formation in a Socialist Community. *The Economic Journal* 43 (170): 237–250.

Hayek, F. A. [1931] 1967. *Prices and Production*. 2nd ed. New York: August M. Kelley.

————. 1933. The Trend of Economic Thinking. *Economica* 40: 121–137.

————, ed. 1935. *Collectivist Economic Planning*. London: Routledge and Kegan Paul.

————. [1937] 1948. Economics and Knowledge. In *Individualism and Economic Order*. Chicago: University of Chicago Press, chapter 2.

————. 1940. Socialist Calculation: The Competitive 'Solution'. *Economica* 7 (26): 125–149.

————. 1944. *The Road to Serfdom*. Chicago: University of Chicago Press.

————. 1945. The Use of Knowledge in Society. *The American Economic Review* 35 (4): 519–530.

————. [1946] 1948. Individualism: True and False. In *Individualism and Economic Order*. Chicago: University of Chicago Press.

————. [1946] 1948. The Meaning of Competition. In *Individualism and Economic Order*. Chicago: University of Chicago Press, chapter 5.

————. [1948] 1980. *Individualism and Economic Order*. Chicago: University of Chicago Press.

————. 1960. *The Constitution of Liberty*. Chicago: University of Chicago Press.

————. 1973. *Law, Legislation, and Liberty, Vol. 1: Rules and Order*. Chicago: University of Chicago Press.

————. 1976. *Law, Legislation and Liberty, Vol. 2: The Mirage of Social Justice*. Chicago: University of Chicago Press.

————. 1979. *Law, Legislation and Liberty, Vol. 3: The Political Order of a Free People*. Chicago: University of Chicago Press.

————. 1988. *The Fatal Conceit: The Errors of Socialism, the Collected Works of F. A. Hayek*. Ed. W. W. Bartley, III. Chicago: University of Chicago Press.

Hume, David. [1777] 1985. Of the Independency of Parliament. In *Essays Moral, Political and Literary*, ed. Eugene F. Miller, Indianapolis: Liberty Fund.

Kaldor, Nicholas. 1932. The Economic Situation of Austria. *Harvard Business Review* 11 (10): 23–34.

Kirzner, Israel M. 1992. Entrepreneurship, Uncertainty, and Austrian Economics. In *Austrian Economics: Tensions and New Directions*, ed. Bruce Caldwell and Stephan Böhm. Boston: Kluwer Academic Publishers.

————. 2017. The Entrepreneurial Market Process—An Exposition. *Southern Economic Journal* 83 (4): 855–868.

Knight, Frank. 1936. The Place of Marginal Economics in a Collectivist System. *American Economic Review* 26 (1): 255–266.

Lange, Oskar. 1936. On the Economic Theory of Socialism. *Review of Economic Studies* 4 (1): 53–71.

————. 1937. On the Economic Theory of Socialism: Part Two. *Review of Economic Studies* 4 (2): 123–142.

Lavoie, Don. 1985. *National Economic Planning: What is Left?* Cambridge, MA: Ballinger.

Lerner, Abba P. 1934. Economic Theory and Socialist Economy. *Review of Economic Studies* 2 (1): 51–61.

————. 1935. Economic Theory and Socialist Economy: A Rejoinder. *Review of Economic Studies* 2 (2): 152–154.

————. 1936. A Note on Socialist Economies. *Review of Economic Studies* 4 (1): 72–76.

Mises, Ludwig von. [1920] 1935. Economic Calculation in the Socialist Commonwealth. In *Collectivist Economic Planning*, ed. F.A. Hayek and Trans. S. Alder, 87–130. London: Routledge.

————. [1922] 1981. *Socialism: An Economic and Sociological Analysis.* Indianapolis: Liberty Fund.

Schumpeter, Joseph A. 1942. *Capitalism, Socialism, and Democracy.* New York: Harper Perennial Modern Classics.

Smith, Adam. [1776] 1976. *An Inquiry into the Nature and Causes of the Wealth of Nations.* Oxford: Oxford University Press.

Taylor, Fred M. 1929. The Guidance of Production in a Socialist State. *American Economic Review* 19 (1): 1–8.

6

The False Promise of Socialism and *The Road to Serfdom*

Introduction

It has been over 70 years since Hayek published *The Road to Serfdom* (1944) and since that time Hitler was defeated, ending WWII, with victory for the Western democracies. Following their wartime alliance, the Cold War emerged between the Western democratic states and the Soviet Union and its satellite countries, ensuing roughly between 1945 and 1991. The constitutional democracies of the West were transformed into social democratic states as governments in these countries grew in size and expanded their scope between 1945 and 1980. In the intellectual realm, the ascendancy of Keynesian macroeconomic theory and policy of demand management was matched by the development of microeconomic market failure theory and policies regulating commerce and industry. With the breakdown of the Keynesian consensus in the 1970s with stagflation, the deregulation of commerce and industry in the 1980s, and the collapse of communism in the 1990s, it seemed to many that Hayek's ideas put forth in *The Road to Serfdom* were at least superficially vindicated by history.

© The Author(s) 2018
Peter J. Boettke, *F. A. Hayek*, Great Thinkers in Economics,
https://doi.org/10.1057/978-1-137-41160-0_6

Hayek's most famous work is often read as a policy book and a political tract for its time. It is also often read as little more than a "slippery slope" argument, and thus, one wrong step leads one down a road from a free society to the gulag. Alves and Meadowcroft have argued in a recent article that "Hayek's slippery slope argument set out in *The Road to Serfdom* is empirically false" (2014, 859). Their claim is based on illustrating a *positive* relationship between government spending as a percentage of GDP in the Western democracies and data from the Economic Freedom Index and Freedom House ratings on political freedom. While the authors are careful not to draw any causal link between government spending and economic and political freedom, their claim is that these figures are prima facie evidence that Hayek's argument failed to anticipate the reality of the post-WWII Western democracies. This chapter counters those claims by explaining that Hayek's book is part of a broader project on *The Abuse of Reason* dealing with the institutional infrastructure within which economic activity takes place. His argument, rather than being a slippery slope, is an immanent critique of the socialist program as advocated by British socialists, who were his primary target in the 1940s. Understood this way, Hayek was *not* making a claim about the "inevitability" of totalitarianism from implementing central planning. Rather, Hayek's slippery slope argument was a claim about the instability between the organizational logic of planning and its effect on liberal institutions.

Hayek would be joined in his effort to warn intellectuals about the growth of government interference in the market economy by Milton Friedman (popular) and James Buchanan (analytical) in the second half of the twentieth century. Buchanan's works, such as *The Calculus of Consent* (Buchanan and Tullock 1962) and *The Limits of Liberty* (Buchanan 1975), sought to grapple with the analytical questions of how to structurally bind the government to minimize the predatory state and empower the protective and productive state. Buchanan's work had a wide academic influence, but limited popular appeal. On the other hand, Friedman's works, such as *Capitalism and Freedom* ([1962] 2002) and *Free to Choose* (Friedman and Friedman 1980), had an amazing popular appeal and practical impact in the world of public affairs. All three— Hayek, Friedman, and Buchanan—would be recognized with the Nobel Prize for their contributions to economic *science*, and all three would also serve as President of the Mont Pelerin Society, reflecting their stature as leading modern representatives of classical liberalism.

The three critical events to highlight this would be the shift of policy focus in China under Deng Xiaoping, in the UK under Margaret Thatcher, and in the USA under Ronald Reagan. Let me state clearly that the rhetoric of these policy shifts always outdistanced their reality. As Xiaoping has quipped, it may not matter what color the cat is as long as it catches the mouse, but it matters that the party maintains central control. Thatcher and Reagan may have respectively slowed the growth of government, but they did not reverse it in either the UK or the USA, respectively. Still the *relative* move toward policies of economic freedom in the 1980–2005 period as compared to the policies of economic regulation from 1945 to 1980 resulted in a series of significant improvements in the economic well-being of billions of individuals across the globe—as documented in Andrei Shleifer's article "The Age of Milton Friedman" (2009). Moreover, Hayek's *The Road to Serfdom* has witnessed a renaissance in popularity, not only among transitional political reformers in post-Soviet Russia, such as Anatoly Chubais (Shapiro 2001, 18), but also political commentators, such as Glenn Beck, Rush Limbaugh, and Mark Levin (see Farrant and McPhail 2010, 2012; Boettke and Snow 2012).

However, it would be absurd to claim a direct causal link between the publication of *The Road to Serfdom* and improvements in the standard of living throughout the world (with the notable troubling locations of Africa and Latin America). It might even be absurd to claim much of a causal link between the publication and the practical affairs of public policy—as if policy is directly about ideas, rather than interests that form and coalesce around certain public policies. But ideas *frame* the policy debate, and in so doing, can indirectly impact the tide of human affairs.

Hayek's work, I want to suggest, had such an indirect influence—not only *The Road to Serfdom* (1944) but also *The Constitution of Liberty* (1960). Rather than allow these works to be relegated to coffee table status, I will focus here on discussing the intellectual context and substantive argument that Hayek puts forth in *The Road to Serfdom*. I contend that rather than making a claim of "inevitability," Hayek's slippery slope argument was a claim about the instability between the organizational logic of planning and its effect on liberal institutions.

The Misesian Roots of Hayek's Argument

Though Hayek himself had regarded *The Road to Serfdom* as a political book, such a labeling requires clarification. The political consequences of central planning, which Hayek explicates, follows from Mises's *economic* critique of socialism. Hayek's argument cannot be taken outside the context of the Socialist Calculation Debate, which followed from Mises's critique, ensuing between the 1920s and 1940s. Understood this way, *The Road to Serfdom* picks up where Hayek's edited volume *Collectivist Economic Planning* (1935) left off. By that, I mean simply that Hayek operated under the impression that the works by the economists he reprinted in *Collective Economic Planning* had decisively demonstrated the failure of socialist plans to centrally plan the economy. In particular, the work of Ludwig von Mises had demonstrated the theoretical *impossibility* of the socialist economic planner to engage in rational economic calculation. Without this ability to engage in rational economic calculation, the socialist planner will be unable to meet socialist objectives by way of socialist means. The project suffered from a devastating internal contradiction.

This was Hayek's theoretical touchstone and must never be forgotten in understanding the nature of the argument as developed in *The Road to Serfdom*. Mises is right, but intellectuals and practical men of affairs are not listening. They are proceeding as if they have either answered Mises's objection, or successfully side-stepped it. Therefore, Hayek is demonstrating what happens when folks pursue a policy path that has been demonstrated to be logically incoherent, but pursue it anyway. The intellectual autopsy that he performs thus shows how this effort resulted in the death of the aspirational dreams of its advocates.

The Road to Serfdom plays out this scenario. It is important to remember as well that the British market socialists—who, in the decade after *Collectivist Economic Planning,* had thought they had successfully designed schemes to counter Mises—also were committed to the proposition that their version of socialism would be completely compatible with the British traditions of individualism, democratic freedom, and the rule of law. So, in his autopsy, Hayek was determined to show

British intellectuals that this compatibility was also a figment of their imagination in the same way that their schemes to address (or side-step) the Misesian challenge were. But, as Hayek argued, "democratic socialism, the great utopia of the last few generations, is not only unachievable, but that to strive for it produces something so utterly different that few of those who now wish it would be prepared to accept the consequences, many will not believe until the connection has been laid bare in all its aspects" (1944, 31).

Mises's argument established that the socialist ends of increased material progress cannot be achieved through socialist means due to the inability to engage in rational economic calculation. We should be careful here because: (a) definitions matter, so a claim about means-ends relies on consistency in the meaning of the terms; and (b) establishing that something is logically incoherent does not establish that individuals will not attempt to pursue this path anyway. Socialism, at the time of Mises's writing, had a specific meaning in the context of economic policy. It was to rationalize production to such an extent that mankind would experience a burst of productivity and propel it from the "Kingdom of Necessity" to the "Kingdom of Freedom." Rationalizing production would eliminate the waste of capitalism that results due to the groping efforts of errant entrepreneurs in their quest for profits, even under favorable conditions, as well as eliminating monopoly power and macroeconomic volatility. By curbing the monopolistic tendencies and the inherent instability of capitalism, rationalizing production through socialist economic planning would result in a new level of material progress that will not only provide the basis for the end of class conflict, but also usher in a new era of peaceful and harmonious relations between all men. That is the desired goal of the socialists, but we still have to be clear on the means of socialist economic planning.

The means are the abolition of private property in the means of production, the establishment of collective ownership, the substitution of administered prices for the free fluctuation of prices dictated by the exchange relations in the market, and the development of economic plans that were based on the idea of production for direct use rather than production for profit. Mises iterated his challenge by simply asking the following: are the socialist means of collective ownership of the means of production, such as administered prices and production for direct use, capable of achieving the socialist ends of rationalizing production, producing advanced material progress, and harmonizing the social relations between the classes? His answer was NO, the reason being the inability of socialist planners to engage in rational economic calculation of the alternative use of scarce productive resources. Production under socialism would be rudderless and would, in fact, be little more than steps in the dark. Without private property, there are no market prices, and without market prices, there can be no rational calculation. It is that simple and that profound. Economic calculation is critical to the efficient operation of an economy because it is precisely that mechanism that enables economic actors to sort out from the numerous array of technological feasible projects those which are economic viable.

Following our line of argument, *The Road to Serfdom* that Hayek describes is the by-product of the truth of the Misesian argument biting against socialist aspirations. As Hayek argued in *The Counter-Revolution of Science* ([1952] 1979, 68–69):

> The problems which they [social sciences] try to answer arise only insofar as the conscious action of many men produce undersigned results, insofar as regularities are observed which are not the result of anybody's design. If social phenomena showed no order except insofar as they were consciously designed, there would be indeed be no room for theoretical sciences of society and there would be, as is often argued, only problems of psychology. It is only insofar as some sort of order arises as a result of individual action but without being designed by any individual that a problem is raised which demands a theoretical explanation.

The problems Hayek identifies are the unintended and undesirable (from the point of view of the advocate) by-product of the policymaker attempting to pursue socialist policies and confronting the reality of the Misesian critique.

Hayek's Journey from Technical Economist to Political Economist

It was during the Socialist Calculation Debate that Hayek, along with Mises, began "a process of improved self-understanding" (Kirzner 1988, 3), not only of the entrepreneurial market process but, more importantly, of the institutional conditions within which the market process generates tendencies toward the mutual adjustment of decentralized decision-makers (Hayek [1937] 1948, 53). Economic analysis proceeds on the basis of the establishment of clearly defined and strictly enforced private property rights. This is the basis of exchange relationships in the market that give us the price system, as well as the complex division of labor that emerges as prices guide production decisions. Since the institutional infrastructure was fixed and given, it was too easily glossed over by modern economists in their analysis of alternative economic systems. Hayek sought to correct this oversight. Though Hayek began his career as a technical economist focused on the problem of imputation, intertemporal coordination, and industrial fluctuations, his debate with other economists over the viability of socialism led him increasingly to explore the institutional foundations of the market economy, and the underlying philosophical issues that clouded their understanding of those foundations.

However, it is important to note that Hayek intended *The Road to Serfdom* to be part of a larger project that he never completed, dubbed *The Abuse of Reason*, out of which he also published *The Counter-Revolution of Science* ([1952] 1979). Moreover, the emphasis on the rule of law and spontaneous order that were prefigured in *The Road to Serfdom* would later be stressed in Hayek's later works, such as *The Constitution of Liberty* (1960) and *Law, Legislation, and Liberty* (1973, 1976, 1979).

Putting *The Road to Serfdom* in the context of this larger project also provides further evidence against not only the inevitability thesis in Hayek's slippery slope argument, but also against the notion that Hayek was trying to generate point predictions about the future of the Western democracies. As Bruce Caldwell states:

Hayek denied this reading both in the book itself and in subsequent responses to his critics. That the book was originally intended as part of the

Abuse of Reason project provides further evidence in Hayek's favor. One of the major themes of the "Scientism [and the Study of Society]" essay is that the historical search for general laws that would allow one to predict the future course of history is chimerical. Would it make sense for the author of such an essay to then turn around later in his work and attempt to predict the future course of history? (2004, 241, fn. 4)

While the empirical data that Alves and Meadowcroft provide are factually correct, it takes Hayek's argument out of its proper theoretical context, in which Hayek was trying to render intelligible or explain why countries like Russia, Italy, and Germany had gone down the road to serfdom. Hayek was not attempting to establish any "scientistic" point predictions about a one-to-one relationship between government spending and freedom—both economic and political—as Alves and Meadowcroft would argue. Rather, Hayek was inferring backward, from the desired goals of the socialists, those institutional changes that had been implemented to pursue such goals. Given such institutional changes, Hayek demonstrates that a consistent pursuit of such goals would generate systematic tendencies that the socialists had never desired, such as the rise of totalitarianism that had occurred in Nazi Germany and Soviet Russia. Hayek was not predicting the "inevitability" of totalitarianism. Rather, taking totalitarianism as it existed in the 1940s, Hayek was trying to explain how this historical tragedy manifested itself unintendedly from the desire of socialists decades prior to the rise of Hitler and Stalin.

As Hayek transitioned from a technical economist in the 1920s and 1930s, to the political economist, to, dare we say, the social philosopher that he would be for the rest of his career, it is vital to remember the underlying economics in his argument. The basic economic calculus persists throughout his work, and the idea of the epistemic properties of alternative institutional arrangements remains his analytical focus. When Hayek decides to write *The Road to Serfdom*, he is ready to deploy his basic economic mode of analysis to address the institutional questions that real-world socialist economies would need to face, and the logic of the situation that socialist decision-makers must confront.

Not only would he make the Misesian argument that socialist means are incoherent with respect to socialist ends, but that the metamorphosis of the system that occurs in the attempt to pursue this impossible task results in a political and economic reality from which the socialist thinker would recoil. The logic of the situation and the logic of organization under socialist planning is such that democracy and the rule of law are unsustainable, and the system, if pursued to its logical end, would result in the concentration of political power in the hands of men least capable of constraining the abuse of power. The worst of us, it seems, will end up on top, a result confirmed by the coincidence of the three leading political mass murders of the twentieth century rising to the top of socialist systems—Hitler, Stalin, Mao—and also reflected in the practice of more recent socialist leaders such as Pol Pot, Castro, and Chavez. Hayek's argument is not an argument of inevitability (more on that in the next section), but merely a simple application of the principle of comparative advantage to the realm of politics.

Similarly, Hayek's analysis of the compatibility of socialism with democratic freedoms and the rule of law relies on his analysis of the logic of the situation. Socialism requires a level of political agreement to operationalize its policies that is far greater in detail than what is required under liberalism. Liberalism only requires agreement on the general rules by which we interact with each other. "Don't hurt people and don't take their stuff" is rather straightforward. But questions of a more detailed nature are progressively more difficult to resolve in such a straightforward manner. As Hayek (1944, 91–92) puts it:

> The question raised by economic planning is, therefore, not merely whether we shall be able to satisfy what we regard as our more or less important needs in the way we prefer. It is whether it shall be we who decide what is more, and what is less, important for us, or whether this is to be decided by the planner. Economic planning would not affect merely those of our marginal needs that we have in mind when we speak contemptuously about the merely economic. It would, in effect, mean that we as individuals should no longer be allowed to decide what we regard as marginal.

And in the next paragraph, he continues:

> The authority directing all economic activity would control not merely the part of our lives which is concerned with inferior things; it would control the allocation of the limited means for all our ends. And whoever controls

all economic activity controls the means for all our ends and must therefore decide which are to be satisfied and what not. This is really the crux of the matter. Economic control is not merely control of a sector of human life which can be separated from the rest; it is the control of the means for all our ends. And whoever has control of the means must also determine which ends are to be served, which values are to be rated higher and which lower—in short, what men should believe and strive for.

Earlier, in *The Road to Serfdom*, Hayek had already made the argument that since any idea of coherent planning requires it to be comprehensive and based on agreement at each of the successive stages—an agreement that democracy cannot guarantee—the logic of the situation will agitate toward a move beyond the process of democratic deliberation and instead a concentration of power will be entrusted to the responsible authorities, unfettered by democratic procedures (1944, 67).

The organizational logic of planning is to concentrate decision power; the situational logic of such an organization incentivizes those who have a comparative advantage in exercising political power over others to rise to the top of the decision authority. "Just as the democratic statesman who sets out to plan economic life will soon be confronted with the alternative of either assuming dictatorial powers or abandoning his plans," Hayek tells his reader, "so the totalitarian dictator would soon have to choose between disregard of ordinary morals or failure. It is for this reason that the unscrupulous and uninhibited are likely to be more successful in a society tending toward totalitarianism" (1944, 135).

This Is Not a Slippery Slope

The counter-reaction to the Mises-Hayek critique by British socialists was to argue that socialist policy and economic and political freedom were compatible. E. F. Durbin, in a review article on *The Road to Serfdom*, published in the *Economic Journal* (1945, 358), argued that Hayek was wrong because: "We all wish to live in a community that is as rich as possible, in which consumers' preferences determine the relative output of goods that can be consumed by individuals, and in which there is freedom of discussion and political association and responsible government." Durbin also states that: "Most of us are socialist in our economics because we are 'liberal' in our philosophy." Even Hayek's close friend and comrade in the debate with market socialists, Lionel Robbins, came to argue in *The Economic Problem in Peace and War* ([1947] 1950, 28) that: "An individualist who recognizes the importance of public goods and a collectivist who recognizes the desirability of the maximum of individual freedom in consumption will find many points of agreement in common. The biggest dividing line of our day is, not between those who differ about organization as such, but between those who differ about the ends which organization has to serve."

It is our contention that both Durbin and Robbins are led down this argumentative alley because (a) they misinterpret Hayek as having abandoned (correctly in their estimation) Mises's "impossibility of rational economic calculation" thesis, and (b) read Hayek as making a slippery slope argument rather than what we will call the "instability" argument. In the argument we have been putting forth, we have an organizational logic and a situational logic going hand in hand to produce an instability in the policy space as a consequence of the incoherence of socialist policy means with socialist policy ends. As Hayek states in the quote we provided earlier, the decision authority must choose to go further along the amassing of centralized power, or abandon the policy agenda being pursued (Boettke 2005, 1048).

There is no ironclad inevitability in Hayek's argument, as presented in *The Road to Serfdom*. The argument, instead, is a warning of a tragic possibility that would be viewed as abhorrent from the point of view of those who believe they are "socialists in their economics because they are liberals in their philosophy." What Hayek was addressing to socialists of the time, particularly in England, was the lagging link between socialist ideas and how such socialist ideas would later demand institutional changes that are inconsistent with liberal principles, transforming democratic institutions into instruments of totalitarian rule:

> I know that many of my English friends have sometimes been shocked by the semi-Fascist views they would occasionally hear expressed by German refugees, whose genuinely socialist convictions could not be doubted. But

while these English observers put this down to their being Germans, the true explanation is that they were socialists whose experience had carried them several stages beyond that yet reached by socialists in this country. It is true, of course, that German socialists have found much support in their country from certain features of the Prussian tradition... But it would be a mistake to believe that the specific German rather than the socialist element produced totalitarianism. It was the prevalence of socialist views and not Prussianism that Germany had in common with Italy and Russia – and it was from the masses and not from the classes steeped in the Prussian tradition, and favoured by it, that National-Socialism arose. (1944, 9)

The connections that Hayek said must be laid bare are done so by this link between organizational logic and situational logic against the backdrop of Mises's impossibility thesis. Hayek's "economic calculus" does not rely on maximizing agents with full and complete information operating in a frictionless environment. Such omniscient automatons are not what Hayek (or Mises) are working with in their development of the economic way of thinking. The stumbling and bumbling actors that populate the analytical framework of Hayek are also not forever clueless; they are capable, but fallible human actors engaged in economic activity within specified organizational and institutional contexts.[1]

The market socialist writers of the 1930s and 1940s were ignoring the vital theoretical point about context mattering. They were instead myopically pursuing economic reasoning as if institutions did not matter, and that resource decisions were purely technical ones. They were misled in this endeavor by a preoccupation with an equilibrium state of affairs where, by definition, all the work that institutions have to do in shaping and guiding economic decisions is in fact done. But absent those very institutions that were now being ignored, economic forces that would be *at work* would in fact be different. This is where Hayek's organizational logic and situational logic enter back into the analysis. Institutions structure the incentives one faces in making decisions, and dictate the flow

---

[1] See Hayek, *Individualism and Economic Order* ([1948] 1980, 11–13) for a discussion of what we now might term his open-ended model of human choosing, and how this feeds into his appreciation of the institutions of secure property rights, the transference of those property rights through consent, and the keeping of promises via contract for the operation of a free economy that is able to harness productive specialization and produce peaceful cooperation.

and quality of information available to guide those decisions. In a world of scarcity, trade-offs abound, and decision-makers must have a means to negotiate those trade-offs. If it is not the institutions of property, prices and profit/loss that are aids to the human mind, something else must serve to structure incentives and guide decisions (see Boettke and Candela 2015).

Absent the institutional infrastructure of a liberal economy, you cannot get the results generated by that infrastructure. Liberalism may indeed be a philosophy, but it has an institutional embodiment and that institutional embodiment has an imprint. In short, you cannot be a socialist in economics and realize the philosophical goals of individual autonomy, productive specialization, and peaceful social cooperation. As Hayek made his institutional turn, starting with his 1937 paper, "Economics and Knowledge," but gaining in momentum through the 1940s and 1950s, the argumentative focal point moved decidedly off the behavioral assumptions of the individual actors and to the alternative institutional contexts within which they acted. Same players under different rules produce different outcomes.

So rather than postulating a slippery slope determinacy, it is better to read Hayek as making a radical argument for a form of pattern prediction indeterminacy—not unlike the sort of theorizing in the social sciences later argued for by Russell Hardin (see his *Indeterminacy and Society* 2005) as well as Vernon Smith (2003) in arguing for "ecological rationality" in contrast to "constructivist rationality." Depending on the institutional context, the situational logic will produce systemic tendencies in this, or that, direction. If the political decision-maker, when confronted with the failure of their socialist plans, chooses to abandon those plans and instead institute more liberal economic policies, then the organizational logic and situational logic will work in one way. But if not, and instead, our socialist planner pushes for further command and control measures, then the organizational logic and the situational logic will go in a different direction.

This pattern-predictive indeterminacy style of reasoning that Hayek's work reflects should also put to rest the mythology that the failure of Britain to devolve into Stalin's Gulag, or for Sweden to avoid that fate, somehow demonstrates the weak predictive power of Hayek's argument in *The Road to Serfdom*. First, Hayek did not make a deterministic slippery slope argument. He made an indeterminate instability argument—a choice must be made; if the wrong choice is made, the organizational logic and the situational logic will produce another decision node in which the frustration of failed plans forces a choice upon those in authority. Second, while the organizational logic and situational logic produce strong tendencies within the alternative institutional contexts, the fact that Hayek wrote *The Road to Serfdom* and that it has had such widespread success (even among its critics) meant that his ideas were part of the endogenous public choosing influences (Witt 1992). That Hayek's warning might have successfully done its job in stopping the realization of his worse prediction in Britain and the USA cannot be dismissed so easily out of hand.

Economic patterns are not invariant to institutional context. The fact that "sophisticated" social science ever thought they were, is a sign of the intellectual bedlam that can result when philosophical currents and methodological fashion are allowed to cloud basic economic theory.

Conclusion

As we reflect on the seven plus decades since Hayek published *The Road to Serfdom*, we should be amazed at the intellectual and practical progress that has been made. The Western democracies have gone through a period of relative opening up of markets compared to the over-regulation of those economies during the 1950–1980 period. The "great social experiment" with communism came to an end as these unfortunate countries suffered under the yoke of economic deprivation and political tyranny. The relative freedom experienced by the economies of East and Central Europe and the former Soviet Union, as well as that of East Asia, India, and China has led to rapid improvements in the material conditions of mankind across the globe.

But we cannot simply be satisfied with the triumph of the ideas one finds in Hayek (and also, Friedman and Buchanan). The reality of the democratic West is that the fiscal situation has largely been undisciplined after the ascent of Keynesian policies and this has produced an era of economic illusion that has yet to be reckoned with (Buchanan and Wagner 1977; Wagner 2012). Hayek's discussions of democracy and decision, of security and freedom, of economic freedom and political freedom are as relevant to our discussions today as they were at the time he sat down to write *The Road to Serfdom*. It was not Hitler and Stalin that concerned Hayek; it was the totalitarians in our midst that animated his effort. We face that same problem today, and we must be ever vigilant. As economists and political economists, we must be capable of competently deploying the technical economic principles that are necessary to analyze how alternative institutional arrangements impact the system's ability to realize the gains from productive specialization and peaceful social cooperation. In addition, to put it frankly, we must also be willing to expose and critically explore the fundamental philosophical issues that are too often smuggled in whenever we discuss the appropriate scope of governmental activities.

In the wake of the Global Financial Crisis, however, the old-time Keynesian narrative about the instability of capitalism has not gone unchallenged, and thus has not been able to wrest hold of the intellectual *zeitgeist* the way it did after the Great Depression. But the bad news is that in the policy space, the old-time Keynesian remedies still are reflected in the tacit presuppositions of political economy throughout the Western world. Our work as Hayekian economists and political economists remains cut out for us. We have indeed, as Hayek argued in his Nobel Lecture, made a mess of things in the twentieth century, and we are doing our best to make matters worse in the twenty-first century by blowing the opportunity of learning from the lessons of the twentieth century about the failure of the alliance of scientism and statism. But perhaps that just means that the challenge we face today is that same one that Hayek identified in the concluding words of *The Road to Serfdom*:

> If they [the 19th century liberals] had not yet fully learned what was necessary to create the world they wanted, the experience we have since gained ought to have equipped us better for the task. If in the first attempt to create a world of free men we have failed, we must try again. The guiding principle that a policy of freedom for the individual is the only truly progressive policy remains as true today as it was in the nineteenth century. (1944, 240)

Bibliography

Alves, André Azevedo, and John Meadowcroft. 2014. Hayek's Slippery Slope, Mixed Economy and the Dynamics of Rent Seeking. *Political Studies* 62 (4): 843–861.

Boettke, Peter J. 2005. Hayek and Market Socialism: Science, Ideology, and Public Policy. *Economic Affairs* 25 (4): 54–60.

Boettke, Peter J., and Rosolino A. Candela. 2015. What Is Old Should Be New Again: Methodological Individualism, Institutional Analysis and Spontaneous Order. *Sociologia* 2: 5–14. Available at SSRN: https://ssrn.com/abstract=2602906.

Boettke, Peter J., and Nicholas A. Snow. 2012. The Servants of Obama's Machinery: F. A. Hayek's *The Road to Serfdom* Revisited?—A Reply. *Eastern Economic Journal* 38 (4): 428–433.

Buchanan, James M. 1975. *The Limits of Liberty: Between Anarchy and Leviathan*. Chicago: University of Chicago Press.

Buchanan, James M., and Gordon Tullock. 1962. *The Calculus of Consent: Logical Foundations of Constitutional Democracy*. Ann Arbor: University of Michigan Press.

Buchanan, James M., and Richard E. Wagner. 1977. *Democracy in Deficit: The Political Legacy of Lord Keynes*. New York: Academic Press.

Caldwell, Bruce J. 2004. *Hayek's Challenge: An Intellectual Biography of F. A. Hayek*. Chicago: University of Chicago Press.

Durbin, E.F. 1945. Professor Hayek on Economic Planning and Political Liberty. *Economic Journal* 55 (220): 357–370.

Farrant, Andrew, and Edward McPhail. 2010. Does F. A. Hayek's *Road to Serfdom* Deserve to Make a Comeback? *Challenge* 53 (4): 96–120.

———. 2012. The Servants of Obama's Machinery: F. A. Hayek's *The Road to Serfdom* Revisited? *Eastern Economic Journal* 38 (4): 423–427.

Friedman, Milton. [1962] 2002. *Capitalism and Freedom*. Chicago: University of Chicago Press.

Friedman, Milton, and Rose Friedman. 1980. *Free to Choose*. New York: Mariner Books.

Hardin, Russell. 2005. *Indeterminacy and Society*. Princeton: Princeton University Press.

Hayek, F.A., ed. 1935. *Collectivist Economic Planning*. London: Routledge and Kegan Paul.

———. [1937] 1948. Economics and Knowledge. In *Individualism and Economic Order*. Chicago: University of Chicago Press, Chapter 2.

———. 1944. *The Road to Serfdom*. Chicago: University of Chicago Press.

———. [1948] 1980. *Individualism and Economic Order*. Chicago: University of Chicago Press.

———. [1952] 1979. *The Counter-Revolution of Science*. 2nd ed. Indianapolis: Liberty Fund.

———. 1960. *The Constitution of Liberty*. Chicago: University of Chicago Press.

———. 1973. *Law, Legislation, and Liberty, Vol. 1: Rules and Order*. Chicago: University of Chicago Press.

———. 1976. *Law, Legislation and Liberty, Vol. 2: The Mirage of Social Justice*. Chicago: University of Chicago Press.

———. 1979. *Law, Legislation, and Liberty, Vol. 3: The Political Order of a Free People*. Chicago: University of Chicago Press.

Kirzner, Israel M. 1988. The Economic Calculation Debate: Lessons for Austrians. *Review of Austrian Economics* 2 (1): 1–18.

Robbins, Lionel. [1947] 1950. *The Economic Problem in Peace and War*. London: Macmillan.

Shapiro, David L. 2001. Hayek's Slippery Slope: Is There a Third Way? *Journal of Private Enterprise* 16 (2): 16–29.

Shliefer, Andrei. 2009. The Age of Milton Friedman. *Journal of Economic Literature* 47 (1): 123–135.

Smith, Vernon L. 2003. Constructivist and Ecological Rationality in Economics. *American Economic Review* 93 (3): 465–508.

Wagner, Richard E. 2012. *Deficits, Debt, and Democracy: Wrestling with Tragedy on the Fiscal Commons*. Northampton: Edward Elgar.

Witt, Ulrich. 1992. The Endogenous Public Choice Theorist. *Public Choice* 73 (1): 117–129.

7

A Genuine Institutional Economics

Introduction

Commercial life always exists inside of an *institutional framework*. Whether social life exhibits Adam Smith's human propensity to "truck, barter, exchange" or Thomas Hobbes's human capacity to "rape, pillage, plunder" is a function of the *institutional framework* within which social life is played out. It is the *framework* that determines the marginal benefit/marginal cost calculus that individuals face in pursuing sociability. If the marginal benefits for productive specialization and peaceful cooperation exceed the marginal benefits of predation and confiscation, then that society will tend toward the Smithian expansion of commercial and civil society. But if the calculus tends toward the other way, then Hobbes's depiction of life as being "nasty, brutish and short" comes to dominate. Most of human history, in fact, is best characterized as Hobbesian. But starting with the "Great Enrichment,"[1] as Deirdre McCloskey has dubbed it, the history of humanity took a different turn. McCloskey puts great emphasis on the ideas that generated this transformation. We do not

---

[1] The Great Enrichment refers here to increase in income per capita by a factor of 40 to 100 that began first in northwestern Europe around 1800. See McCloskey's *The Bourgeois Virtues* (2006), *Bourgeois Dignity* (2010), and *Bourgeois Equality* (2016).

© The Author(s) 2018
Peter J. Boettke, *F. A. Hayek*, Great Thinkers in Economics,
https://doi.org/10.1057/978-1-137-41160-0_7

disagree with the primacy of ideas, but our focus is on the *framework* that these ideas legitimated, and the practices that were engendered by that *framework*. As the great Austrian School economist Ludwig von Mises put it:

> Saving, capital accumulation, is the agency that has transformed step-by-step the awkward search for food on the part of savage cave dwellers into the modern ways of industry. The pacemakers of this evolution were the ideas that created the *institutional framework* within which capital accumulation was rendered safe by the principle of private ownership of the means of production. Every step forward on the way toward prosperity is the effect of saving. The most ingenious technological inventions would be practically useless if the capital goods required for their utilization had not been accumulated by saving. (emphasis added, [1956] 2006, 24)

This emphasis on the *institutional framework* was lost in the first half of the twentieth century due to the rise of formalism in economic reasoning. The classical political economists—from Smith to Mill—were also philosophers and historians, as well as political and legal theorists. They also sought to produce logically sound arguments, rather than merely logically valid ones. This meant that realism of assumptions mattered greatly in the theoretical systems being constructed. They sought to steer an intellectual course between purely free-floating abstractions and momentary concrete description. Political economy was a theoretical edifice consisting of realistic abstractions that aided and guided empirical investigations. But understanding human society is complex; there are no constants. As a result, there was (and always will be) scope for varied interpretations of events. This was often mistaken in the late nineteenth century and early twentieth century as a sign of the immaturity of the science, and due to the nature of verbal reasoning. Ambiguity resulted because the same words were being used to mean different things, or because different words were being used to mean the same thing. As a result, disputes about fundamental issues seemed to be repeated without resolution. So, this could all be cleared up, the thought was, by substituting mathematical models for verbal chains of reason.

Now, hidden assumptions would be eliminated, and the ambiguity of words would be replaced by the clarity and precision of mathematical expression.

There was some resistance to this transformation of economic science for the first few decades of the twentieth century, precisely because it was understood that this transformation moved critical reasoning in the social sciences from a quest for logical soundness to a quest for logical validity. Thus, early twentieth-century thinkers who resisted formalism continuously stressed the lack of realism of assumptions as a problem. The formalistic turn required simplifying assumptions—that is different than the earlier use of abstract reasoning in the construction of theory. But as advances were made in statistical analysis, the belief was that these statistical techniques could effectively sort between the array of logically valid models those which were empirically meaningful from those that were empirically useless. Thus, modern neoclassical economics was born, and classical political economy was discarded.

One of the key casualties of this transformation was the explicit recognition and analysis of the *institutional framework*. In fact, a formalistic rendering of the structure of economic reasoning in the 1930–1960s strove to be *institutionally antiseptic*.[2] First, the *framework* was assumed to be given and fixed for the purposes of analysis. Second, its very "givenness" eventually resulted in the *institutional framework* being forgotten.[3] As Hayek states:

---

[2] See Francis Bator (1957, 31), where he states that the theorems of welfare economics are "antiseptically independent of institutional context." Furthermore, he argues that the optimality conditions are "technocratic" and that the theorist seeks to avoid any "institutional overtones," Bator is in the intellectual line of economic thinking that developed from Lange-Lerner, to Samuelson-Bergson, and eventually to Arrow-Hahn-Debreu. The flip side to this evolution was the rebirth of classical political economy and the rise of neoclassical institutionalism between 1950 and 2000 that we are highlighting.

[3] Barry Weingast (2016) recently identified what he dubbed the "neoclassical fallacy." First, the standard economists treats the institutional framework as given and fixed for analysis, and thus eventually forgets the central role in the analysis and assessment of alternative economic systems that institutions must play. Second, upon realizing this intellectual error, the standard economist will acknowledge the importance of institutions, but remain silent on the analysis of the working mechanisms of those institutions for their maintenance, stability, and/or fragility. In our narrative, exposing and correcting the "neoclassical fallacy" is one way to think about the Austrian-inspired law and economics revolution in the second half of the twentieth century.

It is regrettable, though not difficult to explain, that in the past much less attention has been given to the positive requirements of a successful working of the competitive system than to these negative points. The functioning of competition not only requires adequate organization of certain institutions like money, markets, and channels of information – some of which can never be adequately provided by private enterprise – but it depends, above all, on the existence of an appropriate legal system, a legal system designed both to preserve competition and to make it operate as beneficially as possible. ... The systematic study of the forms of legal institutions which will make the competitive system work efficiently has been sadly neglected. (1944, 87)

The classic example demonstrating this neglect of institutional analysis was in the debate in the 1920s–1940s over the possibility of economic calculation under socialism—with the Austrians, particularly Mises and Hayek, emphasizing the importance of private property rights and freedom of contract, and the market socialists—namely, Oskar Lange and Abba Lerner—insisting that optimality conditions could be established through judicious economic planning and effective public administration. This debate, we will argue, played an essential role in the rediscovery of the *institutional framework* in the post-WWII era. But before we walk through that argument, let us put in context the contributions of Austrian economics to law and economics, which is the study of endogenous rule formation, or the spontaneous evolution of social institutions, going back to the founder of the Austrian School, Carl Menger.

While the Austrian emphasis on the spontaneous evolution of institutions was born out of the *Methodenstreit,* a methodological battle engaged against the German Historical School, Hayek's unique contribution to law and economics emerged directly from the socialist calculation debate. This debate, we will argue, played an essential role in Hayek's rearticulation of the legal institutions necessary for a market economy. In the aftermath of the socialist calculation debate, the earlier Mengerian emphasis on the spontaneous emergence and evolution of the rules that govern economic and social interaction was reemphasized by F. A. Hayek, who in turn, influenced the early pioneers of law and economics, particularly Aaron Director, Ronald Coase, and Bruno Leoni.

From Smith to Menger to Mises:
The Refinement of Invisible Hand Theorizing

Classical political economy consists of a set of ideas about how to understand the social order that follows from the Scottish Enlightenment
moral philosophers, David Hume and Adam Smith, and was further
developed by the French liberals, such as J. B. Say, and the British utilitarians, such as Jeremy Bentham, David Ricardo, and John Stuart Mill.
From Hume, we learn that the foundation of civil society is to be found
in property, contract, and consent. In order for the human condition to
be characterized by productive specialization and peaceful cooperation,
that society must have security and stability of possession, the keeping of
promises, and the transference of property by consent (see Hume [1739]
2000, Book III, Part 2, Sec. II–IV: 311–331).

Smith's argument in *An Inquiry into the Nature and Causes of the Wealth
of Nations* must be understood in a two-stage manner. Yes, the greatest
improvements in the material conditions of mankind are due to the
refinement in the division of labor. But, as Smith pointed out, the division of labor is limited by the extent of the market. The division of labor
is a proximate cause of development. The fundamental cause is what gives
rise to the expansion of the market, and thus the refinement of the division of labor. That fundamental cause—as mentioned already by Mises—
are the ideas that gave rise to the institutional *framework* that make
savings and capital accumulation safe. As Smith ([1795] 1982, 322)
stated: "Little else is requisite to carry a state to the highest degree of
opulence from the lowest barbarism but peace, easy taxes, and a tolerable
administration of justice; all the rest being brought about by the natural
course of things." Unpacking precisely the institutional infrastructure
that produces those consequences has been one of the central tasks of
political economists and social philosophers ever since Smith.

The early neoclassical economists in the wake of the marginal revolution in value theory did not see their tasks as all that radically different
than Smith's. They just had a new set of analytical tools to utilize in
explaining value, exchange, and productive activity within the market
economy. The Austrian economist Carl Menger was one of the founders

of the marginal revolution—alongside co-discoverers Leon Walras and William Stanley Jevons. Yet, what distinguished Menger from the other founders of the marginal revolution was in applying invisible hand theorizing, as emphasized by his predecessors in classical political economy, to the analysis of social institutions. In distinguishing Menger from his counterparts in the marginal revolution, Bruce Caldwell writes the following:

> The marginal concept was only a small part of a much larger contribution, namely, a theoretical demonstration that individuals, acting in their own self-interest, give rise to social institutions that have effects that no one intended and that are in many cases benign. (2004, 73–74)

All the early neoclassical theorists from the founders to Wicksell, Wicksteed, Clark, and Knight possessed a deep appreciation of the *institutional framework* within which economic activity takes place. However, most theorists simply began their analysis by assuming well-defined and strictly enforced property rights. Taking the next step and analyzing the emergence of the rules that govern social interaction, the enforcement of those rules, and the effect of changes in those rules was unique to Menger and his junior colleagues in Vienna—Eugen Bohm-Bawerk and Friedrich Wieser.

The label—the Austrian School of Economics—was given to this group of thinkers by their intellectual opponents, the German Historicists. Originally, Menger thought he was contributing to the German-language scientific tradition by providing the theoretical grounding for the historical and institutional analysis that the German Historical School claimed they wanted to conduct. Menger's point, for our purposes, was rather a basic one—you can do historical and institutional analysis guided by an articulated and defended theory, or you can do it with an unarticulated and non-defended theory, but what you cannot do is conduct the analysis without any theory. The German School rejected the classical political economists because they found the theory too abstract, based on an unrealistic theory of human nature, and for ignoring the historical and institutional details of the situation. So while the older German Historical School of Roscher would have perhaps met Menger's overture with gratitude, the "younger" German Historical School of Schmoller violently rejected such an effort to provide theoretical foundations. Menger was dismissed as "the Austrian"; thus was born the first school of neoclassical institutional economics—what later became known as New Institutionalism, of which the entire field of law and economics is a part.

Menger responded to Schmoller and the German Historical School's rebuff by engaging in the *Methodenstreit* and followed up his *Principles of Economics* ([1871] 1981) with *Investigations into the Method of the Social Sciences* ([1883] 1996). While Menger's work was grounded in economic theory, this book discusses general sociology, politics, jurisprudence, and history. In addition to technical economics, students studied jurisprudence, sociological theory, political theory, and history. Economics was a branch, though the most developed branch, of a more general theory of social interaction. But the Austrian economists argued that the most scientifically productive way forward in this general social theory was to ground the analysis in *methodological individualism*. As Menger put it in *Principles of Economics* ([1871] 1981, 108), man "is himself the point at which human economic life begins and ends." The analytical focus was on the rational actor's arrangement of scarce means to satisfy unlimited wants in the most efficacious manner possible. These actors were acting in an uncertain world and with very limited knowledge, so errors of judgment and errors of execution could plague their efforts, but the basic structure of striving to achieve the most for the least is not deterred by this recognition of man's imperfections. In fact, it is precisely our imperfections and the possibilities for change that motivate and lead acting man to learn through time how better to pursue his purposes individually and through exchange with others.

The Austrian School of Menger, Bohm-Bawerk, and Wieser divided economic science into three branches: pure or exact theory; applied theory or institutionally contingent theory; and empirical examination (both historical and contemporary public policy). Critics thought incorrectly that the classical political economist and Austrian School economists worked exclusively in the realm of pure theory. As Buchanan ([1996] 2001, 290) notes, "to Adam Smith, the 'laws and institutions,' the political-legal framework within which persons interact, one with another, are important and necessary elements in the inclusive 'constitution' for the political economy." Or consider how Hayek (1978, 124–125) summed up Smith's position: "Adam Smith's decisive contribution was the account of a self-generating order which formed itself spontaneously if the individuals were restrained by appropriate rules of law."

The interaction of pure theory of the logic of choice with the institutional context that defined the logic of the situation simply was missed by critics and the formalists. This is perhaps because the critics among the German Historicists and the American Old Institutionalists believed there was an ideological commitment to reform, and one of the serious implications of the classical political economists and the early neoclassical Austrians was that reform faced its own set of constraints.[4] Note we did not say reform was impossible. Rather, we just merely said that it faced constraints, but that was enough to invoke the ire of the would-be reformists who, like Adam Smith's "man of systems," were very wise in their "own conceit" and thus believed they could "arrange the different members of a great society with as much ease as the hand arranges the different pieces upon a chessboard" (Smith [1759] 1984, 234). Stressing the play between context and choice, and understanding intended and unintended consequences—the seen and the unseen; immediate effects and long-run effects—is essential to analyzing the impact of reform measures. Such an analysis was too irksome to the aspirations of the reformers, and too nuanced and subtle in the institutional contingencies for the formalists.

Mises, Hayek, and the Link Between the Early Austrian School and the Modern Austrian School

The Austrian School economists were caught between historicism and formalism as twentieth-century economics was evolving throughout Europe and the USA. Between WWI and WWII, a new generation of

---

[4] On the reform mentality of the Old Institutionalist thinkers, see Thomas Leonard's *Illiberal Reformers* (2016).

theorists emerged to carry the banner, such as Ludwig von Mises and F. A. Hayek. They would be involved as primary actors in three intellectual dramas during those years: the debate over socialist calculation; the debate over business cycles; and the debate over the methodology of economics. For our purposes, what matters most is how each of these debates were interconnected and resulted ultimately in Hayek's turn in the post-WWII era to an explicit focus on the institutional *framework* as seen in *The Constitution of Liberty* (1960) and *Law, Legislation and Liberty* (1973, 1976, 1979).

In both the socialist calculation debate and the business cycle debates, the unique "Austrian" contribution was the guiding role of relative prices in the processes of exchange and production. The coordination of economic plans was guided by relative prices in those respective markets. And the very existence of those relative prices is based on private property rights. Prices without property is a grand illusion, since property, as we saw from Hume, is the basis of exchange and contract. Without private property in the means of production, Mises argued, there would be no market for the means of production, and without a market, there would be no relative prices established in the means of production. And without those relative prices, there could be no rational economic calculation of the alternative use of scratch resources (Mises [1920] 1935, 111, [1922] 1951, 119; see also Boettke 1998, 134). Prices guide production; calculation aids coordination of complex economic arrangements. Advanced material production and wealth creation is only possible within the context of the private property market economy.

But during the interwar years, economic science had taken a turn toward excessive formalism and excessive aggregation and, in the process, tended to cloud our understanding of the subtleties of economic coordination. In the socialist calculation debate, the absence of private ownership in capital goods did not cause concern; instead, a planning procedure of trial and error could easily substitute to achieve the optimality conditions of general equilibrium. In the business cycle dispute, the manipulation of money and credit would not be seen as generating a costly malinvestment in the capital structure, and any errors that were induced could easily be corrected within the model. The problem with macroeconomic volatility was not seen as a bug, but a feature of a more realistic rendering of the market economy, where agent optimism and pessimism and prices do not play a guiding role in exchange and production activity. In short, the conclusion by the end of the 1930s was that models of market socialism were workable and that the market economy was inherently unstable.

The teachings of classical political economy, as well as the early neoclassical school of economics, was overturned not by historicism and institutionalism. Instead, they were overturned by a formalistic version of neoclassicism that drew attention away from the institutional context, and an excessive aggregation that detracted from the active choices of individual actors. Recall our emphasis from Adam Smith on a "tolerable administration of justice." One simply cannot do political economy without addressing the institutional infrastructure within which economic activity takes place. Yet, during the period of 1940–1960, the economics profession turned increasingly away from paying attention to institutions.

The pockets of resistance to this trend are seen in particular developments during this period, especially in the 1950–1970 period of property rights economics, public choice economics, and law and economics associated with names such as Armen Alchian, James Buchanan, and Ronald Coase, respectively. These economists, as Buchanan argued, were "not be content with postulating models and then working within such models." Rather, the economist's task "includes the derivation of the institutional order itself from the set of elementary behavioral hypotheses with which he commences. In this manner, *genuine institutional economics becomes a significant and an important part of fundamental economic theory*" (emphasis added, [1968] 1999, 5).

But Mises and Hayek actually ignited this intellectual trend during the debates over socialism, business cycles, and methodology. They entered into the last debate because of the communicative frustration experienced in the first two. As Mises would often stress, nothing in his proposal for praxeology should be seen as new, but instead as the methodology that was followed by all the leading economists, past and present. And besides the emphasis on the pure logic of choice, Mises's praxeological analysis required the economist to take into account the *institutional framework* within which economic activity takes place. This is the basis of his comparative institutional analysis of the unhampered market economy, socialism, interventionism, as well as his examination of bureaucracy, the war economy, and the total state. The pure logic of choice does not change in each of these institutional settings, but the manifestations and consequences of that choice will vary depending on the institutional context.

The fact that many in the economics profession at the time found Lange persuasive, and even found Hayek and Robbins's respective rebuttals to be wanting, shows that the insidious influence of formalism was already taking hold by the end of the 1930s. Institutionless economics resulted in purging not only law, politics, history, sociology, but ultimately, also the human decision-maker and the agony of choice the human decision-maker must embrace in trying to sort through the uncertainty of the future. However, as Hayek pointed out in his paper "Economics and Knowledge" ([1937] 1948), the optimality conditions of the market were a by-product of the competitive process, and *not* an assumption going into the analysis. Competition is an activity, not a description of a state of affairs where all activity has ceased. Hayek, in particular, tended to blend his institutional turn in research in the 1940s with his *epistemological* turn in research. Institutions do not just structure the incentives that actors face in making their decisions, but they also impact the quality of information and the flow of new knowledge that decision-makers have at their disposal. Much of the most important knowledge that must be utilized is contextual in nature and simply ceases to exist outside of specific institutional contexts. Social scientists are still struggling to catch up to Hayek's fundamental insights in his papers on the utilization of knowledge within an economic system and the role that alternative institutions play in that analysis.

Hayek, the Institutional Turn, and the Emergence of Law and Economics

In the 1940s, Hayek published *The Road to Serfdom* (1944), which was a further elaboration of a monograph entitled *Freedom and the Economic System* (1939). In those works, Hayek turned his attention to the rule of law and democracy, and how the economic system interacts with legal and political institutions. For example, in *The Road to Serfdom*, the reader is first introduced to the argument that comprehensive economic planning will be inconsistent with the rule of law and democracy. This is the rationale for the title of the work, which is meant to capture a tragic tale. Remember, Hayek was addressing his book to his colleagues in Britain who believed they could combine socialist economic planning with liberal democratic institutions. The suppression of individual freedom and the erosion of democratic institutions that Hayek envisioned as the logical outcome of efforts to substitute comprehensive economic planning for the market economy was a tragic warning to his colleagues. Their vision of a rational economic order would result in a political nightmare as the rule of law and democracy would prove to be incompatible with the organizational logic of economic planning. In his subsequent works dealing with the interaction of legal, political, and social institutions and the operation of the economic system, such as *The Constitution of Liberty* (1960) and *Law, Legislation and Liberty* (1973, 1976, 1979), Hayek examines how alternative institutional arrangements impact the economic forces at work, and how the tools of basic economic reasoning can be deployed to analyze the institutional logic of proposed rule changes.

Hayek's line of reasoning was directed at the aspirations to remake the economic system via the political order. One of his main points of emphasis was how political control over economic means was not merely control over material factors, but necessarily control over the means by which we pursue our most lofty goals. "Economic control," Hayek wrote, "is not merely control of a sector of human life which can be separated from the rest; it is the control of the means for all our ends. And whoever has sole control of the means must also determine which ends are to be served, which values are to be rated higher and which lower, in short, what men should believe and strive for" (1944, 127). Freedom of speech, religion, and the press, for instance, is an empty phrase unless we also have the ability to own the means of the press. Human rights are ultimately property rights. Coming from the grand debate in economic theory over rational economic planning under socialism, Hayek moved the conversation from the technical arguments concerning the price system and the allocation of scarce resources to the institutional environment that would need to compliment that planning task.

The rule of law and democratic institutions are the means by which individuals are able to pursue a great variety of purposes. They provide the institutional impediments to the necessary power and discretion of the planners, making it possible for individuals to pursue their individual plans with a fair degree of certainty as to how government officials will exercise their coercive power. The rule of law allows for the mutual adjustment of conflicting plans through voluntary exchange via market prices as guides to production and consumption. However, the rule of law is inconsistent with political discretion, for government planning can only succeed through the suppression of individual plans by political actors willing to exercise force. At this point, Hayek develops a slightly different argument. In his chapter on "Why the Worst Get On Top," Hayek explains how the selection process among leaders of the planning effort will take place. In this, he follows Frank Knight (1932, 1938), and simply uses an argument about the comparative advantage in exercising discretion and power over fellow citizens and the characteristics of such a person. In short, Hayek argues that even if someone of the character of Mother Teresa was to be put in charge of the planning bureau, she would either have to change her character to be more ruthless, or she would lose out in the political struggle for leadership. As Knight put it, only a certain type of character can survive to control the whip on a plantation; it is not a job for everyone. The same is true for those placed in charge of executing comprehensive economic plans.

The fields of public choice and law and economics from a Hayekian perspective should be seen as intertwined and as two sides of the same effort to refocus economists' attention on the *institutional framework*. The work of various sociologists during this same era—including Peter Berger, Rodney Stark, and James Coleman—also sought to integrate social institutions such as norms, mores, beliefs, and so on into this focus on the *framework* in a way consistent with the basic economic way of thinking. The consensus in this research, however, is less solidified than in public choice and law and economics, so the integration is not as easily envisioned.

Methodologically, the approach to the study of political and legal institutions works initially in a rather straightforward linear fashion. An animating rational actor initiates that inquiry, that actor finds themselves interacting within an institutional filter defined by the formal and informal rules of social interaction and their enforcement, and that institutional filter structures the incentives and provides the knowledge that actors need to act on the incentives. This in turn results in certain equilibrating tendencies. As Buchanan often stressed, same players, different rules, produce different games. The explanatory thrust in this approach is to be found not in the behavioral attributes we assign to the individual actors, but in the alternative institutional *frameworks* within which they operate.

As Robert Van Horn (2013) has documented, the relationship between Hayek and Aaron Director in the decades before and after the publication of *The Road to Serfdom* was indeed a deeply committed one. They saw themselves as "comrades in arms" against the collectivist threat to the competitive order. Director was a student at the LSE in the 1930s, and viewed Hayek as his teacher. Director would use his connections to push for the publication of Hayek's *The Road to Serfdom* by the University of Chicago, and he would review the book extremely favorably in the *American Economic Review*. In addition, when private donors approached Hayek to lead the effort to establish a program at the University of Chicago to study in depth the private enterprise system, Hayek recommended that they work with Director instead, and they did. The project—sometimes referred to as the "Hayek project"—was housed at the University of Chicago Law School. The focus of the project was the analysis of alternative legal institutions which aid, or hinder, the operation of the competitive system.

Ronald Coase was another product of the LSE in the 1930s, and his research program sought to examine the *institutional framework* that made possible the workings of firms, markets, and economies. Coase is sometimes referred to as an advocate of a pragmatic-empirical brand of economics. However, Coase was not an old-style institutionalist. He was trapped, as Hayek was, between historicism and formalism. Moreover, like Hayek (and Plant and Robbins), Coase in good LSE fashion was trained in basic economic reasoning and price theory. He was a neoclassical institutionalist and, as such, focused on exchange and the institutions within which exchange takes place. This is seen not only in his development of the transaction cost theory of the firm, which he developed directly from his reflections on the socialist calculation debate as taught to him by Arnold Plant, but in the development of the "Coase Theorem" as articulated in his paper, "The Federal Communications Commission" (1959), and then more fully developed in "The Problem of Social Cost" (1960). It is not necessary to repeat here the arguments in those papers about the allocation of resources and the initial distribution of rights under the assumption of zero transaction costs, or in the face of positive transactions costs. Suffice to say, Coase pioneered comparative institutional analysis, for which he was later awarded the Nobel Prize in Economic Sciences in 1991. He argued that in making the comparison, one must take into account that in moving the decision arena away from the market sphere, one must recognize that they will have to forgo the monetary calculation of benefits and costs, the division of knowledge throughout the economy, and account for the additional costs of vested interest groups (see Coase 1959, 18)

From Hayek, one can draw a direct line of influence to the founding of the law and economics movement after WWII and its development in the 1940–1960s by Aaron Director and Ronald Coase. We do not contend that this development was linear, but instead, it went in a variety of new and interesting directions. But the influence was direct nevertheless, and it was seen as a corrective to the disregard for the *institutional framework* by mainstream economists in the 1930s–1950s that had resulted from fundamental confusions about that operation of the competitive market order, and the vital role that legal institutions play in its effective operation.

Hayek, Leoni, and Endogenous Rule Formation

One point of emphasis in the Hayekian perspective on the institutional *framework* that has caused confusion is the question of the origin and maintenance of this *framework*. Alexander Hamilton in *Federalist* #1 put the puzzle as follows: will we base our constitutions on accident and force, or on reflection and choice? The obvious answer to this question is to rely on reflection and choice. Hayek is simply pointing out that we cannot just design institutions out of thin air and implement them. We are constrained in our quest for rational institutional design by the historical path we are on. But that does not mean we cannot engage in positive reform of the rules and in efforts at institutional design. The critical rationalist is permitted, and in fact, must, challenge all of society's values, but they cannot challenge all of them at once. Hayek's position cannot be considered "conservative" since he wants to hold nothing as sacred, yet Hayek is not a "constructivist" because he argues we cannot design society from nothing according to our will. It is a subtle and nuanced dance of evolution and design that makes up the spontaneous order of society and the institutional *framework* that shapes that order. Hayek makes this point in *Law, Legislation, and Liberty*:

> At the moment our concern must be to make clear that while the rules on which a spontaneous order rests, may also be of spontaneous origin, this need not always be the case. Although undoubtedly an order originally formed itself spontaneously because the individuals followed rules which had not been deliberately made but had arisen spontaneously, people gradually learned to improve those rules; and it is at least conceivable that the formation of a spontaneous order relies entirely on rules that were deliberately made. (Hayek 1973, 45)

The crucial step in Hayekian analysis was to argue that not only was the pattern of social interaction within the *framework* a result of spontaneous order, but that the very *framework* itself was the product of another spontaneous process of ordering. This focus on endogenous rules, rather than processes within exogenous rules, is what separated Hayek from the earlier Austrians (except Menger) and the later New Institutionalists (except Elinor Ostrom).

The Italian classical liberal political economist Bruno Leoni was one of the earliest writers to see the connection between the socialist calculation debate and this focus on the endogenous evolution of law. In his now classic work *Freedom and Law* ([1961] 1972), Leoni argues that the theoretical impossibility of economic central planning is considered only a small part in a more general problem.

> [T]his demonstration [that a centralized economy does not work] may be deemed the most important and lasting contribution made by the economists to the cause of individual freedom in our time. However, its conclusion

may be considered only a as a special case of a more general realization that no legislator would be able to establish by himself, without some kind of continuous collaboration on the part of all the people concerned, the rules governing the actual behavior of everybody in the endless relationships that each has with everybody else. No public opinion polls, no referenda, no consultations would really put the legislators in a position to determine these rules [...]. The actual behavior of people is continuously adapting itself to changing conditions. (Leoni [1961] 1972, 18–19)

In correspondence with Hayek after the publication of *Freedom and the Law*, Leoni summed up his argument as follows: "I think that the underlying idea of such a theory is that there is a market of the law as well as there is a market of goods. The rules correspond to the prices: they are the expression of the conditions requested for the exchange of actions and behaviours, just as the prices are the expression of certain conditions requested for the exchange of the goods. And the rules, as well as the prices are not imposed, but found out. I said before that the rules are found out by some special kind of people. But even this is true only partially. Everybody can find out a rule under given circumstances: this happens whenever people exchange their actions, their behaviours etc. at certain conditions without being compelled to consult anybody" (quoted in Masala 2003, 228). Just as market coordination through the price system requires competition to sort out errors and provide corrective adaptations and adjustments, a working legal system requires competition to discover errors in judgment and rulings, to adapt and adjust to changing circumstances, to minimize conflicts, and to promote productive specialization and peaceful social cooperation. The law, like the market, is a discovery procedure. Legislation, like centralized planning, curtails learning and thus becomes an impediment to progress in social intercourse and economic well-being.

The contrast is most starkly seen in spontaneous order within a framework of law versus spontaneous order of the framework of law itself in the presentations of Hayek and Buchanan. For our purposes, we want to stress that the contrast is overblown. Hayek's emphasis on the spontaneous order of common law versus the constructivist rationalism of legislation led to confusion about the role of constitutional construction in Hayek's system. But drawing on the discussion of conservativism and constructivism, we argue that while there is no doubt a tension, this tension need not be a source of confusion, but instead a source of inquiry. Constitutional construction is a constrained intellectual exercise, but a necessary one for the maintenance of the liberal order. Law evolves, but it can also be improved upon when this evolution is derailed in perverse directions in relationship to liberalism. Hayek stresses constitutional construction from the bottom up, but there is nothing in his system that would prevent constitutional design on the margins.

On the other hand, one of the most challenging research questions law and economics scholars have puzzled over in the past quarter of century has been how does one "grow" a rule of law. As Rajan (2004) so eloquently put it, you cannot proceed under the assumption of well-defined and enforced property rights in a world that has completely fallen apart institutionally. The reason why these societies are dysfunctional is precisely because they lack the *institutional framework* that more functional systems possess. We must, as Rajan put it, "Assume Anarchy" if we are going to make any progress. That is our starting point of analysis, and the question is how law develops. As Peter Leeson (2014) has stressed repeatedly, one cannot just assume that you can impose a working Western-style government. In such a dysfunctional environment, the most likely outcome is an abusive dysfunctional government that will predate on the people, rather than be constrained. So, one possible avenue of research that has been opened by this is the role of *informal* institutions in providing the impetus for development.

To tie this back to Buchanan, consider the conclusion that Buchanan and Tullock are led to in *The Calculus of Consent* (emphasis added, 1962, 80–81) concerning social cleavages:

> The evolution of democratic constitutions from the discussion of rational individuals can take place only under certain relatively narrowly defined conditions. The individual participants must approach the constitution-making process as 'equals' in a special sense of this term. The requisite 'equality' can be insured only if the existing differences in external characteristics among individuals are accepted without rancor and if there are no clearly predictable bases among these differences for the formation of permanent coalitions. On the basic of purely economic motivation, individual members of a dominant and superior group (who consider themselves to

be such and who were in the possession of power) would never rationally choose to adopt constitutional rules giving less fortunately situated individuals a position of equal partnership in governmental processes. On noneconomic grounds the dominate classes might choose to do this, but, as experience has so often demonstrated in recent years, the less fortunately situated classes will rarely interpret such action as being advanced in their favor. *Therefore, our analysis of the constitution-making process had little relevance for a society that is characterized by a sharp cleavage of the population into distinguishable social classes or separate racial, religious, or ethnic groupings sufficient to encourage the formation of predictable political coalitions and in which one of these coalitions has a clearly advantageous position at the constitutional stage.*

So, if we take them at their word, either Buchanan and Tullock's analysis is irrelevant, or we have to embrace the challenge of studying endogenous rule formation in the field of law and economics and public choice.

So What Is "Austrian" About a Hayekian Genuine Institutional Economics?

The term "Austrian" in the Austrian School of economics can be interpreted in one of two ways. First, it could be understood as a cultural founding of a certain approach to economics in *fin-de-siècle* Vienna. This Viennese intellectual and artistic culture was a unique period of human creativity, and the discipline of economics was no different. This time period is worthy of study for anyone intrigued by intellectual history (see, e.g. Dekker 2016). On the other hand, the term "Austrian" also designates a certain approach to the study of economics and a set of methodological and analytical propositions, as I laid out in my essay for *The Concise Encyclopedia of Economics* and the introduction to *The Contemporary Handbook of Austrian Economics*. The interaction of these two is quite fascinating for scholars of economics, political economy, and social philosophy. At the University of Vienna, the economics faculty was located within the School of Law. And the Austrian economists in their economic analysis always placed great importance on the institutional framework of property, contract, and tort.

As we have seen, in the second half of the twentieth century, law and economics emerged from combining two fields of study into one. There was the traditional economic analysis of exchange relationships and competitive behavior within a given set of institutions. And there is the application of the rational choice tools of analysis to study the institutional rules themselves. There are subtle and important differences between an approach that attempts to examine how alternative institutional arrangements impact the operation of an economic system, and the use of economic reasoning to address the efficiency, or possible efficiency, of a set of institutional arrangements.

From Carl Menger to Mises and Hayek, Austrian law and economics study the evolution of legal rules as a prime example of spontaneous order analysis. *"How can it be,"* Menger (emphasis original, [1883] 1996, 146) famously asked, *"that institutions which serve the common welfare and are extremely significant for its development come into being without a common will directed toward establishing them?"* Hayek ([1952] 1979, 69) went further and argued that to the extent that the social institutions are a result of deliberate design, there would be no necessity for theoretical inquiry in the sciences of man and society. It is only because we are dealing with institutions that are the result of human action, but not of human design, that we, as social scientists, have a need for theoretical sophistication and refinement.

In this, as in many other ways, the modern Austrian School was simply updating the political economy and social philosophy of the Scottish Enlightenment philosophers by refining economic theory that followed from the marginalist revolution and the development of the subjective theory of value. The equilibrium approach that also emerged in the first half of the twentieth century often clouded the fundamental relationship between the institutional framework and economic performance, as well as the study of that institutional framework itself. "Nothing is solved," Hayek famously wrote, "when we assume everybody to know everything and that the real problem is rather how it can be brought about that as much of the available knowledge as possible is used. This raises for a competitive society the question, not how we can 'find' the people who know best, but rather what institutional arrangements are necessary in order that the unknown persons who have knowledge suited to a particular task are most likely to be attracted to that task" (Hayek [1948] 1980, 95).

This argument of Hayek's was deployed to examine the coordinating role played by prices in a competitive economy, and the consequences of distortions to that guiding role. But the broader point about the evolution of an institutional environment that is conducive to economic growth would be a persistent theme in Hayek and was developed in *The Road to Serfdom*, *The Constitution of Liberty* and *Law, Legislation and Liberty*. These works that form the classic writings in Austrian law and economics emphasize individual choice not only against constraints, but in an environment of ignorance and uncertainty. The coping function of institutions is to deal with uncertainty by providing predictability and stability, while maintaining a mix of coherence and flexibility to enable the necessary adaptations and dynamic adjustments to the rules.

The Spontaneous Order Approach

Hayek's social theory project is the advancement and refinement of a tradition of social analysis that dates back to the Scottish Enlightenment and thinkers such as David Hume and Adam Smith. Hayek develops that tradition by interpreting it in light of the economic and social theory tradition handed down to him via his intellectual mentors, Carl Menger and Ludwig von Mises. It is his Austrian perspective that leads him to question the ability of modernist economics to understand spontaneously grown, complex social orders. As Hayek states:

> Even two hundred years after Adam Smith's Wealth of Nations, it is not yet fully understood that it is the great achievement of the market to have made possible a far-ranging division of labour, that it brings about a continuous adaption of economic effect to millions of particular facts or events which in their totality are not known and cannot be known to anybody.... A system of market-determined prices is essentially a system which is indispensable in order to make us adapt our activities to events and circumstances of which we cannot know.... [N]eoclassical economics, never clearly brought out what I call the "guide" or "signal function" of prices. That was due to the survival of the simple causal explanation of values and prices, assuming that values and prices were determined by what had been before rather than as a signal of what people ought to do. (1983, 19, 35–36)

It is this understanding of the spontaneous emergence of a complex, and beneficial, social order that informed Adam Smith's arguments for economic liberty and against the restraints of trade. The voluntary action of thousands of individuals, each pursuing his own interests, generates and utilizes economic information that is not available to any one individual or group of individuals in its totality. Economic coordination relies upon the utilization of "local" or contextual knowledge (or what Hayek later terms knowledge of particular time and place) and not abstract "data." It is this emphasis on the use of contextual knowledge that underlies the critical defense of the liberal order from Smith to Hayek.

"A real understanding of the process which brings this about was long blocked," Hayek has argued, "by post-Smithian classical economics which adopted a labour or cost theory of value" (1983, 19). In addition, with David Ricardo's reformulation of Smith, the emphasis came to be much more concentrated on the long-run static equilibrium outcome of economic activity. This trend became all the more apparent after the marginalist revolution in the 1870s with the rise of Walrasian general equilibrium and Marshallian partial equilibrium. Among the founders of the marginalist revolution, however, Carl Menger was unique in his emphasis on the spontaneous ordering of economic activity. Menger, for example, devotes all of Book 3 of his *Investigations* ([1883] 1996) to examining social institutions that emerge spontaneously. "We can observe," he wrote, "in numerous social institutions a strikingly apparent functionality with respect to the whole. But with closer consideration they still do not prove to be the result of an intention aimed at this purpose, i.e., the result of an agreement of members of society or of positive legislation. They, too, present themselves to us rather as 'natural' products (in a certain sense), as the unintended results of historical development" ([1883] 1996, 130). The examples of money, law, language, markets, and communities are presented to demonstrate the prevalence of "organically" grown social institutions.

For the proper study of these institutions, Menger emphasized, the social analyst cannot borrow the methods of the natural sciences. Rather, social theory requires the development of its own methods. Social institutions "simply cannot be viewed and interpreted as the product of purely mechanical force effects. They are, rather, the result of human efforts, the efforts of thinking, feeling, acting human beings" ([1883] 1996, 133).

Social institutions arise either due to a "common will directed toward their establishment" or as "the unintended result of human efforts aimed at essentially individual goals." In the second case, complex social phenomena "come about as the unintended result of individual human effort (pursuing individual interests) without a common will directed toward their establishment" ([1883] 1996, 133).

While recognizing the importance of social institutions that emerge out of conscious design, Menger ([1883] 1996, 146) did argue that it is in explaining institutions which arise spontaneously that social theory is dealing with the most noteworthy problem of the social sciences. Moreover, Menger went on to argue that:

> The solution of the most important problems of the theoretical sciences in general and of theoretical economics in particular is thus closely connected with the question of theoretically understanding the origin and change of 'organically' created social structures. ([1883] 1996, 147)

In order to demonstrate the power of spontaneous order explanations, Menger utilizes the example of the origin of money. A common medium of exchange emerges not as a product of anyone's design, but as a result of individuals striving to better their condition.

Ludwig von Mises, who remarked that it was upon reading Menger's *Principles* that he became an economist (1978, 33), argues that Carl Menger's theory of the origin of money represents "the elucidation of fundamental principles of praxeology and its method of research" ([1949] 1966: 405). Mises's vast contributions to economic science derive from his consistent application of what he called subjectivism to all areas of economic theory. This perspective is perhaps most vivid in his work on economic calculation and the importance of the institutions of private property and freely fluctuating money prices. Hayek's research has elaborated on this economic calculation insight, both in its positive form of the ability of the market process to convey the necessary economic knowledge for successful plan coordination and its negative form of socialism's impossibility and interventionism's ineffectiveness at doing so. And none of these insights emerge unless economics evolves as a genuine institutional economics—grounded in the logic of choice, but also detail-oriented with respect to the institutional context of human action and social interaction.

Human Agency, Meaning, and Social Theory

The human sciences begin with: "what men think and mean to do: from the fact that the individuals which compose society are guided in their actions by a classification of things or concepts which has a common structure and which we know because we, too, are men" (Hayek [1952] 1979, 57).

The data of the human sciences, in fact, "are what the acting people think they are" (1952, 44). Indeed, as Hayek puts it, the human sciences, and economics, in particular, could be described

> as a *meta*theory, a *theory about* the theories people have developed to explain how most effectively to discover and use different means for diverse purposes. (1988, 98, emphasis in original)

We interpret the meaning individuals place on events because we "interpret the phenomena in light of our own thinking" ([1952] 1979, 135). These interpretations are not perfect and may not even be correct in any particular case, Hayek points out, but it is:

> the only basis on which we ever understand what we call other people's intentions, or the meaning of their actions; and certainly the only basis of all our historical knowledge since this is all derived from the understanding of signs or documents. ([1952] 1979, 135)

We rely upon our understanding of others, that we derive from our self-understanding, to theorize and also to orient our actions to those of others. The pre-theoretical understanding of others, enables us to cooperate socially with those who confront us anonymously. As Hayek states:

> All people, whether primitive or civilised, organise what they perceive partly by means of attributes that language has taught them to attach to groups of sensory characteristics. Language enables us not only to label objects given to our senses as distinct entities, but also to classify an infinite variety of combinations of distinguishing marks according to what we expect from them and what we may do with them.... all usage of language is laden with interpretations or theories about our surroundings. (1988, 106)

Our common-sense understanding of "the other," which comes to us through language, provides an invaluable source of knowledge in social understanding, both at the theoretical level and in our day-to-day existence. "It would be impossible," Hayek says, "to explain or understand human action without making use of this knowledge" ([1952] 1979, 43–44). Try to imagine, Hayek argues, what the social world would look like:

> if we were really to dispense with our knowledge of what things mean to the acting man, and if we merely observed the actions of men as we observe an ant heap or a beehive. In the picture such a society study could produce there could not appear such things as means or tools, commodities or money, crimes or punishments, or words or sentences; it could contain only physical objects defined either in terms of the sense attributes they present to the observer or even in purely relational terms. And since the human behavior toward physical objects would show practically no regularities discernible to such an observer, since men would in a great many instances not appear to react alike to things which would to the observer seem to be the same, nor differently to what appeared to him to be different, he could not hope to achieve an explanation of their actions unless he had first succeeded in reconstructing in full detail the way in which men's senses and men's minds pictured the external world to them. The famous observer from Mars, in other words, before he could understand even as much of human affairs as the ordinary man does, would have to reconstruct from our behavior those immediate data of our mind which to us form the starting point of any interpretation of human action. ([1952] 1979, 105)

Interpretation and understanding is only possible because we possess a pre-theoretical understanding of what it means to be human. In other words, it is only because we can attribute meaning to human action that we can understand the diverse patterns of actions that make up the social world. The key question for the social theorist is how the various and diverse images of reality that individual minds develop could ever be coordinated to one another. The social institutions that arise through the voluntary association of thousands of individuals guide individuals in the process of mutual accommodation. The voluntary interaction of individuals reveals their various subjective patterns of trade-offs and utilizes this knowledge to promote plan coordination.

Market participants, for example, do not possess knowledge of the real underlying economic factors in the economy. On the basis of understanding, individuals interpret the meaning of economic changes and orient their behavior accordingly. They rely on the freely established exchange ratios in the market to inform them about (1) current market conditions, (2) the appropriateness of past decisions, and (3) the future possibilities of pure profit. The market system provides *ex ante* information in the form of money prices reflecting the relative scarcities of goods. The market system also provides *ex post* information through the system of profit and loss to inform market participants about the appropriateness of their past actions. If they bought cheap and sold dear, they are rewarded, whereas if they bought dear and sold cheap, they suffer losses. The array of market prices, however, also possess information about the possibility of pure entrepreneurial profit. The discrepancy between the current array of prices and the possible future array generates the discovery of ever new and fresh ways to shuffle or reshuffle resources. The market system as a whole, in its *ex ante*, *ex post* and discovery capacity, generates and utilizes economic knowledge "so tens of thousands of people whose identity could not be ascertained by months of investigation, are made to use the material or its products ... in the right direction" (Hayek 1945, 87).

Social life, however, is not restricted to the market but encompasses a vast array of complex structures, which enable us to successfully plan our actions. The same procedure by which we understand successful plan coordination on the economic scene is applicable to other areas of our social existence. As Hayek has pointed out:

> While at the world of nature we look from the outside, we look at the world of society from the inside; while, as far as nature is concerned, our concepts are about the facts and have to be adapted to the facts, in the world of society at least some of the most familiar concepts are the stuff from which the world is made. Just as the existence of a common structure of thought is the condition of the possibility of our communicating with one another, of your understanding what I say, so it is also the basis on which we all interpret such complicated social structures as those which we find in economic life or law, in language, and in customs. (1943, 76)

Though the complex structures of society are the composite of the purposive behavior of individuals, they are not the result of conscious human design. The intentional, that is, meaningful, behaviors of individuals affirm or reaffirm the overall order in society. But social order is not the result of conscious design and control. Perhaps the greatest source of misunderstanding in our social world is the failure to view society as an interpretive process which translates meaningful utterances of the human mind into socially useful knowledge, so that the various anonymous actors may come into cooperation with one another, regardless of whether this was their intention. As Hayek states:

> We still refuse to recognize that the spontaneous interplay of the actions of individuals may produce something which is not the deliberate object of their actions but an organism in which every part performs a necessary function for the continuance of the whole, without any human mind having devised it. In the words of an eminent Austrian economist [Mises], we refuse to recognize that society is an organism and not an organisation and that, in a sense, we are part of a 'higher' organised system which, without our knowledge, and long before we tried to understand it, solved problems the existence of which we did not even recognise, but which we should have had to solve in much the same way if we had tried to run it deliberately. (1933, 130–131)

Much of Hayek's work, including his work on the common law and on the co-evolution of reason and tradition, follows directly from his exploration of Mises's discussion of the foundation of a social order based on the division of labor. The Hayekian research program extends the spontaneous order approach beyond the realm of economic explanation to all realms of social interaction, including science, law, and history. Hayek's economics has sought to articulate the discovery role of the competitive market process, his legal philosophy has sought to examine the discovery process of the common law, and his philosophical anthropology explores the discovery process of history.

Hayek, Rationalism, and the Law of Association

Law and principles of just conduct evolve over time and take on new meaning as they are applied in new circumstances to resolve social conflicts. The recognition of the spontaneous ordering of social cooperation does not demean reason; in fact, it upholds man's reason in ordering his own affairs. Much of Hayek's work should be seen as an attempt to defend reason against its abuse under the guise of scientism or Cartesian rationalism. Consider the following statements from Hayek's work on the liberal society:

> Complete rationality of action in the Cartesian sense demands complete knowledge of all relevant facts. A designer or engineer needs all the data and full power to control or manipulate them if he is to organize the material objects to produce the intended result. But the success of action in society depends on more particular facts than anyone can possible know. And our whole civilization in consequence rests, and must rest, on our believing much that we cannot know to be true in the Cartesian sense. (1973, 12)

> What we have attempted is a defense of reason against its abuse by those who do not understand the conditions of its effective functioning and continuous growth. It is an appeal to men to see that we must use our reason intelligently and that, in order to do so, we must preserve the indispensable matrix of the uncontrolled and non-rational which is the only environment wherein reason can grow and operate effectively. (1960, 69)

What Hayek's work does deny is that the complex order of society is a result of rationalist construction and human design. The order that emerges under a system of division of labor and private property was not the result of anyone's design or intention, but was the composite of all the separate striving of individuals to realize their purposes and plans.

Much controversy surrounds Hayek's recent attempts to reformulate this principle and his use of cultural evolution in the explanation of the principle. For example, David Ramsey Steele (1987) has argued that Hayek has abandoned the social theory project of the Scottish Enlightenment and embraced a holistic approach to social analysis that is alien to both that tradition and Hayek's earlier work on methodological individualism. Hayek's theory of group selection and cultural evolution is, at best, incorrect, and quite possibly damaging to the classical liberal project. Hayek is reduced, Steele argues, by the logic of his own argument, to a naive conservative.

Viktor Vanberg (1986) raised a very similar criticism of Hayek's theory of cultural evolution. "A closer examination of Hayek's writings on this topic," Vanberg (1986, 83) argues, "reveals that, in actual fact, he neither systematically elaborates nor consistently pursues such an individualistic, evolutionary approach to the question of why it is that rules can be expected spontaneously to emerge that increase the efficiency of the group as a whole and that provide solutions to 'problems of society'" (Vanberg 1986, 83). There is, Vanberg concludes, a tacit shift in Hayek's work from his earlier methodological individualism to the quite different emphasis on social rules which are followed because of the benefits that accrue to the group. This shift, to Vanberg, is undesirable and unjustified, and undermines our attempt to grapple with the problem of rule formation in social processes.

James Buchanan (1977, 1986a) has also reiterated these criticisms. However, Buchanan's criticism is more fundamental. He challenges the very idea of extending the spontaneous order paradigm beyond the realm of economics. While the discovery process of competitive markets tends to produce some optimality conditions (suboptimalities are eliminated in the pursuit of pure profit), there is no guarantee that legal processes yield the same result, and certainly, the discovery process of history cannot be relied upon. Buchanan finds Hayek's arguments about diffuse knowledge and the discovery process of the market convincing, but the extension of the argument to other social institutions creates problems, he believes, for grappling with what he calls the constitutional level of political economy. Hayek's conservativism does not allow for the deliberate reform of the rules of society. "There is no room left," Buchanan argues, "for the political economist, or for anyone else who seeks to reform social structures, to change laws and rules, with an aim of securing increased efficiency in the large" (1986a, 76).

Even Israel Kirzner, perhaps the leading representative of the modern Austrian School, follows Buchnan's 'equilibrium' criticism of Hayek. Kirzner is concerned that Hayek's extension of the spontaneous order approach beyond economics may lead us astray and undermine the defense of economic liberty. "The extraordinary power of arguments rooted in market theory should not be compromised," Kirzner warns, "by well-meaning but unhelpful reference to other kinds of spontaneous order" (1987, 46). Kirzner distinguishes between traditional spontaneous order explanations found in the writings of Adam Smith and others, which assumed individuals acting with regard to their self-interest within a given institutional framework, and the more recent literature on spontaneous order, which emphasizes the plausibility of social coordination emerging out of the self-interested behavior of individuals within an environment without any given institutional framework. While the earlier work was able to demonstrate, Kirzner argues, that within a certain institutional environment, the decentralized decisions of economic actors could be coordinated in a manner which allocated resources in an "objectively" efficient manner, the later work does not possess such a logic—there are no equilibrium conditions in law, language, and custom.

Both Buchanan and Kirzner explicitly rely on the neoclassical description of competitive markets as Pareto Optimal. Buchanan, for example, argues that there are three reasons to adopt spontaneous order explanations: political, aesthetic, and economic. Political, because a proper understanding of the spontaneous ordering of economic activity in a competitive market will possess tremendous import for economic policy decisions. Aesthetic, because spontaneous order explanations are intellectually more satisfying than expectations from design. Economic, because an understanding of spontaneous order allows us to "say that the workings of the market generate Pareto-efficient results" (Buchanan 1977, 29). But this third reason for adopting spontaneous order explanations of social coordination also limits their normative application beyond technical economics. We simply cannot say that either the legal or historical process possesses any logic which generates Pareto-efficient results. While the competitive market harbors tendencies to equilibrate, and thus eliminate socially undesirable states of affairs, "the forces of social evolution ... contain within their workings no guarantee that socially efficient results will emerge over time." The social institutions that emerge "need not be those which are the 'best'" (Buchanan 1977, 31). Or, as Kirzner has put it:

> There is no guarantee that the English language my children learn at their mother's knee will be a 'better' language for purposes of social intercourse than, say, French—or Esperanto. The demonstration that widely accepted social conventions can emerge without central authoritarian imposition does not necessarily point to any optimality in the resulting conventions.

What is demonstrated in the spontaneous order explanation of free market process, on the other hand, "is that there does exist a spontaneous tendency toward social optimality under the relevant conditions." (1987, 48)

The Achilles heel of these criticisms, however, is their continued reliance on the neoclassical notion of optimality. The Hayekian program has become increasingly disillusioned with any idea of optimality conditions and equilibrium states as these concepts proved to frustrate our understanding of social interaction, as Buchanan himself has recognized (1986b, 73–74). As Hayek expressed this point:

> I am afraid that I have become—with all aesthetic admiration for the achievement—more and more sceptical of the instructive value of the construction by which at one time I was greatly fascinated, that beautiful system of equations with which we can show in imagination what would happen if all these data were given to us. But we often forget that these data are purely fictitious, are not available to any single mind, and, therefore, do not really lead to an explanation of the process we observe. (1983: 36)

The modern Austrian School, following Hayek, has sought to consistently advance an alternative approach to the study of economic activity. The Austrian theory of the market process stands in stark contrast to the more traditional equilibrium analysis of mainstream neoclassical economics. This theoretical perspective has developed, which is built around both a deep appreciation of the subjective nature of the economic world and a recognition of how social institutions work through the filter of the human mind. This economic process is neither an evolutionary natural selection process that assures the survival of the "best" or "fittest," nor is it a chaotic and random walk. The discovery process of the competitive market is a learning process—a process of trial and error and experimentation in which the key component is the ability to reveal error and motivate the discovery of new knowledge about economic opportunities.

As Kirzner and Buchanan have demonstrated, the market process does not lead to any optimal state. The market process is misspecified if presented as an equilibrium system. Free market processes are characterized by continuous suboptimalities—in fact, this is what generates the process of learning and discovery. The superiority of the market process lies not in its ability to produce optimal results, but rather in its ability to mobilize and effectively use knowledge that is dispersed throughout the economic system.

Moreover, the criticisms of Hayek's project on the grounds of his abandonment of methodological individualism, moreover, are misplaced for two reasons. First, Hayek is mainly talking about the co-evolution of reason and tradition in the epoch when man was first emerging from his prehuman condition. Hayek's thesis is that our reason developed because we followed certain rules, not that we followed certain rules because of our reason. As he writes, cultural evolution "took place not merely after the appearance of Homo sapiens, but also during the much longer earlier existence of the genus Homo and its hominid ancestors. To repeat: mind and culture developed concurrently and not successively" (1979, 156). This leads to a position which challenges the sort of isolated and atomistic methodological individualism characteristic of much economics. Social inquiry must begin with a recognition of the social embeddedness of the mind.

Second, the best way to understand what Hayek is trying to do in *The Constitution of Liberty, Law, Legislation and Liberty* and *The Fatal Conceit* is to restate and elaborate from a consistently non-rationalist perspective, Mises's argument concerning the Law of Association, or social cooperation under the division of labor. "We have never designed our economic system," Hayek states. "We were not intelligent enough for that" (1979, 164). Hayek building on, as John Gray (1986, 130) points out, on the critical rationalist tradition of the Scottish Enlightenment, which is a "more humble, sceptical and modest form of liberalism," not the Cartesian rationalist tradition of the French Enlightenment. Building on the Scottish Enlightenment tradition of Ferguson, Hume, and Smith, Hayek writes in *The Fatal Conceit*:

> To understand our civilization, one must appreciate that the extended order resulted not from human design or intention but spontaneously: it arose from unintentionally conforming to certain traditional and largely moral practices, many of which men tend to dislike, whose significance they usually fail to understand, whose validity they cannot prove, and which have nonetheless fairly rapidly spread by means of an evolutionary selection—the comparative increase of population and wealth—of those groups that happened to follow them. (1988, 6)

The institution of private property, which man stumbled into, according to Hayek, made possible the growth of civilization. By following certain rules, which he could not justify nor even state, man cultivated his social world. "Such activities in which we are guided by a knowledge merely of the principle of a thing," Hayek states, "should perhaps better be described by the term cultivation than by the familiar term 'control'" (emphasis in original, 1955, 19).

Hayek argues that the coincidence of opinion concerning just rules of conduct will emerge through the purposive and meaningful dialogue of human interaction. Implicit rules of conduct will be respected among the various individuals in the social world before agreement is reached on articulated rules. It is these implicit rules through which the law of association operates to bring about the liberal extended order. "It is only as a result of individuals observing certain common rules," Hayek argues, "that a group of men can live together in those orderly relations which we call society" (1973, 95). Man does not need to consciously recognize the benefits of society as a whole, but merely the benefits to him. Out of a process by which individuals strive to improve their lot in life, the rules of the extended order come to be respected. Neither do we need to live in a world where every other man believes as we do about fundamental values in order to live in harmony. All we need are rules or social institutions (conventions, symbols, etc.) that produce mutually reinforcing sets of expectations to maintain a degree of social order, and these rules or institutions must serve as guides to individuals so they may orient their actions. The rules of social intercourse must be rigid enough so as to confirm our expectations, but flexible enough to allow for changing circumstances and creative human potential. "Living as members of society and dependent for the satisfaction of most of our needs on various forms of cooperation with others," Hayek writes, "we depend for the effective pursuit of our aims clearly on the correspondence of the expectations concerning the actions of others on which our plans are based with what they really do" (1973, 36).

Civilization can be cultivated through the judicious use of reason, but its complexity lies beyond the ability of human reason to design or control in fine detail.

Conclusion

There exists a bidirectionality between purposive human action and institutions; between agency and structure. Hayek sought to examine how alternative institutional arrangements impact economic performance *and* how the tools of economic reasoning help us better understand the operation of institutions. He studied law as the product of evolutionary processes, and thus a quintessential example of a spontaneous order *and* the constitutional structures that are most effective at constraining the predatory capacities of the state. Hayek's theory of spontaneous order and cultural evolution is precisely at the core of his effort to develop a genuine institutional economics.

The Austrian School of economics in its historical and contemporary embodiment, as well as the various thinkers that it influenced along the way, such as Alchian, Buchanan, Coase, Director, and Leoni, contributed significantly to the development of property rights economics, law and economics, political economy, and market process economics in the post-WWII era, and continues today into the twenty-first century with a new generation of scholars. It is in following the spontaneous order approach developed by Ferguson, Hume, and Smith in the eighteenth century, and Hayek in the twentieth century that scholars in the social sciences and humanities can continue to productively refine our study of how alternative institutional arrangements either hinder or promote productive specialization and peaceful cooperation among diverse individuals who often have divergent plans.

Bibliography

Bator, Francis M. 1957. The Simple Analytics of Welfare Maximization. *The American Economic Review* 47 (1): 22–59.

Boettke, Peter J. 1998. Economic Calculation: *The* Austrian Contribution to Political Economy. *Advances in Austrian Economics* 5: 131–158.

Buchanan, James M. [1968] 1999. The Demand and Supply of Public Goods. In *The Collected Works of James M. Buchanan Volume 5*. Indianapolis: Liberty Fund.

———. 1977. *Freedom in Constitutional Contract.* College Station: Texas A&M University Press.

———. 1986a. Cultural Evolution and Institutional Reform. In *Liberty, Market and State: Political Economy in the 1980s*, ed. James M. Buchanan. New York: New York University Press.

———. 1986b. Order Defined in the Process of Its Emergence. In *Liberty, Market and State: Political Economy in the 1980s*, ed. James M. Buchanan. New York: New York University Press.

———. [1996] 2001. Adam Smith as Inspiration. In *The Collected Works of James M. Buchanan, Volume 19: Ideas, Persons, and Events.* Indianapolis: Liberty Fund.

Buchanan, James M., and Gordon Tullock. 1962. *The Calculus of Consent: Logical Foundations of Constitutional Democracy.* Ann Arbor: University of Michigan Press.

Caldwell, Bruce J. 2004. *Hayek's Challenge: An Intellectual Biography of F. A. Hayek.* Chicago: University of Chicago Press.

Coase, Ronald H. 1959. The Federal Communications Commission. *Journal of Law and Economics* 2: 1–40.

———. 1960. The Problem of Social Cost. *Journal of Law and Economics* 3: 1–44.

Dekker, Erwin. 2016. *The Viennese Students of Civilization: The Meaning and Context of Austrian Economics Reconsidered.* New York: Cambridge University Press.

Gray, John. 1986. *Hayek on Liberty.* 2nd ed. Oxford, UK: Blackwell.

Hayek, F.A. 1933. The Trend of Economic Thinking. *Economica* 40: 121–137.

———. [1937] 1948. Economics and Knowledge. In *Individualism and Economic Order.* Chicago: University of Chicago Press, chapter 2.

———. 1939. Freedom and Economic System. *Public Policy Pamphlet* (29): iv–38.

———. 1943. The Facts of the Social Sciences. *Ethics* 54 (1): 1–13.

———. 1944. *The Road to Serfdom.* Chicago: University of Chicago Press.

———. 1945. The Use of Knowledge in Society. *The American Economic Review* 35 (4): 519–530.

———. [1948] 1980. *Individualism and Economic Order.* Chicago: University of Chicago Press.

———. [1952] 1979. *The Counter-Revolution of Science*, 2nd ed. Indianapolis: Liberty Fund.

———. 1955. Degrees of Explanation. *The British Journal for Philosophy of Science* 6 (23): 209–225.

———. 1960. *The Constitution of Liberty.* Chicago: University of Chicago Press.

———. 1973. *Law, Legislation, and Liberty, Vol.1: Rules and Order.* Chicago: University of Chicago Press.

———. 1976. *Law, Legislation and Liberty, Vol. 2: The Mirage of Social Justice.* Chicago: University of Chicago Press.

———. 1978. *New Studies in Philosophy, Politics, and Economics and the History of Ideas.* London: Routledge and Kegan Paul.

———. 1979. *Law, Legislation, and Liberty, Vol. 3: The Political Order of a Free People.* Chicago: University of Chicago Press.

———. 1983. *Knowledge, Evolution and Society.* London: Adam Smith Institute.

———. 1988. *The Fatal Conceit: The Errors of Socialism.* The Collected Works of F. A. Hayek W. W. Bartley, III (ed.). Chicago: University of Chicago Press.

Hume, David. [1739] 2000. *A Treatise of Human Nature.* Oxford: Oxford University Press.

Kirzner, Israel M. 1987. Spontaneous Order and the Case for the Free Market. In *Ideas on Liberty: Essays in Honor of Paul L. Poirot*, 45–50. Irvington-on-Hudson: Foundation for Economic Education.

Knight, Frank. 1932. The Newer Economics and the Control of Economic Activity. *Journal of Political Economy* 40 (4): 433–476.

———. 1938. Lippmann's *The Good Society. Journal of Political Economy* 46 (6): 864–872.

Leeson, Peter T. 2014. *Anarchy Unbound: Why Self-Governance Works Better Than You Think.* New York: Cambridge University Press.

Leonard, Thomas C. 2016. *Illiberal Reformers: Race, Eugenics, and American Economics in the Progressive Era.* Princeton: Princeton University Press.

Leoni, Bruno. [1961] 1972. *Freedom and the Law.* Los Angeles: Nash Publishing Company.

Masala, Antonio. 2003. *Il Liberalismo di Bruno Leoni.* Milan: Rubbettino.

McCloskey, Deirdre Nansen. 2006. *The Bourgeois Virtues: Ethics for an Age of Commerce.* Chicago: University Press.

———. 2010. *Bourgeois Dignity: Why Economics Can't Explain the Modern World.* Chicago: University Chicago Press.

———. 2016. *Bourgeois Equality: How Ideas, Not Capital or Institutions Enriched the World.* Chicago: University of Chicago Press.

Menger, Carl. [1871] 1981. *Principles of Economics.* New York: New York University Press.

———. [1883] 1996. *Investigations into the Method of the Social Sciences.* Auburn: Ludwig von Mises Institute.

Mises, Ludwig von. [1920] 1935. Economic Calculation in the Socialist Commonwealth. In *Collectivist Economic Planning*, ed. F.A. Hayek, trans. S. Alder, 87–130. London: Routledge.

———. [1922] 1951. *Socialism: An Economic and Sociological Analysis*. New Haven: Yale University Press.

———. [1949] 1966. *Human Action: A Treatise on Economics*, 3rd ed. New Haven: Yale University Press.

———. [1956] 2006. *The Anti-Capitalist Mentality*. Indianapolis: Liberty Fund.

———. 1978. *On the Manipulation of Money and Credit: Three Treatises on Trade-Cycle Theory*. Indianapolis: Liberty Fund.

Rajan, Raghuram. 2004. Assume Anarchy? Why An Unorthodox Economic Model May Not Be the Best Guide For Policy. *Finance and Development* 41 (3): 56–57.

Smith, Adam. [1759] 1984. *The Theory of Moral Sentiments*. Indianapolis: Liberty Fund.

———. [1776] 2014. *An Inquiry into the Nature and Causes of the Wealth of Nations*. London: Edwin Cannan, ed. 1904. Available online from Library of Economics and Liberty.

———. [1795] 1982. *Essays on Philosophical Subjects with Dugald Stewart's Account of Adam Smith*. Indianapolis: Liberty Fund.

Steele, David Ramsay. 1987. Hayek's Theory of Cultural Group Selection. *Journal of Libertarian Studies* 8 (2): 171–195.

Van Horn, Robert. 2013. Hayek's Unacknowledged Discipline: An Exploration of the Political and Intellectual Relationship of F. A. Hayek and Aaron Director (1945–1950). *Journal of the History of Economic Thought* 35 (3): 271–290.

Vanberg, Viktor. 1986. Spontaneous Market Order and Social Rules: A Critical Examination of FA Hayek's Theory of Cultural Evolution. *Economics & Philosophy* 2 (1): 75–100.

Weingast, Barry. 2016. Exposing the Neoclassical Fallacy: McCloskey on Ideas and the Great Enrichment. *Scandinavian Economic History Review* 64 (3): 189–201.

8

The Political Economy of a Free People

Ideas, Institutions, Performance

At the time of this writing, true liberalism is in perilous times as new threats from right and left authoritarian populism have arisen in rhetoric and in policy throughout Europe, North America, and Latin America. The gains made throughout the world due to liberalizing economies and polities since the collapse of communism are being questioned. This is perhaps because, as Ronald Coase remarked in his Nobel Prize Address, of a neglect of economists' understanding of the market, "or more specifically the institutional arrangements which govern the process of exchange" ([1992] 2016, 66). Globalization, rather than being recognized as a force behind the miracle of lifting the desperately poor from the miserable existence of living on less than $2/day, is accused of ushering in a new gilded age of inequality and insecurity for all except the privileged few with the corresponding charge that liberal democratic governance is corrupted by wealth and

© The Author(s) 2018
Peter J. Boettke, *F. A. Hayek*, Great Thinkers in Economics,
https://doi.org/10.1057/978-1-137-41160-0_8

power.[1] These disputes are ultimately empirical in nature, but our understanding of these "facts" depends on the utilization of sound theory—what I have recently taken to referring to as "mainline economics."[2] The "facts" do not speak directly to us, but it is also the case that you cannot satisfactorily answer empirical questions philosophically. The true liberal must engage the challenges from the right, left, and center with the tools of reason and evidence.

In stressing reason and evidence, I do not mean to suggest dull and dispassionate analysis. No, as Hayek stressed years ago in his 1949 essay "The Intellectuals and Socialism," if true liberalism is going to gain wider acceptance:

> We must make the building of a free society once more an *intellectual adventure, a deed of courage*. What we lack is a liberal Utopia, a program which seems neither a mere defense of things as they are nor a diluted kind of socialism, but a *truly liberal radicalism* which does not spare the susceptibilities of the mighty (including the trade unions), which is not too severely practical, and which *does not confine itself to what appears today as politically possible*. We need intellectual leaders who are prepared to resist the blandishments of power and influence and who are willing to work for an ideal, however small may be the prospects of its early realization. (emphasis added, 1949, 432)

---

[1] In 2015, the World Bank estimated that for the first time in human history, less than 10% of the world's population was living in conditions of extreme poverty. As Deaton states, "the fall in absolute numbers of poor has been driven in large part by the rapid growth in China, so that, at least in the past ten years, the absolute number of non-Chinese poor has continued to increase" (Deaton 2015, 46), such as in sub-Saharan Africa (Deaton 2015, 45). This is the "Great Escape" as Angus Deaton terms it, yet it occurred without much notice while Stiglitz's "Great Divide" and the concern with inequality domestically and internationally continues to shape the contemporary intellectual discourse. On the importance of Deaton's work and his Nobel, see my article: http://www.politico.eu/article/a-humane-nobel-economist-angus-deaton/ Boettke (2015). On questions of global justice in general, see Loren Lomasky and Fernando Teson, *Justice at a Distance* (2015).

[2] Mainline Economics refers to the set of substantive propositions that can be found in the works of thinkers from Adam Smith to F. A. Hayek about how the world works. It is to be contrasted with "mainstream" economics which I argue is a more sociological designation of what is currently considered scientifically fashionable. Sometimes, the mainline and the mainstream align; other times, they diverge significantly from one another. See Boettke, *Living Economics* (2012). Also see Boettke, Haeffele-Balch, Storr, ed., *Mainline Economics: Six Nobel Lectures in the Tradition of Adam Smith* (2016) and Mitchell and Boettke, *Applied Mainline Economics: Bridging the Gap Between Theory and Public Policy* (2017).

And, Hayek continued, the main lesson to be learned from the triumph of socialist ideas in the previous generation was "their *courage to be Utopian* which gained them the support of the intellectuals and therefore an influence on public opinion which is daily making possible what only recently seemed utterly remote." The socialist had shifted the tacit presuppositions of political economy, which in effect shifts the argumentative burden. So, whereas to Mill, who certainly was no enemy of government intervention in the economy, the argumentative burden still rested with those who wanted to deviate from the laissez-faire principle, by the time of Keynes that argumentative burden had been reversed. As Hayek summed up the situation in 1949, "*Unless we can make the philosophic foundations of a free society once more a living intellectual issue,* and its implementation a task which challenges the ingenuity and imagination of our liveliest minds the prospects of freedom are indeed dark" (emphasis added, Hayek 1949, 432).

Hayek (1960, 410–411) argued that this task constitutes, first and foremost, building the intellectual system in a political economy that cultivates an appreciation for how freeing "the process of spontaneous growth from the obstacles and encumbrances that human folly has erected" in the hope that this can persuade and gain the support of those "progressive" intellectuals that while their goals of eradicating poverty, ignorance, squalor and, most of all, injustice, are laudable, the methods are in the wrong direction. The least advantaged are not better served by erecting more obstacles and encumbrances to the free play of the competitive economy. But Hayek also warns the readers of *The Constitution of Liberty* that they must not interpret his arguments as related in the least to a political platform. Again, this emphasis by him should be seen as part of his focus on the *tacit presuppositions of political economy* as in "The Intellectuals and Socialism" because it is there that we find where the argumentative burden is to rest. Quoting Adam Smith, Hayek argues that political programs must be left to "that insidious and crafty animal, vulgarly called a statesman or politician, whose councils are directed by the momentary fluctuations of affairs." This is not him, or those his message is directed toward. That audience was political philosophers and political economists, and their task can only be accomplished effectively if they are "not concerned with what is now politically possible," but instead they consistently defend "the general principles which are always the same."

Today we face new versions of the old intellectual threats critical of the market economy and the private property order upon which the market is based. There are also new practical challenges in the realm of public policy on the free flow of capital and labor, the freedom of trade, freedom of association, and the innovative spirit. We are confronted with the "sickness of the over-governed society" to use Walter Lippmann's phraseology ([1937] 2005, 40), and we must seek relief in the form of greater freedom, as he put it, to avoid disaster.

Liberalism, correctly understood, is little more than the persistent and consistent applications of the principles of economics of the affairs of men, be they domestic or international. Since the time of Adam Smith, economists have understood that the precondition for mutually beneficial exchange is both the recognition of private property rights and a general agreement on the rules of just conduct between parties. Adam Smith and his contemporaries never argued that individual pursuit of self-interest will always and everywhere result in the public interest, but rather that individual pursuit of self-interest within a specific set of institutional arrangements—namely well-defined and well-enforced private property rights—would produce such a result. Smith's examples of classroom instruction in Scotland, where professors were paid directly from student fees, and in Oxford, where professors were paid from an endowment independent of student feedback, provides a clear example ([1776] 1981, 759–761). Professors in both environments are "self-interested," but only in one environment are the incentives aligned in a way that transforms that self-interest into a harmony of interests between teachers and students. So, as Robbins writes, "You cannot understand their attitude to any important concrete measure of policy unless you understand their belief with regard to the nature and effects of the system of spontaneous-cooperation" ([1952] 1965, 12).

Alfred Marshall ([1890] 1920) referred to this argument as the Classical Economist's "system of economic freedom" and it can be summed up as an argument that consumers should be free to choose what they believe best satisfies their wants and desires, and producers (including workers, managers, and owners) should be free to use their labor and property in whatever manner in which in their judgment would result in the highest monetary reward or greatest satisfaction as measured along some non-monetary dimension. Market forces would provide the mechanism to bring about the harmony of the various interests in this interaction such that the common welfare would be enhanced. This, of course, is Adam Smith's famous "invisible hand" and the classical theory of economic policy argued that the prime objective of policy was to ensure that trade and industry was free and that any, and all, obstacles to the spontaneous order of the market economy be swept away.

From this perspective, Lionel Robbins's *The Theory of Economic Policy in English Classical Political Economy* ([1952] 1965) is as relevant today as it was when it was first presented as a series of lectures in the late 1930s, and revisited after WWII in the early 1950s. Robbins makes it crystal clear that the classical theory of economic policy must be seen not in juxtaposition to a positive theory of state action, but must always be seen "in combination with the theory of law and the functions of government which its authors also propounded; the idea of freedom *in vacuo* was entirely alien to their conceptions" ([1952] 1965, 12). This system of spontaneous cooperation, or economic freedom, does not come about absent a "firm framework of law and order." The "invisible hand," according to the classical economists, "is not the hand of some god or some natural agency independent of human effort; it is the hand of the law-giver, the hand which withdraws from the sphere of the pursuit of self-interest those possibilities which do not harmonize with the public good" (Robbins [1952] 1965, 56).

In many ways, the classical economists' position was simply the commonly accepted wisdom of nineteenth-century Western political philosophy. In 1854, Abraham Lincoln, while decrying the oftentimes "do nothing" view of government, nevertheless summed up the position as follows: "The legitimate object of government, is to do for a community of people, whatever they need to have done, but can not do, at all, or can not, so well do, for themselves—in their separate, and individual capacities" (1953, 220). Lincoln used this argument to then argue for variety of government actions, for instance, bridges and other public work projects. But the presumption at his time was to demonstrate that a community of people could not do for themselves what was necessary. Without that demonstration, the presumption would be for government action to limit itself to the positive agenda associated with the institutional framework. It is important to note that Lincoln's formulation also sets up the correct comparative institutional exercise, for even if individuals cannot do for themselves, or do what is required well for themselves, that still leaves unanswered whether government can do it, or if it can do it better than what a community of individuals would do for themselves. We can never be content with just assuming that government can do something, or do it well, simply because we have demonstrated that individuals would have difficulty doing the delineated task. Assuming otherwise runs into the same difficulty that assuming that, there will always be a natural harmony of interest if individuals are left to their own devices. In other words, as Milton and Rose Friedman put in *Free to Choose* (1980, 292), there is an "invisible hand" explanation in politics which runs the opposite of Smith's famous "theorem" in markets—namely that individuals who intend only to promote the general interest are led by an invisible political hand to promote a special interest that was no part of their intention.[3]

Progress in the theory of economic policy, as James Buchanan and Gordon Tullock taught us, is made when we reject behavioral asymmetry and adhere strictly to behavioral symmetry. Same players, different rules, produce different outcomes for us to study. The focus is not on the characteristics of the specific players, but the institutional environment within which they interact. Furthermore, progress in comparative

---

[3] In a reference work edited with Peter Leeson, *The Economic Role of the State* (2015), we go through the various presumptions in the debate: the perfect market, the market failure, the government failure, and the anarchy presumption. These presumptions or tacit presuppositions of political economy held by theorists dictate that conversation. What we insist is that any effort to curb the potential of private predation by the establishment of a public entity of coercion, by definition, has now created the potential for public predation. This is way too often forgotten in the standard perspective of economists. In a debate with Richard Musgrave, for example, James Buchanan once asked him whether he would put a muzzle on his tiger if he was taking him for a stroll in the park. Musgrave responded, no, what if my tiger wanted to eat the grass. Buchanan was appropriately exacerbated by such a response. Remember also Keynes's response in a letter dated June 28, 1944, to Hayek's *The Road to Serfdom*—while in deep moral agreement, he nevertheless thought that clearly men like Hayek and him could be entrusted to centrally plan an economy. Reprinted in John Maynard Keynes, *Activities 1940–1946. Shaping the Post-War World: Employment and Commodities*. In Donald Moggride, ed. (1980). *The Collected Works of John Maynard Keynes*, Vol. 27.

political economy follows directly from rejecting the assumptions of omniscience, omnipotence, and benevolence. We are, instead, very imperfect beings interacting with other imperfect beings in a very imperfect world stumbling upon ways for us to live better together than we ever could in isolation.

Elinor Ostrom (1990, 25–26) described concisely why this approach is important in the policy sciences. As she put it:

> As an institutionalist studying empirical phenomena, I presume that individuals try to solve problems as effectively as they can. That assumption imposes a discipline on me. Instead of presuming that some individuals are incompetent, evil, or irrational, and others are omniscient, I presume that individuals have very similar limited capabilities to reason and figure out the structure of complex environments. It is my responsibility as a scientist to ascertain what problems individuals are trying to solve and what factors help or hinder them in these efforts. When the problems that I observe involve lack of predictability, information, and trust, as well as high levels of complexity and transactional difficulties, then my efforts to explain must take these problems overtly into account rather than assuming them away.

So, as we have seen, neither in the approach of classical political economy nor in our approach will we assume perfect markets populated by perfectly rational actors. Moreover, we will not assume a perfect government under the command of omniscient, omnipotent, and benevolent social planners. There will be problems to deal with daily; there will be tensions in human affairs at each moment in time. But institutional problems demand institutional solutions. The answer is never better people need to populate our models, and thus our communities in order for our policy solutions to work their magic. Our world is characterized instead by erring entrepreneurs *and* bumbling bureaucrats, so we are forever obliged to ask the comparative institutional question about the impact of alternative configurations of the rules of the game on the playing of the game. To do that, we have the basic tools of economic reasoning—namely, incentive alignment and information processing.

The first question of any policy proposal to ask is whether the policy is *incentive compatible*. If it cannot pass this simple test and would require instead a transformation of individuals within the economy to act in ways not consistent with the ordinary business of economic life, they will fail, regardless of how pleasing they may be in the abstract in terms of lofty goals such as justice and equality. The second question that must be raised in the theory of economic policy, assuming the first question is satisfactorily answered, is whether there is an incentive compatible *political strategy* for implementing the policy recommendation. Again, if the policy proposal would require politicians to act in violation of the ordinary, yet peculiar, business of politics, then we can reasonably expect a failure at the implementation stage, and thus inconsistent and sometimes counter-productive policy changes. The presumption of behavioral symmetry as well as dispersed knowledge, which can never be held in a single political official's mind, leads Hayek to argue the following:

> I think people are quite likely to agree on general rules which restrict government, without quite knowing what it implies in practice. And then I think if that is made a constitutional rule, they will probably observe it. You can never expect the majority of the people to regain their belief in the market as such. But I think you can expect that they will come to dislike government interference. If you can make it clear that there's a difference between government holding the ring and enforcing certain rules, and government taking specific measures for the benefit of particular people— That's what the people at large do not understand. ([1978] 1983, 212)

If the proposed policy can answer these two questions, we have an additional set of questions raised by the informational constraints that economic and political actors face in their respective domains. As a disciplinary constraint on our efforts, we are not permitted to assume that the theorist advising government policy knows more than the economic actors on the ground. Actors on the ground do not possess the theoretical knowledge of the policymaker, but the policymaker does not have access to the "on the ground" knowledge of the particular circumstances of time and place that economic actors are in possession of. Both face a "knowledge problem" that must be solved, and they need mechanisms endogenous to their respective arenas that provide them the knowledge necessary to learn from, adjust, and adapt their behavior. Economic actors rely on the price system—relative price movements, along with the lure of pure profit and the disciplining penalty of loss—in making their private choices. Political decision-makers must rely on the context of politics—voting and bureaucracy—to make their public choices. How well does the decentralized system of the market do in coping with inevitable errors in comparison with more centralized systems of government planning and management?[4] For much of the twentieth century, it became a common presumption that a professionalized bureaucracy was synonymous with modernity.

The vision of bureaucratic public administration as synonymous with modernity has been an article of faith for the establishment elite since Weber and Wilson. But consider the following from Hayek's *The Road to Serfdom* (emphasis added 1944, 94–96):

The assertion that modern technological progress makes planning inevitable can also be interpreted in a different manner. It may mean that the complexity of our modern industrial civilization creates new problems with which we cannot hope to deal effectively except by central planning… What they generally suggest is that the increasing difficulty of obtaining a coherent picture of the complete economic process makes it indispensable that things should be coordinated by some central agency if social life is not to dissolve in chaos. This argument is based on a complete misapprehension of the working of competition. Far from being appropriate only to comparatively simple conditions, it is the very complexity of the division of labor under modern conditions which makes competition the only method by which such coordination can be adequately brought about. There would be no difficulty about efficient control or planning were conditions so simple that a single person or board could effectively survey all the relevant facts. It is only as the factors which have to be taken into account become so numerous that it is impossible to gain a synoptic view of them that decentralization becomes imperative. But, once decentralization is necessary, the problem of coordination arises – a coordination which leaves the separate agencies free to adjust their activities to the fact which only they

---

[4]And it is always important to remember Milton Friedman's warning in *Capitalism and Freedom* that any public policy arrangement where a sincere error on the part of a few can threaten the entire economic system is perhaps a public policy arrangement we cannot afford ([1962] 2002, 50). Also see Vincent Ostrom's *The Intellectual Crisis of American Public Administration* ([1973] 1989) and more recent work on "expert failure" by David Levy and Sandra Peart, *The Escape from Democracy* (2017) and Roger Koppl, *Expert Failure* (2017).

can know and yet brings about a mutual adjustment of their respective plans...This is precisely what the price system does under competition, and which no other system even promises to accomplish. It enables entrepreneurs, by watching the movement of comparatively few prices, as an engineer watches the hands of a few dials, to adjust their activities to those of their fellows. The important point here is that the price system will fulfill this function only if competition prevails, that is, if the individual producer has to adapt himself to price changes and cannot control them....It is no exaggeration to say that if we had to rely on conscious central planning for the growth of our industrial system, it would never have reached the degree of differentiation, complexity, and flexibility it has attained. Compared with this method of solving the economic problem by means of decentralization plus automatic coordination, the more obvious method of central direction is incredibly clumsy, primitive, and limited in scope.

Hayek's political economy ran counter to all the trends of his time—methodologically, analytically, and social philosophically. The discipline of economics was transformed during this period from a branch of moral philosophy to a tool for social control. Economics became a form of "social physics," and to fit that image relied increasingly on mathematical modeling and statistical analysis. There is nothing wrong in principle with mathematics and statistics, but there is something wrong if to utilize those tools, a variety of critical issues for human understanding are pushed aside—such as human purposes and plans, subjectivism of value and expectations, time and ignorance, and the social relationships formed in exchange. If these very human elements are purged in the study of human affairs, we run the risk of transforming a human science into a mechanical one.

The cost of this intellectual transformation was to avoid, rather than address, the essential complexity of social life. Excessive aggregation and excessive formalism went hand in hand, and resulted in turning a blind eye to the complexity, the diversity, and the dynamics of the governing dynamics in a self-regulating modern commercial society. The *economy* became something to be managed and planned, rather than being the subject of study and reflection. Just imagine how strange it must have been to read Hayek's counter-claims to the Progressive mind of the mid-twentieth century.

In addition to these points raised by Hayek about the economic system, it is important to remember that in the realm of politics, another critical point related to the normative "ought" of reform, and the positive analysis of "can." Even if we philosophically speculate about what *ought* to be done by a governmental authority, we still have to answer the points I have raised about incentives and information, only after which we can answer the question of whether we *can* accomplish what we claim we ought to do. Similarly, if it can be established that the government *can* do X, Y, or Z, that does not establish directly that it *ought* to do it. Ought does not imply can, and can does not imply ought.

In thinking about this relationship between ought and can in the theory of economic policy, it is critical to remember a point stressed by James Buchanan—any work in public economics implicitly relies on a political theory or social philosophy. This is true because questions of public economics and public finance turn on questions of the scale and scope of government in society. So, it would be better if all economists are required to state and defend their political philosophical position, rather than be allowed to sneak it into the analysis without any critical analysis. In addition, no matter what political philosophical position one adopts, there is a technical constraint that public authorities must pursue— namely *fiscal equivalence*—if they are striving for the efficient use of resources in the public sector. We are defining the term in two ways to describe what an ideal tax would do, and to help delineate governmental responsibilities between the different levels of government (local, state, federal). With respect to delineation of responsibilities, a general rule of thumb would be to match the magnitude of the externality identified with the governmental unit responsible. Externalities that are small in magnitude, such as garbage collection, would be dealt with at the local level, while externalities larger in magnitude, such as national security, would be dealt with at the federal level. And the financing of these public activities would be from taxes and fees charged to citizens. In an ideal arrangement, citizens would be charged that tax rate that would reflect the value they place on the use of that governmental service. Citizen preferences would be matched with the delivery of the public services or goods, just as they would in a competitive market setting *if* a competitive market could exist for the good or service under investigation.

This formal similarity between the optimality conditions of the market, and the optimality of resource use and demand revelation in the public sector must be recognized as a background constraint in the analysis of economic policy. The question is whether any particular policy can meet this test in implementation, or will the administrative costs of the policy result in significant deviations from this ideal benchmark, such that the costs of the policy exceed the benefits of the policy.[5] Citizen frustration, say with public safety in cities, often result due to these sort of considerations where the externality is not matched with the governmental unit, the preferences of citizens are not accurately taken into account, and the administrative costs of the policy far exceed the benefits of the policy. The machinations of politics often take into account voter preferences, but then produce public policies that are divorced from those preferences.

The challenges to the competitive economy presume that, due to problems of monopoly, externalities, public goods, and inequality, the government had to play a more active role in the operation of the economy, either through price controls, regulations, or taxation and subsidization. We are leaving nationalization out of our discussion at the moment. The government might also need to play an active role in the economy due to macroeconomic instability, and will do so with the tools of macroeconomic management and a host of counter-cyclical policy measures. Monetary policy and fiscal policy provide the basic tools, but intervention in the labor market to provide a strong countervailing power to labor versus business interests is often relied on as well. However, a critical examination of these activist policies will reveal that rather than providing the appropriate tools to organize a vibrant and growing economy, they are often the primary source of the problems they purport to solve. In short, it is government policies that distort the economic incentives and economic signals that actors use to coordinate their behavior, and they destabilize the economic environment within which decisions are made.

---

[5] See Milton Friedman's review essay on Abba Lerner's *The Economics of Control* published originally in the *Journal of Political Economy* (1947). Friedman brilliantly diagnoses Lerner's proposals from a comparative institutional approach and stresses that Lerner ignores the administrative costs of his policies and that these costs cannot be ignored.

True liberals have tended to respond to criticisms of the market economy in one of two ways—conceptual clarity and/or robustness and resiliency. There is no necessary conflict between them, but they do place a different emphasis on the argument. In stressing conceptual clarity, the liberal economist seeks to capture the actual costs and benefits that actors are facing and not the imaginary costless transition from one institutional arrangement to another. This approach was practiced to perfection in many ways by George Stigler, an economist of the post-WWII Chicago School and the 1982 Nobel Laureate in Economic Sciences (see Boettke and Candela 2017). Alternatively, the liberal could focus on how individuals in the face of conflicts and tensions engage in various bargains and adjustments to ameliorate the conflict and tension. This approach was practiced to perfection in many ways by Ronald Coase. In working out our understanding of the economic policy of a free society, we must deploy both, but emphasize the importance of institutional change, entrepreneurial alertness, and creativity. Property rights incentivize and create expectations, relative prices guide us in our decision-making, pure profits lure us, and losses discipline us. Restrictions on property, prices, and profit/loss will distort and pervert the decisions of economic actors, including not just their initial actions, but the adaptations and adjustments they will make as they learn throughout the process of economic activity. In other words, bad public policy not only prevents learning the "right things," but engenders learning the "wrong things." Error, rather than being selected out, is actually embedded into the system and with that, waste and misuse of resources, including talents.

We must be steady in our scientific exploration of comparative institutional analysis, and steadfast in upholding the lessons learned from that scientific exploration for public policy. Same players, but different rules produce different outcomes. The history of the twentieth and now twenty-first century has demonstrated that while there are many ways for people to play the social game, there are few ways to play the social game that produces generalized wealth and prosperity, capable of lifting humanity from the miserable existence of extreme poverty. To realize such wealth-creating social games, we must not only resist the urge of command and control in public policy, but also jettison the scientistic prejudices that strangled scientific progress in economics during significant portions of the twentieth century.

The damage done to our understanding of the economic policy for a free society, and thus to true liberalism was a result of an intellectual alliance of statism and scientism that was the defining characteristic of progressivism and socialism. The new threats to liberalism from the right, left, and center may be expressed in populist rhetoric, but when implemented in the realm of public policy, they invoke the statist and scientism alliance once more. As Hayek put it in his Nobel Prize lecture:

> If man is not to do more harm than good in his efforts to improve the social order, he will have to learn that in this, as in all other fields where essential complexity of an organized kind prevails, he cannot acquire the full knowledge which would make mastery of the events possible. He will therefore have to use what knowledge he can achieve, not to shape the results as the craftsman shapes his handiwork, but rather to cultivate a growth by providing the appropriate environment, in the manner in which the gardener does this for his plants. There is danger in the exuberant feeling of ever growing power which the advance of the physical sciences has engendered and which tempts man to try, 'dizzy with success,' to use a characteristic phrase of early communism, to subject not only our natural but also our human environment to the control of a human will. The recognition of the insuperable limits to his knowledge ought indeed to teach the student of society a lesson of humility which should guard him against becoming an accomplice in men's fatal striving to control society—a striving which makes him not only a tyrant over his fellows, but which may well make him the destroyer of a civilization which no brain has designed but which has grown from the free efforts of millions of individuals. ([1974] 2016, 38–39)

Our understanding of the nuances and subtleties of the economic policy of a free society begins only once we accept this essential message from Hayek. The true liberal is a student of civilization and never its savior; we are at best lowly philosophers and never high priests. The creative powers of free civilization flow from cultivating an institutional environment that exhibits neither discrimination nor dominion. General rules of just conduct, and rather than particular privileges and status, define the institutional infrastructure of a thriving society. Economic freedom gives rise to generalized prosperity and to human flourishing.

Institutional Problems Demand Institutional Solutions

As we had discussed throughout, the Hayekian move was to place at the center of analysis in political economy that set of institutions that enable the utilization and learning of the relevant knowledge to realize the gains from social cooperation under the division of labor. In his mind, the project from Adam Smith onward was for the political economist—in their joint role as discoverer of governing dynamics in the world, and as institutional craftsman of improvements in the social world—to explore what could occasionally be achieved not when individuals were on their best behavior, but what configuration would prevent individuals from doing great harm when they are at their worst. The idea was to find that institutional configuration where bad actors could do least harm to the political and economic system.

This exercise means that one must think through the logic of choice and the situational logic of social interactions without recourse to assumptions of benevolence or omniscience. For if the social system relied for its functioning on selecting only the good and the wise to rule, or on all of humanity becoming "better" versions of ourselves, then the system would be quite vulnerable to failure due to our ignorance or our opportunism. Instead of relying on a mechanism to select only the good and the wise, we can grant freedom to all if, and only if, we can find a set of institutions that makes use of individuals in their given variety—sometimes bad; sometimes good; sometimes smart; sometimes stupid. And as Hayek points out, the classical political economists and moral philosophers found that the liberal order of private property and the rule of law did provide such an institutional system. It was never perfect by any stretch of the imagination, but it worked to simultaneously provide greater individual freedom, more generalized economic prosperity, and peaceful social interaction. Reform was to be sought through continually marginal adjustments consistent with private property and the rule of law, not a wholesale institutional change in an effort to replace the private property system, as the socialists and progressives did.

The socialist and progressive experiments in the democratic West, according to Hayek, threatened the very viability of the liberal order. This is what he was getting at when in *The Road to Serfdom*, he argued that: "The supreme tragedy is still not seen that in Germany it was largely people of good will, men who were admired and held up as models in the democratic countries, who prepared the way for, if they did not actually create, the forces which now stand for everything they detest" (1944, 3). Unless we start to understand this, Hayek fears, we will not see the vulnerabilities in the system created by our "fatal conceit"—a conceit that creates scope for loss of liberty, prosperity, and peace due to ignorance and/or opportunism. And, as he states: "Is there a greater tragedy imaginable than that in our endeavor consciously to shape our future in accordance with high ideals we should in fact unwittingly produce the very opposite of what we have been striving for?" (1944, 5).

The best way to understand Hayek's efforts in articulating a political economy of a free people would be to first understand to the full extent possible what he meant by the rule of law, and then, to think through the implications of passing all proposals through this rule of law check. According to Hayek, the rule of law refers to the absence of political or legal privilege among market actors, the corollary of which is also an absence of arbitrary discretion among political actors. It is a political-legal principle, whereby the governing authority of a particularly society is restricted to enforcing laws applied equally to all and not intended to benefit one particular party at the expense of another. Any violation of the rule of law implies that political-legal privileges cannot be granted without simultaneously granting discretionary power to those political actors who are in the position to grant such privileges. For Hayek, the rule of law does not imply a law of rules, but a norm of generality such that individuals are seen as one another's equals before the law, regardless of birth, race, ethnicity, or religion. This generality norm meant that the political and legal structures we would exist under in a true liberalism would exhibit neither discrimination nor dominion. Liberalism and the rule of law are inherently intertwined, since the "essence of the liberal position," according to Hayek, "is the denial of all privilege, if privilege is understood in its proper and original meaning of the state granting and protecting rights to some which are not available on equal terms to others" (Hayek 1944, 46).

"The conception of freedom under the law," Hayek argued in *The Constitution of Liberty* (1960, 153), "that is the chief concern of this book rests on the contention that when we obey laws, in the sense of general abstract rules laid down irrespective of their application to us, we are not subject to another man's will and are therefore free." Laws and not men rule. He continues, "Because the rule is laid down in ignorance of the particular case and no man's will decides the coercion used to enforce it, the law is not arbitrary. This, however, is true only if by 'law' we mean the general rules that apply equally to everybody. This generality is probably the most important aspect of that attribute which we have called its 'abstractness'. As a true law should not name any particulars, so it should especially not single out any specific persons or group of persons" (1960, 153–54).

We live together in groups, and we must choose together in groups how we will live with one another. Throughout most of human history, this question was answered rather straightforwardly—those in position of power and privilege decided, and those without that status suffered the fate of subjects. They were not free. Jean-Jacques Rousseau famously asked—how can a man be free while subject to wills other than his own? This in essence was the puzzle to be solved by liberalism. Can rules be crafted and instantiated that are based on contract and consent, rather than status and force?

Hayek's objections to socialism and progressivism were not only philosophical, but technical as well. Technically, the arguments for planning and interventionism were flawed because the policy means chosen could be demonstrated to be ineffective at achieving the policy goals sought *from the point of view of the planner or the intervener*. This is the tragedy he talked about in *The Road to Serfdom*, where high ideals crash against the hard reality of economic analysis. Nothing in this discussion committed Hayek to a normative disagreement with socialist and progressives. In fact, he was in agreement with the high ideals and desired a social system that addressed the social ills of poverty, ignorance, and squalor with just as much fervor as those to which he addressed his argument. The problem was that once an analyst recognizes the constraints, in particular the necessity of choice against constraints, and the complexity, in particular the necessity of coping with our ignorance, then the calm and dispassionate analysis of means-ends efficiency produces disturbing results to the zealot reformer. They cannot achieve what they hope to achieve pursuing the path they have chosen to pursue. But Hayek's argument went farther and explained that not only would they fail to achieve what they sought to achieve, but they would create the conditions for the establishment of everything they detest.

In order to pursue the socialist and progressive vision, the reformers have adopted means which, by necessity, undermine any notion of freedom under the law. Discrimination and dominion are reintroduced and reinforced with abandon. Hayek, in this sense, anticipated the literature on the "New Class" in studies of the real existing socialist systems, and the "Losing Ground" studies of the social democratic welfare state. His argument begins in *The Road to Serfdom*, matures with *The Constitution of Liberty*, and is given one last presentation in *Law, Legislation and Liberty*. His final work *The Fatal Conceit* goes back into the fundamental philosophical problem with socialism, and in many ways is a work providing an alternative anthropology as much an alternative vision of political economy. For our purposes, we can focus on the three main works in political economy and social philosophy. I would like to suggest a way to see the evolution of Hayek's argument in *The Road to Serfdom*, *The Constitution of Liberty* and *Law, Legislation and Liberty* that I believe will aid the reader not only in their interpretative quest to understand Hayek's contributions to political economy and social philosophy, but to see the evolutionary potential of the Hayekian argument.

First, *The Road to Serfdom* must be understood as a warning to his fellow liberals in Britain and to others who had been seduced by socialist rhetoric during the depths of the Great Depression. Hayek does not use this book to challenge the dominant narrative that capitalism suffers inherently from inefficiency, instability, and injustice. There are nuggets spread throughout the text countering specific claims along these lines, but that is not the primary purpose of the work. His primary purpose is to demonstrate the situational logic of the effort to plan a modern economy, and the resulting necessary political and legal changes that will undermine the rule of law and democracy.[6] This is critical to the debate of his day because many British intellectuals argued that they were socialist in their economics because they were liberals in their politics. New Liberals argued along these lines in the UK just as the Progressive did in the USA. "There can be no doubt," Hayek (1944, 78–79) argued, "that planning necessarily involves deliberate determination between particular needs of different people, and allowing one man to do what another must be prevented from doing. It must lay down by a legal rule how well off particular people shall be and what different people are to be allowed to have and do." Hayek argues this will return us to the age of status rather than contract, and thus reverse the progress that societies have made in establishing the Rule of Law. It is the Rule of Law that is the safeguard against arbitrary government and guarantees equality before the law. The economic agenda of socialist and progressives, however, relies on strengthening the arbitrary power of government and treating different people differently, and thus results in "the destruction of the Rule of Law." Economic planning not only cannot work to achieve its stated objectives, but it necessitates a destruction of the very institutions that made possible the liberty, prosperity, and peace that civilization had experienced to that point. The move back to a society of status meant reductions in liberty, declines in prosperity, and an increase in conflict. The narrow institutional pathway to liberty that constituted the political and economic experiences Deirdre McCloskey has recently dubbed "The Great Enrichment" is replaced by the road to serfdom.

---

[6] And counter to the "slippery slope" interpretation, Hayek argued in *Law, Legislation and Liberty*, Vol. 1 (1973, 58) that: "What I meant to argue in *The Road to Serfdom* was certainly not that whenever we depart, however slightly, from what I regard as the principles of a free society, we shall ineluctably be driven to go the whole way to a totalitarian system. It was rather what in more homely language is expressed when we way: 'If you do not mend your principles you will go to the devil.' That this has often been understood to describe a necessary process over which we have no power once we have embarked on it, is merely an indication of how little importance of principles for the determination of policy is understood, and particularly how completely overlooked is the fundamental fact that by our political actions we unintentionally produce the acceptance of principles which will make further action necessary."

Second, *The Constitution of Liberty* must be understood as a work that articulates the abstract principles of the Rule of Law. By doing so, it seeks to put them in their historical context in order to provide an ideal picture of a liberal society under a correctly understood Rule of Law, and then use that as a benchmark to judge various concrete policy questions of his era and sentiments of the intellectuals of his era. I would argue that Hayek's purpose in the second half of the book was to see how far a Rule of Law approach could be stretched to accommodate the sentiments of the intellectuals of his day, and yet, maintain the generality and abstract nature of the law. The "hot socialism" of comprehensive central planning, and even the more "modest" model of market socialism that were discussed in *The Road to Serfdom* were now replaced with the "cold socialism" of the social democratic welfare state and the general sentiments of the intelligentsia that was concerned with the abuse of monopoly power, the injustice of unequal bargaining power for labor, the external economies associated with urban dwelling, the necessity of social security and the care of the elderly, the challenges of the decline in agriculture and depletion of natural resources, the structure and nature of education in a free society, and the quest to find the fiscal and monetary policies most consistent with the Rule of Law. The various "concessions" Hayek makes in this book to the welfare state were all deemed to be policies that were consistent with the Rule of Law. Those measures he rejects are based precisely on their violation of the generality norm consistent with the Rule of Law. To allow such measures would entail, he argues, the privileging of some at the expense of others. In the process, he rules out of court a host of policies that the sentiments of that age thought of as enlightened public policy.

One of the most important lessons modern readers can learn from studying Hayek, I would contend, is to learn from the adjustments he continually made to his arguments due to frustrations with earlier efforts. This is most evident in his examination of crafting monetary policy. In the earlier discussions of cyclical fluctuations, I argued that Hayek's theory was made up of constituent theoretical parts—non-neutrality of money, the interest rate as the price that coordinates intertemporal investment decisions, and the capital structure that consists of heterogeneous capital goods that possess multiple specific uses. In the background of this theory is the Misesian theory of rational economic calculation and price theory, and in the foreground is the institutional configuration of a central bank and loanable funds market. Put all these pieces together, the Austrian theory of business cycle follows from the manipulation of money and credit by the central bank.

If the goal of monetary policy, with this narrative in mind, is to minimize monetary induced cyclical fluctuations, then monetary policy must be structured to be as neutral as possible.[7] So, if you study Hayek's monetary theory and policy writings from the 1920s to the 1970s, one can see an endless quest, as well as frustration, with his effort to find the institutional configuration that will simultaneously withstand political manipulation, and be robust against sincere errors by policymakers, and yet, also provide a working monetary system for an modern advanced economy. His frustration with his previous efforts ultimately leads him to argue for the denationalization of money, and a system of free banking. Similar frustrations on this issue of finding the institutional configuration and the monetary policy rules that will ensure a well-functioning modern economy can be found in the works of Milton Friedman and James Buchanan, as discussed in Boettke and Smith (2016).

The questions of the Rule of Law and Democracy are evident in *The Road to Serfdom*, and he argues, as we have seen, that socialist planning is incompatible with both. One of the communication difficulties that Hayek has had through the years is the shifting meaning of democracy in the eyes of the intelligentsia. In an earlier age, democracy had a meaning that was beyond one person-one vote and majority rule. It referred more

---

[7] First, without leading us into a long digression in modern macroeconomics, the Hayekian theory of a *monetary* induced business cycle does not preclude non-monetary factors causing other cyclical fluctuations—often extremely volatile. Non-monetary policy-induced fluctuations are studied in real business cycle theories and empirical research. The key Hayekian push back would only be whether the explanations offered are economic theories or not would rely on their being choice and price theoretic stories, rather than just aggregate demand and supply stories unmoored from human choice and the adjustment of relative prices in the market system. Second, it is important to see the apparent contradiction of insisting that theoretically money by its nature is non-neutral, and that the goal of monetary *policy* to pursue a goal of neutral money is only an apparent and not a real contradiction. Hayek's argument for a neutral monetary policy is basically the same argument as he makes for generality in the Rule of Law. The question is can he find the institutional configuration that will provide the mechanisms to produce a policy of neutral money.

broadly to a way of living with one another and our status as individuals who shared a basic human equality. We are to view ourselves as one another's equals before the law. The one person-one vote, majority rule basis of democracy follows from this broader idea of liberalism, and refers to the machinery by which we collectively decide and peacefully transition power. As Hayek's writings in political theory evolve, he emphasizes the distinction between liberalism and democracy. "Liberalism," he states in *The Constitution of Liberty* (1960, 103), "is a doctrine about what the law ought to be, democracy a doctrine about the manner of determining what will be the law." As he puts it later in that chapter:

> The liberal believes that the limits which he wants democracy to impose upon itself are also that limits within which it can work effectively and within which the majority can truly direct and control the actions of government. So long as democracy constraints the individual only by general rules of its own making, it controls the power of coercion. If it attempts to direct them more specifically, it will soon find itself merely indicating the ends to be achieved while leaving to its expert servants the decision as to the manner in which they are to be achieved. And once it is generally accepted that majority decisions can merely indicate ends and the pursuit of them is to be left to the discretion of administrators, it will soon be believed also that almost any means to achieve those ends are legitimate. (1960, 115–116)

This is how, through a subtle shift in public ideology, the machinery of freedom is transformed step-by-step into a tool of tyranny. Calling this a slippery slope argument is not quite correct. Calling it a warning about the possible abuse of minorities by the majority in an unchecked democracy, and the necessity of adopting the necessary rules to check the administrative state would be more appropriate. Hayek's argument is one where there are decision nodes at each step along the way, and thus subject to revision of the path. But there is a situational logic in play, and without a course reversal, the path laid out is one that results in outcomes that would be counter to the core principles of liberalism and the high ideals that inspired democratic political change. If, in *The Road to Serfdom*, the culprit was the socialist idea of planning, in *The Constitution of Liberty*, the culprit is the administrative state that has been empowered to pursue the goals of the social democratic welfare state.[8]

In *The Constitution of Liberty*, Hayek seeks to find the institutional configuration that would provide the machinery of freedom in the constitutional constraints that were historically associated with the evolution of the common law in Britain and the constitutional founding period of the USA. In his chapter "Economic Policy and the Rule of Law," Hayek begins simply by telling his readers: "The classical argument for freedom in economic affairs rest on the tacit postulate that the rule of law should govern policy in this as in all other spheres." He continues, "We cannot understand the nature of the opposition of men like Adam Smith or John Stuart Mill to government 'intervention' unless we see it against this background" (1960, 220).[9]

The classical political economists did not believe that government had no role whatsoever in the economic system. There was, in fact, a positive program for laissez-faire in their system, and that included not only the enforcement of the common law of property, contract, and tort, but also alterations to these rules or the introduction of new rules so long as they were consistent with the idea of the rule of law—abstract and general rules that apply equally to all, meant to last for an indefinite period. The resistance to government intervention was restricted to those laws and

---

[8] Though Hayek does not stress this, I would say that his argument would apply with equal force to the warfare state as well, though that is perhaps more connected to the American experience than cross-nationally, precisely because post-WWII, the USA took such a lead in global military affairs. On the growth of government as a result of the dynamics in the welfare-warfare state, see Robert Higgs (1987, 2006) and Chris Coyne (2008, 2013) and Coyne and Hall (2018). The problem of the permanent war economy and the military industrial complex is one that true liberals have yet to address with the intellectual force required.

[9] One of the biggest misconceptions in the interpretation of Hayek's writings has been, I believe, with regard to his essay on "The Intellectuals and Socialism" and this idea of the "tacit presuppositions" of political economy. The reason socialists were successful is because they changed these tacit presuppositions, and then, all his other arguments about second-hand dealers in ideas go through. It is not a call to supply the intellectual division of labor with liberal-minded individuals, but a call for philosophers to change the tacit presuppositions once more, and with that, the intellectual division of labor will follow. Liberalism in Hayek's mind, I would argue, does not suffer from either a marketing problem or a network problem. Rather, it suffers from an ideas problem that must be addressed head-on with serious critical reflection and the best and the brightest minds in the particular society attracted to working out the arguments.

acts of government that were intended to address a concrete problem faced by a specific group and for a specific time.

Institutional problems demand institutional solutions. In other words, economic reform is based on a change in the structural rules of the game under which commercial life takes place. These changes are introduced in an effort to provide individuals with a framework more conducive for them to realize productive specialization and peaceful social cooperation. For that to be the case, they must be general and abstract and equally applicable to all. "The case for a free system," Hayek (1960, 228–229) argues, "is not that any system will work satisfactorily where coercion is confined by general rules, but that under it such rules can be given a form that will enable it to work." For the market process to work, the institutional framework must prevent violence and fraud, protect property and the enforcement of contract, and to recognize the freedom of trade and at the freely negotiated prices. But even when such a framework is in place, the "efficiency" of the market system will vary, depending on the particular content of the rules in place.

Hayek invites the contemporary political economist to study the legal order in depth. "The relation between the character of the legal order and the functioning of the market system has received comparatively little study, and most work in the field has been done by men who were critical of the competitive order rather than by its supporters." This needs to change, and it must become recognized by all economists that "[h]ow well the market will function depends on the character of the particular rules" (1960, 229).

Finally, Hayek's effort in *Law, Legislation and Liberty* is threefold. First, Volume 1 of *Law, Legislation and Liberty* (1973) is devoted to restating the basic principles of a liberal theory of justice and political economy, and in clarifying the challenge. The major problem that we face today is the same that liberals have always faced in practical affairs. In the debate over concrete policy action, the expediency of the moment will almost always win out over the principle. As Hayek (1973, 56–57) argues, "[s]ince the value of freedom rests on the opportunities it provides for unforeseen and unpredictable actions, we will rarely know what we lose through a particular restriction on freedom. Any such restriction, any coercion other than the enforcement of general rules, will aim at the achievement of some foreseeable particular result, but what is prevented by it will usually not be known." And the punchline is that the "direct effects of any interferences with the market order will be near and clearly visible in most cases, while the more indirect and remote effects will mostly be unknown and will therefore be disregarded." As a consequence, if "the choice between freedom and coercion is treated as a matter of expediency, freedom is bound to be sacrificed in almost every instance." Freedom, Hayek concludes, can only be preserved if it is treated as a supreme principle that must never be sacrificed.

Second, Volume 2 of *Law, Legislation and Liberty* (1976) reiterates his argument for abstract rules that serve the general welfare rather than particular purposes. But the failure to understand—let alone appreciate—the spontaneous ordering of commercial society has resulted in a general confusion in the intellectual and governing class in the quest for justice. Rather than the rules of just conduct, we get demands for distributive justice. As Hayek pointed out, "The rules of just conduct thus merely serve to prevent conflict and to facilitate co-operation by eliminating some sources of uncertainty. But since they aim at enabling each individual to act according to his own plans and decisions, they cannot wholly eliminate uncertainty. They can create certainty only to the extent that they protect means against the interference by others, and thus enable individuals to treat those means as being at his disposal. But they cannot assure him success in the use of these means, neither in so far as it depends only on material facts, nor in so far as it depends on the actions of others which he expects. They can, for instance, not assure him that he will be able at the expected price to sell what he has to offer or to buy what he wants" (1976, 38).

In moving from a system characterized by rules of just conduct to a system more defined by the quest for social justice, it is often forgotten that the ideal of equality before the law must be sacrificed. There is a great difference in a system where the government treats "all citizens according to the same rules in all the activities it undertakes" and "government doing what is required in order to place the different citizens in equal (or less unequal) material positions" (1976, 82). Treating individuals with a diversity of attributes as one another's equal in the eyes of the law and the polity is not at all consistent with the goal of equality of material outcomes. "Indeed," Hayek argues, "to assure the same material position to people who differ greatly in strength, intelligence, skill, knowledge and perseverance as well as in their physical and social environment, government would clearly have to treat them very differently to compensate for those disadvantages and deficiencies it could not directly alter." The quest for social justice, just like planning, ultimately undermines the rule of law and liberal democracy. The extended order of the "Great Society," Hayek contends, is based on the rules of just conduct embedded in the institutional infrastructure. The quest for social justice through redistribution is "irreconcilable with the rule of law, and with that freedom under the law which the rule of law intended to secure. The rules of distributive justice cannot be rules for the conduct toward equals, but must be rules for the conduct of superiors toward their subordinates" (1976, 86).

Third, Volume 3 of *Law, Legislation and Liberty* is dedicated to exploring these institutional solutions to the institutional problems identified in the first two volumes. There is a lot more going on in all three of these volumes than I have discussed, just as there is a lot more going on in *The Road to Serfdom* and *The Constitution of Liberty*. But remember my purpose—to explore the evolutionary potential of Hayekian ideas by way of examining Hayek's own evolution in his three main contributions to political economy and social philosophy. Hayek's proposed constitutional reforms in *Law, Legislation and Liberty* are, for my purposes, less interesting than his general theoretical point to build contestation into the public sector analogous to competition between individuals and firms in the market economy. Hayek emphasizes that his "stress on coercion being a monopoly of government by no means necessarily implies that this power of coercion should be concentrated in a single central government. On the contrary, the delegation of all powers that can be exercised locally to agencies whose powers are confined to the locality is probably the best way of security that the burdens of and the benefits from government action will be approximately proportioned" (1979, 45–46). In essence, competitive federalism would be the best structure to generate "fiscal equivalence" and the principle of subsidiarity so that the significance of the externality to be dealt with in the public sector was matched to the governmental decision unit entrusted with power. We do not need the federal government in charge of garbage collection, but it might be difficult to imagine the city council being placed in charge of national defense.

Still, Hayek's argument focuses on the need for contestation to keep monopoly power in check, even in the realm of public sector activity. Competition, to Hayek, is the key to the effective delivery of goods and services, even if it does not always, at each point of time, guarantee the most efficient utilization of resources. Competition is a discovery procedure, it is a *learning* mechanism by which individuals come to cooperate and coordinate with one another while exercising their liberty, pursuing productive specialization, and realizing peaceful social cooperation.

> That the 'public sector' should not be conceived of as a range of purposes for the pursuit of which government has a monopoly, but rather as a range of needs that government is asked to meet so long and in so far as they cannot be met better in other ways, is particularly important to remember. (Hayek 1979, 49)

One must keep in mind that government finance and provision of the collective good need not always be the only, let alone, the best alternative. In dethroning politics, Hayek hopes to give his readers a vision of the liberal order that can achieve peace, freedom, and justice. It is a quest for "decent government", which has been rendered impossible once "politics becomes a tug-of-war for shares in the income pie" (1979, 150).

Conclusion

The very first paragraph of *The Constitution of Liberty* explains the journey we have just described. Hayek states clearly: "If old truths are to retain their hold on men's mind, they must be restated in the language and concepts of successive generations. What at one time are their most effective expressions gradually become so worn with use that they cease to carry a definitive meaning. The underlying ideas may be as valid as ever, but the words, even when they refer to problems that are still with us, no longer convey the same conviction; the arguments do not move in a context familiar to us; and they rarely give us direct answers to the questions we are asking" (1960, 1).

There is much to learn from Hayek's effort to provide a new statement of the liberal principles of justice and political economy. His different efforts maybe have the same fate as he judged those from Montesquieu on down—noble, but inspiring, failures in the effort to ensure liberty by constitutional craftsmanship. The key thing I hope contemporary readers take away from this is the inspiring nature of the principles, and the creativity and energy to think through the institutional solutions to the institutional problems in a way that is consistent with the rules of just conduct and the requirements for the achievement of liberty, prosperity, and peace.

Bibliography

Boettke, Peter J. 2012. *Living Economics: Yesterday, Today, and Tomorrow.* Oakland: Independent Institute.

———. 2015. A Humane Nobel Economist Angus Deaton Shows Us How to Be Healthy, Wealthy and Wise. *Politico.eu*, October 13, 2015. Retrieved: https://www.politico.eu/article/a-humane-nobel-economist-angus-deaton

Boettke, Peter J., and Peter T. Leeson. 2015. *The Economic Role of the State.* Northampton/Cheltenham: Edward Elgar.

Boettke, Peter J., and Rosolino A. Candela. 2017. Price Theory as Prophylactic Against Popular Fallacies. *Journal of Institutional Economics* 13 (3): 725–752.

Boettke, Peter J., and Daniel J. Smith. 2016. Evolving Views on Monetary Policy in the Thought of Hayek, Friedman, and Buchanan. *Review of Austrian Economics* 29 (4): 351–370.

Boettke, Peter J., Stefanie Haeffele, and Virgil H. Storr, eds. 2016. *Mainline Economics: Six Nobel Lectures in the Tradition of Adam Smith.* Arlington: The Mercatus Center.

Coase, Ronald H. [1992] 2016. The Institutional Structure of Production. In *Mainline Economics: Six Nobel Lectures in the Tradition of Adam Smith*, ed. Peter J. Boettke, Stefanie Haeffele-Balch, and Virgil Henry Storr. Arlington: Mercatus Center.

Coyne, Christopher J. 2008. *After War: The Political Economy of Exporting Democracy.* Palo Alto: Stanford University Press.

———. 2013. *Doing Bad by Doing Good: Why Humanitarian Action Fails.* Palo Alto: Stanford University Press.

Coyne, Christopher J., and Abigail R. Hall. 2018. *Tyranny Comes Home: The Domestic Fate of US Militarism*. Palo Alto: Stanford University Press.

Deaton, Angus. 2015. *The Great Escape: Health, Wealth, and the Origins of Inequality*. Princeton: Princeton University Press.

Friedman, Milton. 1947. Lerner on the Economics of Control. *Journal of Political Economy* 55 (5): 405–416.

———. [1962] 2002. *Capitalism and Freedom*. Chicago: University of Chicago Press.

Friedman, Milton, and Rose Friedman. 1980. *Free to Choose: A Personal Statement*. New York: Harcourt.

Hayek, F.A. 1944. *The Road to Serfdom*. Chicago: University of Chicago Press.

———. 1949. The Intellectuals and Socialism. *The University of Chicago Law Review* 16 (3): 417–433.

———. 1960. *The Constitution of Liberty*. Chicago: University of Chicago Press.

———. 1973. *Law, Legislation, and Liberty, Vol. 1: Rules and Order*. Chicago: University of Chicago Press.

———. 1976. *Law, Legislation, and Liberty, Vol. 2: The Mirage of Social Justice*. Chicago: University of Chicago Press.

———. 1979. *Law, Legislation, and Liberty, Vol. 3: The Political Order of a Free People*. Chicago: University of Chicago Press.

Hayek, F. A. (interviewee). [1978] 1983. *Nobel Prize-Winning Economist Oral History Transcript*. Los Angeles: Oral History Program, University of California, Los Angeles.

———. [1974] 2016. The Pretense of Knowledge, in *Mainline Economics: Six Nobel Lectures in the Tradition of Adam Smith*, ed. Peter J. Boettke, Stefanie Haeffele-Balch, and Virgil Henry Storr. Arlington: Mercatus Center.

Higgs, Robert. 1987. *Crisis and Leviathan*. New York: Oxford University Press.

———. 2006. *Depression, War and Cold War Studies in Political Economy*. Oakland: Independent Institute.

Keynes, John Maynard. 1980. *Activities 1940–1946: Shaping the Post-War World: Employment and Commodities, The Collected Writings of John Maynard Keynes Vol. 27*, ed. Elizabeth Johnson and Donald Moggridge. Cambridge: Cambridge University Press.

Koppl, Roger. 2017. *Expert Failure*. New York: Cambridge University Press.

Levy, David M., and Sandra J. Peart. 2017. *Escape from Democracy: The Role of Experts and the Public in Economic Policy*. New York: Cambridge University Press.

Lincoln, Abraham. 1953. *The Collected Works of Abraham Lincoln, Vol. 2*, ed. Roy P. Basler. New Brunswick: Rutgers University Press.

Lippmann, Walter. [1937] 2005. *The Good Society.* New Brunswick: Transaction Publishers.

Lomasky, Loren E., and Fernando R. Tesón. 2015. *Justice at a Distance: Extending Freedom Globally.* New York: Cambridge University Press.

Marshall, Alfred. [1890] 1920. *Principles of Economics,* 8th edn. London: Macmillan.

Mitchell, Matthew D., and Peter J. Boettke. 2017. *Applied Mainline Economics: Bridging the Gap Between Theory and Public Policy.* Arlington: The Mercatus Center.

Ostrom, Vincent. [1973] 1989. *The Intellectual Crisis of American Public Administration.* Tuscaloosa: University of Alabama Press.

Ostrom, Elinor. 1990. *Governing the Commons: The Evolution of Institutions for Collective Action.* New York: Cambridge University Press.

Robbins, Lionel. [1952] 1965. *The Theory of Economic Policy in English Classical Political Economy.* London: Macmillan.

Smith, Adam. [1776] 1981. *An Inquiry into the Nature and Causes of the Wealth of Nations,* ed. R. H. Campbell and A. S. Skinner. Indianapolis: Liberty Fund.

9

Hayek, Epistemics, Institutions, and Change

Introduction

Traditional economics examines the choices that individuals make in light of the constraints and costs and benefits that they face. In light of this choice within constraints, economists rightfully tend to talk in terms of *incentives*.

It is important to stress that incentives are not the same as the more psychological concept *motivation*. The conflation of incentives with motivation has been one of the critical blocks to wide-scale understanding of the economic way of thinking. To put it bluntly, self-interest is not the same as selfishness. Individuals can have a wide variety of motivations, but they still are making choices within constraints. Even the most humble and saintly among us must weigh the marginal costs and the marginal benefits they face in making decisions on how to pursue their goals of serving others. They must learn through doing what path is most efficacious and avoid those wrong turns that lead to frustration and failure.

Our point is a rather simple one: in order to learn how to best cope with the constraints we face, we must not only have the incentives to make the right decisions and to learn from our past mistakes, but we also

© The Author(s) 2018
Peter J. Boettke, *F. A. Hayek*, Great Thinkers in Economics,
https://doi.org/10.1057/978-1-137-41160-0_9

must have access to correct the relevant *information* that is specific to the context in which we evaluate our past decisions and make decisions. Incentives and information are by-products of the *institutions* within which individuals make choices, learn from the past, enter and exit relationships with one another, and interact with nature as well as each other. Analysis that seeks to make progress in understanding the social world has to account for the institutional environment within which they are acting in order to understand the incentives they face and the information they are processing. Political economy at its finest is a discipline that examines alternative institutional arrangements and whether they are conducive to, or a hindrance to, the realization of productive specialization and peaceful cooperation among diverse individuals. Institutions determine the wealth and poverty of nations, and incentives and information engendered by those institutions are the first-level mechanisms that explain the connection between those institutional arrangements and the realization of poverty or wealth, and of tyranny or freedom.

The quest to lay bare the foundations of human sociability was not a unique research program to twentieth-century economists, but something that has its roots deep in the Scottish Enlightenment moral philosophers and classical political economy. Hayek's argument is that the alternative perspective on society was what could be termed "the design" or "rationalistic" approach. It is this rationalistic approach that sees all human institutions as a product of design that resulted in the late nineteenth- and twentieth-century arguments for socialism and collectivism. In contrast, the classical political economy tradition from Adam Smith to Lord Acton recognizes that the institutions upon which advanced civilization was based were "the result of human action, but not of human design." Men in this depiction of human progress are not highly rational and able to mold nature to their desire, but are instead highly fallible creatures "whose individual errors are corrected only in the course of a social process, and which aims at making the best of a very imperfect material" (Hayek 1948, 8–9). Hayek best describes this vision of political economy that follows from the Scottish Enlightenment tradition:

> [T]he main point about which there can be little doubt is that Smith's chief concern was not so much with what man might occasionally achieve when he was at his best but that he should have as little opportunity as possible

to do harm when he was at his worst. It would scarcely be too much to claim that the main merits of the individualism which he and his contemporaries advocated is that it is a system under which bad men can do least harm. It is a social system which does not depend for its functioning on our finding good men for running it, or on all men becoming better than they now are, but which makes use of men in all their given variety and complexity, sometimes good and sometimes bad, sometimes intelligent and more often stupid. Their aim was a system under which it should be possible to grant freedom to all, instead of restricting it, as their French contemporaries wished, to 'the good and the wise' (Hayek 1948, 11–12).

In many ways, Hayek's epistemic turn was an attempt to restate and rearticulate these lessons from the Scottish Enlightenment for the twentieth century. In doing so, Hayek would expose and critique the hubris that had taken hold with regard to the economist's perceived capacity not only to centrally plan an economy under socialism, but also to rationally design the institutions that would be required to engage in macroeconomic aggregate demand management in developed "market" economies and development planning in underdeveloped countries.

Hayek's Intellectual Journey

Though he began his career as a technical economist, Hayek was led to address philosophical and ultimately political and legal institutional questions because of his twin debates in the 1930s with the market socialists and the Keynesians. According to Hayek, in both cases, the underlying institutions that enable fallible, but capable, human actors to coordinate their affairs with one another and realize productive specialization and peaceful cooperation had been brushed aside in the analysis. Modern economic theory had proceeded by assuming and taking for granted an idealized institutional order, including an idealized democratic politics that would seamlessly discover and map the collective good into political decisions. The economic model that modern economists had in their head was a radically different one than what had shaped the thinking of the classical political economists. While in many ways this just reflected the scientific progress of a discipline, in certain subtle but critical ways the shift in the way of thinking resulted not in progress, but in a retrogression in thinking.

In the early 1930s, Hayek thought all his fellow neoclassical economists shared his appreciation for institutions, and the incentives and information they constantly provide for economic actors. Consider the following quote from Adam Smith's *The Wealth of Nations* ([1776] 1981, IV.2.10):

> What is the species of domestic industry which his capital can employ, and of which the produce is likely to be of the greatest value, every individual, it is evident, can, in his local situation, judge much better than any statesman or lawgiver can do for him. The statesman who should attempt to direct private people in what manner they ought to employ their capitals would not only load himself with a most unnecessary attention, but assume an authority which could safely be trusted, not only to no single person, but to no council or senate whatever, and which would nowhere be so dangerous as in the hands of a man who had folly and presumption enough to fancy himself fit to exercise it.

But as neoclassical economics evolved from its original period, emphasizing the subjective nature of valuation and choice on the margin, into a formal analysis of the optimality conditions under an equilibrium state of affairs, the emphasis on institutions, incentives and information tended to disappear. During the debates in the 1930s, the formal model of neoclassical microeconomics and Keynesian macroeconomics took on new intellectual life in the effort to combat the inefficiencies and injustice of monopoly power, exploitation of the working class, underconsumption, and the inherent instability of capitalism (Boettke 2012, part III; White 2012). The very neoclassical price theory that Hayek believed had strengthened the classical political economists' agenda for understanding the political and economic order was now utilized as a tool to critically tear asunder the *laissez-faire* presumption that was in the classics from Smith to Mill. Moreover, Hayek's own celebrated insights about the role of information (Hayek 1945) have been widely, but mistakenly, assumed to have been fully incorporated into the neoclassical apparatus (Boettke and O'Donnell 2013).

A new approach to economic policy was becoming dominant. This new approach, labeled by Buchanan ([1982] 2001) as "romantic constructivism," was based on ambitious top-down design and confidence in its ability to obtain the desired outcomes. In the eyes of Hayek (1960, 1973) or Buchanan ([1989] 2001), such an attempt underestimated the complexity of human society and was overly optimistic about the capacity of human reason to avoid unintended consequences. Nonetheless, it found its way into the neoclassical paradigm, and Hayek was caught by surprise in his debates with the market socialists and Keynesians. It is our contention that this intellectual reality set Hayek on the scholarly and scientific path that would define his career from the 1930s to the very end. In our narrative, Hayek did not cease to do economics at any time over the subsequent decades; he was instead seeking to recapture the institutional insights that were the great discovery of the Scottish Enlightenment moral philosophers, which formed the basis of classical political economy. As he put it, the great insight of the classical political economists was to "find a set of institutions by which man could be induced" to "contribute as much as possible to the need of all others" and the set of institutions they identified was "the system of private property" (1948, 13). Hayek's ambitious goal by the end of the 1930s was to synthesize the technical contributions of neoclassical economists with the broader institutional insights of the political economists.

His task proved to be more difficult than he first imagined because the opposite position had already become so ingrained in the professional as well as popular mindset. Only recently has he been followed by other noteworthy economists such as James Buchanan ([1964] 1999; [1989] 2001), Vernon Smith (2007), and Elinor Ostrom (1998). Hayek had to shift the discussion not only with respect to technical economics, but also with regard to what Schumpeter, in his *History of Economic Analysis* (1954), had termed "preanalytic cognitive" material. Hayek's challenge was thus on multiple margins of intellectual life. In our rendering, Hayek's strategy as a technical economist entailed countering both the close-ended model of choice, and the single-exit equilibrium modeling of the market. Rather than being lightening calculators of pleasure and pain, man, to Hayek, was a fallible creature caught between alluring hopes and haunting fears, whose capabilities—to the extent he revealed them—emerged in a social process defined by specific institutions.[1] We must *learn*, and what we learn—as well as our capacity *to* learn—is a function of the institutional environment within which we make decisions and interact with one another. The competitive market economy is one such learning environment, and Hayek ([1968] 2002) would eventually depict the private property market economy as a discovery procedure (see also O'Driscoll 1977). The market process, however, is not the only institutional configuration that must be rethought in terms of learning, but so must the political, legal, and moral infrastructure within which market activity takes place. For our purposes, we are going to limit the discussion to economics and politics. One of the critical reasons why we make this decision is because of the recent emergence of work in what has been called *epistemic democracy*.

Hayek and the Epistemic Turn in Economics

In evaluating the evolution of the argument for socialist economic planning, Mises ([1920] 1935, [1922] 1951, [1949] 1998) actually argues that it was a natural conclusion from the way that the classical political economists had set up the problem of social order and the appropriate role of government in the economic affairs of men. Rather than stress the conflict of interests, the eighteenth-century liberals invoked an almost godlike image of the state that was populated only by rulers that pursued the public interest. In this way, the private property system was justified by the claim that the logic of its operation would produce a result that would be identical to the result that would be desired by a benevolent godlike state.

---

[1] See Hayek's discussion of the wrong-headed interpretation of Adam Smith in relation to the concept of "economic man." As Hayek says, Smith's view was quite distant from this caricature of acting man, and instead viewed man by nature as "lazy and indolent, improvident and wasteful" and that only through the impact on institutional circumstances could "be made to behave economically or carefully to adjust his means to his ends." The intellectual fashion of deriding Smith for his "erroneous psychology" obviously irked Hayek, and thus he concluded this section by stating, "I may perhaps venture the opinion that for all practical purposes we can still learn more about the behavior of men from the *Wealth of Nations* than from most of the more pretentious modern treatises on 'social psychology'" (Hayek 1948, 11).

As Mises summed his point up in *Human Action* ([1949] 1998, 688), the inference that socialist planning was superior to the competitive market was

> logically inescapable as soon as people began to ascribe to the *state* not only moral but also intellectual perfection. The liberal philosophers had described their imaginary state as an unselfish entity, exclusively committed to the best possible improvement of its subjects' welfare. They had discovered that in the frame of a market society the citizens' selfishness must bring about the same results that this unselfish state would seek to realize; it was precisely this fact that justified the preservation of the market economy in their eyes. But things became different as soon as people began to ascribe to the *state* not only the best intentions but also omniscience. Then one could not help concluding that the infallible state was in a position to succeed in the conduct of production activities better than erring individuals. It would avoid all those errors that often frustrate the actions of entrepreneurs and capitalists. There would no longer be malinvestment or squandering of scarce factors of production; wealth would multiply. The "anarchy" of production appears wasteful when contrasted with the planning of the *omniscient* state. The socialist mode of production then appears to be the only reasonable system, and the market economy seems the incarnation of unreason.

As an argumentative strategy during the socialist calculation debate, Mises and Hayek would leave the benevolence assumption untouched, and focus their respective efforts on debunking the omniscience assumption. There are a few reasons for this:

Positive Economics Prior to Positivism

Mises, following Weber, was a strict adherent to the doctrine of value-freedom in economic analysis. Thus, the argumentative strategy was to treat ends as given and limit scientific analysis to an examination of the chosen means with respect to the achievement of given ends. In questions of strictly economic nature, Hayek followed Mises in this strict adherence to value-freedom in social scientific analysis. Benevolence on the part of the political elite was an argumentative construct, not an empirical assessment of the reality of government actors—which were as prone as any governments in history to corruption and violence.

Lange and Questions of Psychology

During his attempted rebuttal of Mises on socialist calculation, Oskar Lange made the interesting intellectual move to conflate questions of incentives with statements about motivation, and to then claim that motivations are questions of psychology and not economic theory. In response, an argument by Mises and Hayek about the incentives faced by socialist economic planners would have been an argumentative non-starter. Debate in science, just as in all forms of debate, is productive only if the parties can agree on the terms of the debate. Lange had ruled out questions of incentives, so the assumption of benevolence was critical not only for the maintenance of value-freedom, but for the debate to be engaged at all.

Knowledge Assumptions in Economic Models

The formal development of the model of perfectly competitive general equilibrium required critical assumptions about the state of knowledge in possession of economic actors. This set of assumptions did not address the acquisition and use of knowledge, nor did it cope with the full logical implications of the assumption of perfect knowledge.

It is this third issue that captured Hayek's intellectual imagination, though we would contend that the first two were critical in attracting Hayek's focus on knowledge. Hayek already is glimpsing the importance of what we discussed earlier as institutions and their impact on incentives and information in his work on the monetary theory of the trade cycle, and perhaps even earlier, in his first works on imputation theory. One must remember that Hayek was impacted greatly by Mises's 1920 article and subsequent 1922 book, *Socialism*. Furthermore, at roughly the same time, he was beginning work on the further development of the Wicksell-Mises theory of the business cycle in his original lectures at the LSE, later published as *Prices and Production* ([1931] 1935), which was based on the central claim that prices are guides to future production activities. It is the price system that enables the coordination of economic activities through time. Prices are not the sum of past costs, but the guide to future action. This is why Hayek would harp on the meaninglessness of concepts such as "price level" and insist that economists focus their analytical attention on relative prices.

Hayek's *epistemic* turn would take shape in the context of a more general theoretical argument about the nature of the market economy and its equilibrium properties. In "Economics and Knowledge" ([1937] 1948), Hayek argued that theorists had been misled by the assumption of perfect knowledge, and therefore sought to redirect theoretical attention to the acquisition of knowledge via competition as an active discovery process. To illustrate his point in a slightly different way, the optimality conditions of price equal marginal cost and production at the minimum of average costs of production were not assumptions of the model, but by-products of the competitive process. Optimality results from the filters of the price system—freely adjusting relative prices and accurate profit-and-loss accounting—working to guide the production plans of some to mesh with the consumption demands of others. Prices guide production, and calculation enables coordination. For neoclassical economists of the time, perfect knowledge came to be regarded as an assumption, which defined the characterization of a competitive equilibrium, but defined away the puzzle of plan coordination in a market economy. "Any approach," Hayek states, "such as that of much of mathematical economics with its simultaneous equations, which in effect starts from the assumption that people's *knowledge* corresponds with the objective *facts* of the situation, systematically leaves out what is our main task to explain" (emphasis in original, 1945, 530). The pre-reconciliation of plans does little to explain the process by which disparate, and often divergent, plans come to be reconciled with one another. Again, the *process* by which the knowledge necessary for this reconciliation of plans comes about is completely ignored in the standard analysis.

Second, Hayek argued that theorists were wrong to highlight behavioral assumptions rather than the institutional conditions that enable the price system to adapt and steer economic actors to coordinate their plans with those of others in a way that results in an equilibrium state of affairs. Markets, in Hayek's rendering ([1946] 1968, [1968] 2002), become learning mechanisms, and how effective they are at teaching is a function of the institutional environment within which they operate. To introduce perhaps a useful metaphor, think of a well-lit classroom with a white board, and black marker—a student (assuming the incentives are aligned for them to desire learning over not) will be able to easily read the information on that white board and add to their knowledge base. On the other hand, imagine that same student finds themselves in a dark classroom with no lights, with a white board and white marker. The information may in fact be written up on the white board, but the student cannot read it, and thus they cannot add to their knowledge base.

Hayek's basic insight is that context matters—both the context within which economic activity takes place, and the context of the decision-maker and their knowledge of unique time and place. The importance of context was lost with the assumption of perfect knowledge and the theoretical apparatus of the perfectly competitive model de-emphasized the learning by economic actors in response to changing circumstances. As Hayek would put it in "The Use of Knowledge in Society," the economic problem that society must address is not the allocation of "given" resources among competing ends. The "data" of the market is never "given" to a single mind or even collection of minds. Rather, the problem is "the utilization of knowledge which is not given to anyone in its totality" (1948, 78). Furthermore, the discovery and use of the relevant knowledge emerges only within the market process itself, as economic actors react and adapt to changing circumstances. "It is," Hayek wrote, "perhaps, worth stressing that economic problems arise always and only in consequence of change" (1948, 82).

The price system is constantly adapting to the ever-changing circumstances of economic reality. The least cost method of production that an enterprise can pursue must be discovered and implemented, just as what flow of goods and services will satisfy the demands of fellow citizens is revealed only in the pattern of exchange and production as it forms over time. The competitive market does not just marshal incentives to efficiently allocate existing resources, but provides a constant spur in the form of pure entrepreneurial profit to be alert to opportunities for mutual gain, and to discover lower cost methods to produce and distribute goods and services as well as discover new goods and services that may better satisfy the demands of consumers. The agitation of the market guided by relative prices, and lured by profit, and disciplined by loss shuffles and reshuffles resources so that the production plans of some mesh with the consumption demands of others. The incentive to discover new methods of cutting down costs *on the relevant margins* only exists in the competitive market environment. The same socialist calculation argument briefly described above also applies to the problem of allocating research and development resources. In the absence of market prices for factors of production, research and development cannot be guided by economic calculation, but only by either ad hoc ("planned chaos" to use Mises's term) or political reasons. The way in which the market system generates new knowledge is by incentivizing entrepreneurs to discover cost-cutting measures along the relevant margins, that is, the margins that give the biggest "bang for the buck" in terms of satisfying consumer demand. It is along those margins that the biggest profit increases can be made, hence the incentive. We thus see how, in this account, information and incentives are embedded in a unified account of entrepreneurial production. Indeed, one of the least well appreciated points of Hayek's (1945) account of the division of knowledge in society is that, absent the system of market prices, knowledge will not be generated at all because the profit incentive is not there. Hence, in a centrally planned system, or even when prices are distorted, we are not dealing just with a failure of aggregating existing knowledge, we are dealing with an *incentive failure* to generate the knowledge that would allow the most efficient cost-cutting developments.

What follows from this argument is that the knowledge communicated and acted upon in this process of adaptation is not the sort of knowledge that can be entered into statistics. The knowledge used in the market economy is knowledge of the "circumstances of time and place" that only individuals actively engaged in the buying (or abstaining from buying) and selling (or abstaining from selling) of goods and services on the market have. And, thus, we must reconceive of "the economic problem of society is mainly one of rapid adaptation to changes in the particular circumstances of time and place" (Hayek 1948, 83) and the price system as the solution to the problem by guiding production plans and coordinating those plans with consumption demands. It is the "higgling and bargaining" of the market economy, as Adam Smith taught, that brings about the coordination of economic activity through time.

Hayek came to focus on this issue of the acquisition of knowledge because the misunderstanding among economists about the limitations of the pure logic of choice and the nature of equilibrium had resulted in theoretical and practical confusion. As he would put it at the end of "The Use of Knowledge in Society," there must be something fundamentally wrong with an approach—no matter how strong its merits—when it leads to the disregard of the fundamental problem under investigation. We are, Hayek stressed, very imperfect creatures interacting with other imperfect creatures in a very imperfect world, and thus the central mystery of social cooperation under the division of labor is how certain institutional patterns will engender a pattern of human interaction where the necessary knowledge for plan coordination is constantly communicated and utilized by actors within the economic system. Hayek argues, "I am far from denying that in our system equilibrium analysis has a useful function to perform. But when it comes to the point where it misleads some of our leading thinkers into believing that the situation which it describes has direct relevance to the solution of practical problems, it is high time that we remember that it does not deal with the social process at all and that it is no more than a useful preliminary to the study of the main problem" (1948, 91).

Hayek's contention in this passage is that equilibrium properties of the competitive system should be in the background of an analysis of the competitive market process, rather than in the foreground. To counter the dominance of perfect knowledge assumption and equilibrium modeling, Hayek argued in "Economics and Knowledge" that "we must explain by what process they will acquire the necessary knowledge" (1948, 46). In this effort, the pure logic of choice is a necessary, but certainly not sufficient, component of the explanation of market coordination. The optimality conditions of competitive equilibrium must be understood as a by-product of the economic process under conditions of private property and freedom of contract; they should never be treated as the assumptions from which the analysis proceeds.

Hayek's "epistemic turn" in economics was precisely due to the tendency among his contemporaries to evade the critical questions of the institutional infrastructure, or what more recently has been dubbed the "ecology" within which human decisions and economic activity transpires (Smith 2007). The assumption of "quasi-omniscient" individuals does little to help us make progress even in understanding fundamental propositions in economics such as the law of one price. Economic science emerges, Hayek argued, from the tendency of the subjective plans of economic actors to dovetail over time with the objective facts of the economic situation. To clarify, we can refer to the "objective facts" of the situation as the existing state of tastes, technology, and resource availability. The market process guided by relative prices and the lure of profit and the penalty of loss will tend to produce a situation where the pattern of exchange and production corresponds with the external facts. Rather than solving this central mystery of economics through the assumptions of perfect knowledge and perfect markets, Hayek argued that we must explore (1) the institutional conditions under which the tendency exists, and (2) the process by which the knowledge that individuals are acquiring and utilizing changes to bring about this dovetailing of economic plans through time.

Public Choice and the Epistemic Turn

Public choice economics emerged in the 1960s as a counter to the then dominate market failure theory (Buchanan and Tullock 1962, chapter 5; Buchanan [1979] 1999, [1987] 2001; Ostrom and Ostrom 2004). The terms under which the socialist calculation debate was conducted by Mises-Hayek and Lange-Lerner had shifted considerably. Remember that in that earlier debate, Lange had ruled out questions of the incentive issues that would need to be addressed by socialist economic planners as matters of psychology and not pure economic theory. To counter Lange's solution, both Mises and Hayek respectively sought mainly to challenge the assumption of omniscience, while granting the assumption of benevolence. Nonetheless, Mises and Hayek were willing to grant, for the sake of argument, the assumption[2] that economic planners, bureaucratic agents, state-owned enterprise managers, and the workers in the farm and the factory were all rightly motivated to do the right thing to achieve the public interest. The question was how they would *know* what the right thing to do would be in order to realize the public interest in a complex economic order with shifting tastes, technology, and resource availability.

It is important to stress that both the market socialist model as well as the more modest market failure argument were committed to the economic system achieving the full utilization of resources to maximize economic well-being. The rationalization of production would lead to a burst of productivity, the efficient intervention into the market economy would align private marginal benefits/costs with social marginal benefits/costs, and macroeconomic demand management would eradicate instability and maintain full employment. The promise of scientific management of the economy by trained experts in economics was not a trivial matter. The claims made were strong—markets cannot be left to their own device, they are not self-regulating, and instead "fail" to produce optimal results due to monopoly, externalities, public goods, and macroeconomic instability. Left uncorrected, the capitalist order will be both inefficient and unjust. Power will favor the few, and the rest will be forced to fend for themselves amid the vagaries of economic circumstances. On the other hand, through the judicious use of government policy tools, the trained economic experts can fight monopoly power, align private costs/benefits with social costs/benefits, provide the necessary public goods, and managed aggregate demand to maintain full employment levels of output.

As we have seen, the strategy that Mises and Hayek pursued was to leave the benevolence assumption alone and focus on examining the consequences of relaxing the omniscience assumption. Public choice economics originally did seem to do the opposite—leave the omniscience assumption alone, but challenge the benevolence assumption. What incentive, public choice economists asked, do public officials face in

---

[2] This is of course a rather unrealistic assumption. The same factors that generate market failures also generate principal-agent problems in organizations (Miller 1992).

making and implementing public policy? By systemically examining the incentives within the political process, public choice economists were able to identify sources of systemic government failure associated with the vote motive, special interest politics, rent-seeking, and bureaucratic red tape (Shughart and Razzolini 2001; Tullock et al. 2002; Mueller 2003; Simmons 2011). Markets may indeed fail, but the proposed governmental remedy might exacerbate that failure, rather than provide the solution (Winston 2006).

In developing the theory of government failure, public choice economists relied upon the consistent and persistent application of neoclassical economics to examine the arena of politics. The result was a theory that tended to emphasize interests rather than ideas in understanding political outcomes (Rubin 2001). In short, public choice reproduced the same tensions in the analysis of politics that Hayek had identified in the neoclassical model of the market. Rational choice theory morphed into a close-end model of decision science, and the examination of politics as exchange morphed into a single-exit model of a structure-induced political equilibrium.

James Buchanan (1969, [1989] 2001, [1993] 2001) sought to resist this direction of public choice. His own development of the constitutional level of analysis was one such attempt to offer an alternative that accounted for human decision-makers engaged in bargaining activity, and transforming situations of conflict into opportunities for cooperation through constitutional craftsmanship. The team of Elinor and Vincent Ostrom (1971, 2004), however, argued that to truly grasp the importance of constitutional craftsmanship, one had to make intellectual moves similar to the ones that Hayek had suggested with respect to market theory, though they would not have stated it exactly as we just did. Nevertheless, a critical part of their work was the rejection of the assumption of omniscience, and the belief that there was a one-size-fits-all solution to social dysfunctions (Ostrom 1998, 2005, 2014). Their work stressed moving beyond the markets and states dichotomy, and instead, embracing what they dubbed polycentricity (Ostrom 1999, 2010; Ostrom and Ostrom 1971).

The epistemic turn in public choice is best understood in the context of constitutional political economy of which the Ostroms have been prominent practitioners. As Buchanan ([1989] 2011, 268) put it, the pattern of outcomes in an economic system "emerge from the whole set of interdependent choices made by individuals as these choices are constrained by the *structure* of the economy." One individual's choice *within* a given structure can exert only negligible effects upon the overall, aggregated, pattern of outcomes. As such, to the extent that "the pattern of results is subject to deliberative change," this can only happen "through effective changes in structure, i.e. in the set of rules that constrain the exercise of individual choices within the rules" (Buchanan [1989] 2011, 270). But once again, assuming, especially within a democratic context, that "the individual can exercise no influence on the structure of the economy as he chooses separately and independently among the options that he confronts," it follows that "any choice among alternative sets of rules must be, and can only be, collective." Once this is established, the questions about knowledge and incentives are now moved to the level of the collective. Under what institutional system does the collective most effectively use available information and learn from past mistakes? To put it differently, what incentives do individuals have, under alternative institutions, to search for new ideas about how to change the structure of the economy such that the aggregated pattern of outcomes is improved according to the opinion of as many members of the community?

In a political world populated by heterogeneous and diverse actors, the question is how to communicate knowledge so as to coordinate plans and successfully engage in collective action. The first critical step is acknowledging the heterogeneity of values. As Hayek (1960, 170) notes, "the current theory of democracy suffers from the fact that it is usually developed with some ideal homogeneous community in view and then applied to the very imperfect and often arbitrary units which the existing states constitute." Or, to quote Buchanan ([1989] 2011, 271):

> [T]he presumption that there is a unique, and agreed-on, objective, or objective function, for an economy ... reflects a carryover from idealism into political philosophy. ... [T]here is no agreed-on objective for the participants in an economic nexus, each one of whom seeks only to pursue his or her own privately defined aims (which may or may not reflect narrowly defined economic interest). Absent such agreement, there is simply no external standard by which alternative structures can be evaluated.

But how can one then avoid *both* the "presumed existence of an ideal standard" and "the nihilism implied by the absence of agreement" ([1989] 2011, 272)? Buchanan's answer, further elaborated by Vincent Ostrom (1997), is that we can avoid these two extremes only by applying to the issue of constitutional choice the same logic of mutually beneficial voluntary exchange. A structure of the economy populated by heterogeneous individuals is able to satisfy the values of as many of those individuals as possible, the closer the process of constitutional choice gets to the contractarian scenario of individuals agreeing under consensus to the system of rules. The alternative, in which the heterogeneity of values is denied, in the name of "some idealized standard (efficiency, justice, liberty)" (Buchanan 1989, 271), represents a more or less transparent attempt to offer a "legitimizing cover for the efforts of some persons and groups to impose their own purposes on others" ([1989] 2011, 275). In other words, the normative ideal of self-governance, the rejection of political dominance, and the emphasis on a process of contractarian constitutional choice follow from the extension of the standard economic assumption of the subjectivity of values to the realm of values used to evaluate the pattern of outcomes of an economy.

The incipient theory of "public entrepreneurship" can be seen as trying to map the individual level benefits that political actors may get as a result of changing the structure of rules in a direction of increased self-governance (Oakerson and Parks 1988; Klein et al. 2010). This is different from the more well-known theory of political entrepreneurship and rent-seeking, according to which political actors only cater to various special interests while harming less well-organized groups in society (Wagner 1966; Olson 1982).

One can further complicate the theory by acknowledging not only heterogeneity, but also the malleability of values and opinions (Katznelson and Weingast 2007). Preferences need not be assumed as given. Ideas come to serve as focal points, not just private interests, and as such, ideas guide actions. Words and deeds are ultimately shaped by ideas in the political realm. As Boettke and Coyne (2009) note, one can provide an entrepreneurial theory of social change by mapping the private benefits that "social entrepreneurs" can get as a result of becoming focal points and facilitating the emergence of a certain uniformity of values and beliefs. The presence of such entrepreneurs makes social coordination easier than one might believe just from a fixed preferences account. V. Ostrom's (1997) emphasis of the importance of "shared communities of understanding" for the emergence of productive social orders follows the same logic.

Vincent Ostrom (1993) summed this epistemic turn best when he challenged his fellow public choice theorists to move beyond envisioning the theory as little more than an appendage to neoclassical price theory. One needs to go beyond simple price theory because, as noted above, individual choices within rules do not affect the structure of the economy, and price theory only describes choices within the given rules. We need to think again in terms of Hayek's concept of competition which does not operate merely against a structure of objectively given costs, but it is instead a discovery procedure of methods for diminishing costs along relevant margins. In the context of our discussion, the costs are those due to existing conflicts over the "proper function" of the economic system. It is social and public entrepreneurs who discover focal points for coordination and changes in rules that eliminate conflicts that had previously seemed unavoidable (or create compensation schemes), hence diminishing the costs of conflicts. The relevant margins here are the reduction of those conflicts that provide the highest returns per dollar spent. Needless to say, we are still far from having a rigorous theory of either social or public entrepreneurship that would (1) explain how such allocations of effort are made, and (2) identify the institutional structure within which such entrepreneurship would operate most effectively.

In the same way that the Hayekian theory of competition as a discovery procedure melds together knowledge and incentive problems in an inseparable whole, so does an entrepreneurial theory of public choice. As argued by V. Ostrom (1993), if in the end, all public choice amounts to is an appendage to price theory ignoring the essential problem of knowledge discovery, then the future progress in public choice analysis is bound to be minuscule at best. But instead, if the future of public choice scholarship is to be found in the puzzling over social dilemmas and agonizing over anomalies, then progress will indeed be possible. It is only by taking the epistemic turn in politics, Ostrom argued, that public choice could be a progressive research program. The epistemic element of institutions in Hayek is best paralleled by Vincent Ostrom in the following statement:

Perhaps the most distinctive characteristics of human beings is their capability for learning. Learning involves the development of an image about the order of events and relationships that occur. Where constraint exists, a learning organism can take advantage of that constraint by inducing variety in its own behavior so as to improve its adaptive potential (1980, 310–311).

Ironically, though not necessarily recognized this way by the Ostroms, Hayek, who had taken an early version of the institutional turn in economics and politics, could also be seen as analyzing the epistemic properties of politics. In *The Road to Serfdom*, Hayek argues forcefully that there are limits to agreement within a democratic system. Heterogeneous and diverse actors may be able to agree on broad principles of the way we should engage each other as equal citizens, but they cannot come to agreement on very specific demands that would be required if socialist economic planning was to be pursued. Socialist planning, Hayek argued, was incompatible with the rule of law, and also with viable notions of liberal democracy.

Liberalism, on the other hand, created a framework that unleashed and utilized the creative power of a free civilization. All that diversity and heterogeneity goes to work in the complex division of knowledge in society. Liberalism creates scope for learning within its operation; in fact, it depends on such learning. But this characteristic of the liberal order also means that the liberal order itself is learning. So just as Hayek had argued with respect to the learning capacity of the market, his theory of the polity is one that emphasizes how individuals come to learn how to live better together than apart.

In the follow-up book, *The Constitution of Liberty*, Hayek wondered about milder forms of government interventions, falling short of full-blown collectivization. What kind of welfare state was *not* subject to the same danger of sliding toward "serfdom"? Hayek's conclusion was that one could have quite extensive interventions, as long as the rule of law was still kept in place. Such interventions would go far beyond what a classical liberal like himself would find preferable, but that was beside the point as he was less interested in promoting his own preference than he was in understanding the conditions under which civilization itself can persist even though, to use Buchanan's (2005) expression, many "are afraid to be free." What kind of political-economic organization should a group of people "afraid to be free" have such that they will continue to enjoy most—if not all—benefits created by the past era of quasi-laissez-faire? Hayek's answer is that they may introduce numerous forms of collective insurance, but they should nonetheless preserve a system in which the same rules apply to everyone. More recently, Buchanan and Congleton (1998) have reached a very similar conclusion. The crux of the argument is that when rule of law is preserved, the possibility of rent-seeking is limited. Hence, markets remain relatively free and Olson's (1982) "decline of nations" is prevented. The question now is what kind of political institutions favor this outcome?

The Epistemic Limits of Democracy

Hayek (1960, 171) noted that although "it is reasonable that [collective tasks] should be decided by the majority ... it is not obvious that the same majority must also be entitled to determine what it is competent to do." This position is currently a hotly debated one. The emphasis on how citizens learn, and how systems process the necessary information for that learning, is now a very deeply discussed aspect of democratic society (Wohlgemuth 2002).

Many recent works, such as Bryan Caplan's *The Myth of the Rational Voter* (2007), have challenged the collective intelligence of democracies, not really on epistemic grounds, but on incentive grounds. In Caplan's theory, when individuals find themselves in an environment where holding wrong beliefs will not be penalized severely, we can expect to see more wrong beliefs being held, sometimes with great passion and even confidence. This, Caplan argues, is the realm of democratic politics, and an environment where it is rational to be irrational about the opinions one holds and the beliefs one cherishes. The systematic biases that result in the political process will not be canceled out in such an environment, and dumb public policies will be adopted. Due to the incentives in the current arrangement of governmental institutions, modern democratic governments suffer from a "garbage in, garbage out" problem.

On the other hand, the political theorist Helene Landemore in her book *Democratic Reason* (2013) attempts to argue by way of the "miracle of aggregation" that the "wisdom of crowds" saves democracy from the sort of problems that Caplan and others have identified about the intelligence of the voters. There is a subtle issue here that we should stress, and that is that Caplan's argument does not necessarily turn on the intelligence of the voters, but on the incentives that they face. In the right institutional environment, Landemore is in fact wildly correct—the knowledge generated in the process will exceed the ability of any one mind or even subgroup of minds to know in any detail. The collectivity will in fact exhibit more intelligence and/or wisdom than any of the individuals within the system. But the critical condition to deriving that conclusion is the *right institutional environment.*

Landemore takes on the hard case of a democratic decision that goes against a cherished belief that she holds. However, upon reflection, she believes the result should give her pause about the correctness of her cherished opinion. Democratic citizenship requires such a willingness to learn from the wisdom of the crowd as much as, if not more than, the capability of contributing to the collective formation of that wisdom through active participation in the democratic process of collective action. But how general is this argument? Caplan deliberately chooses relatively uncontroversial issues for the economist, such as the belief that free trade is beneficial. How many economists are going to change their minds about this issue *because* the presumed "wisdom of the crowds" of the general population goes against it? We presume, very few. Which brings us back to the issue of the institutional environment. The reason why economists should not probably change their minds about such widely accepted issues is because the institutional framework of science is such that it generally leads to the discovery of truth (Polanyi 1962; Tullock 1966). *By comparison*, the institutional environment under which popular opinion forms is less conducive to the discovery of truth. In other words, our confidence in the opinion of professional economists over that of the general public is based on a comparative institutional analysis.

One can see Caplan and Landemore as two incomplete sides of the problem. Caplan analyzes incentives problems in knowledge formation about collective issues, while Landemore notes that under some conditions (of unclear realism), these incentive problems become more or less irrelevant. If one reads Hayek, one is bound to find this debate too static. After noting that "[d]emocracy is the only method of peaceful change that man has yet discovered" (1960, 172), and that "democracy is an important safeguard to individual liberty" because "it can scarcely be to the advantage of a majority that some individuals should have the power arbitrary to coerce others" (1960, 173), he continues by saying that "democracy is the only effective method of educating the majority" and "[d]emocracy is, above all, a process of forming opinion" (1960, 174):

> Its chief advantage lies not in its method of selecting those who govern but in the fact that, because a great part of the population takes an active part in the formation of opinion, a correspondingly wide range of persons is available to select. We may admit that democracy does not put power in the hands of the wisest and best informed and that at any given moment the decision of a government by an elite might be more beneficial to the whole; but this need not prevent us from still giving democracy the preference. It is in its dynamic, rather than in its static, aspects that the value of democracy proves itself.

Interestingly, this dense passage contains a critique of both Caplan and Landemore. On one hand, it accepts Caplan's static argument about the irrationality of the public at each moment in time. In fact, anticipating Caplan's technique of simulating the preferences of an "enlightened public," Hayek explicitly writes that majority decisions do not reflect "what it would be in their interest to want if they were better informed" (1960, 175). This, however, is less important for him than the fact that democracy provides a mechanism for (1) altering public opinion rather than simply responding to it, and (2) fermenting change by offering a certain degree of free entry into the political arena. Point (1) is less well studied than it should be. For example, when one looks back even a few decades ago, one finds not just that some remarkably bad policies were in place (such as extensive price controls), but also that they would be almost unthinkable today. How did the climate of opinion improve? Is Hayek correct that it is the democratic process itself that is responsible?

This being said, point (2) goes against Landemore's approach to defending democracy as Hayek, like Buchanan, rejects the idea that democracy is a truth-seeking enterprise: "there is a convention that the view of the majority should prevail so far as collective action is concerned, but this does not in the least mean that one should not make every effort to alter it" (1930, 175). Moreover, "[o]ne may have profound respect for that convention and yet very little for the wisdom of the majority" (1960, 175).

Instead of relying on the "wisdom of crowds," Hayek's defense of democracy hinges on the idea of peaceful contestation and competition. It dovetails, and actually significantly strengthens, Buchanan's (1954) critique of Arrow's impossibility theorem (Arrow 1951; see also Pettit 2012). For Hayek, majority opinion at any point in time can never be trusted to reflect truth; yet, the process of democratic contestation and competition over time tends to eliminate the most deleterious views as the public learns what to *avoid*. Similarly, Buchanan stressed that (a) one should never expect to be able to aggregate across individuals into a stable social welfare function (see also Riker 1982; Ostrom 1987), and (b) that cyclical majorities is not a problem for democracy, but actually one of its strong points because the existence of such cycling means that no one group is exercising dominion over long periods of time. Instead, we would experience "turn taking" at exerting control over the institutions of political power.

The Hayekian focus on process and the dynamic of collective learning brings to mind further developments, such as Friedman's "Long and Variable Lag" and the "Lucas Critique." Milton Friedman argued that in making public policy decisions to address social ills, government analysts must: (a) recognize the problem at T_0, (b) design a policy response, (c) get that policy response implemented at T_1, and (d) wait for that policy to have an impact on a complex economic system in T_2. This policymaking process takes place through time (T_0 to T_2 in our notation). And that is precisely the potential problem, because (d) may actually be sometime down the road from (a), and in the meantime, things may indeed have changed again such that (b) is no longer the right response to the situation, and in fact may result in new destabilizing results in the economy. Friedman used a variant of this argument to make his case for rules versus discretion in monetary policy; we are suggesting that it may have a much wider application to the world of public policy formation and implementation within a democratic polity. And thus, this simple question of *timing* may impact the epistemic quality of the policy process.

Friedman's long and variable lag problem in policy design and implementation is joined by considerations about credibility and strategic interaction. We cannot go into the credible commitment arguments here in any depth, but want to mention them as another wrinkle in the discovery, conveyance, and use of knowledge within the democratic system to determine the correct policy path.

Moreover, Hayek's focus of the dynamics of collective learning as an outcome of the market process must also take into account the role of expectations with regard to changes in policy, as Lucas (1976) highlighted. Lucas's critique was over the use of econometric models independent of changes in macroeconomic policy. If individuals are presumed to be rational, then individuals will adjust their expectations when governments change economic policies. Therefore, the econometric results under one policy regime will not be valid in predicting the expected outcomes of an alternative set of macroeconomic policies.

To conclude, Hayek's approach to the question of the limits of democratic decision making is quite different from either Caplan's or Landemore's (or of other contemporary proponents of "epistemic democracy"). Because, unlike Landemore, he has little trust in the "wisdom of the crowds," he is emphatic that democratic decision making should be constrained by rule of law requirements. On the other hand, while he actually agrees with Caplan that expanding the realm of markets and limiting the realm of issues decided collectively would be beneficial, he operates under a heterogeneity and subjectivity of values approach that forces him (like Buchanan) to take seriously the fact that many other people assign various non-classical-liberal functions to the economic-political system. As such, he cannot use economic efficiency itself as a universal benchmark for top-down evaluation. All he can do is think about institutional constraints such as the rule of law.

Moreover, while Caplan discusses the incentive problems faced by voters, he does not discuss the incentive problems faced by elites. As such, one may get the (mistaken) impression that Caplan's account is providing support for a move on the margin away from democracy and toward elite rule. Interestingly, as Hayek notes, while at any given moment in time, "the decision of a government by an elite" may be superior to that of majority rule, nonetheless such a system would be problematic over a longer course of time. This is because of two types of incentive problems. On the one hand, along standard public choice lines of analysis, it is hard to establish a ruling elite that has the incentive to care about the general welfare more than a democratically elected political class (Olson 1993). On the other hand, and this is the specifically Hayekian add-on, a ruling elite would also have less of an incentive to discover the proper information about how to improve various public issues (Wohlgemuth 2002).

All in all, the Hayekian perspective on both the defense and the limits of democracy is quite different from the existing literature on epistemic democracy. On the one hand, he offers a comparative institutional defense that does not overly commit itself to exaggerated claims about the efficiency of democracy. On the other hand, he provides an argument for rule of law as a constraint on unlimited democracy without making an ideological (classically liberal) argument. Part III in *Constitution of Liberty* is a unique piece of political theorizing in providing a genuine attempt at a meta-ethical political system, that is, a political framework designed to fit more than just one single political philosophy.

Conclusion

In taking the epistemic turn in economics and politics, Hayek was one of the first modern economic and political theorists to switch attention away from the behavioral assumptions that were employed in the analysis, and instead to reorient that analysis to the institutional conditions within which individuals interact with each other and with nature. Critical to the development of social theory is the recognition that some rules enable diverse groups of individuals to live better together than they would apart. They do so because the rules of the social game they adopt (whether through design or simply by stumbling upon them) are conducive to the realization of the gains from social cooperation under the division of labor. Absent that fundamental achievement of social cooperation, the group will instead be mired in conflict regarding resource use.

The political infrastructure helps to define the ecology of social space. Hayek stressed that it was the liberal order that was most conducive to human flourishing—in commerce, in science, in art, in all variety of human endeavors. The creative powers of a free civilization were unleashed by the ideas and institutional machinery of liberalism in its classic sense. Our argument has simply been that this identification of progress with institutions is conducive to the discovery, communication, and utilization of the unique knowledge of every individual in a society, and was made possible only with Hayek's epistemic turn in economics and politics.[3] And furthermore, that there are great opportunities for those influenced by Hayek's writings to continue pursuing this turn through critical engagement with the emerging literature on epistemic democracy. In short, the Hayekian revolution in the social and policy sciences is far from complete. Economists engaged in a largely failed effort to appropriate Hayek's ideas in formalistic models (see Boettke and O'Donnell 2013) and political scientists have failed to come to grips with the full implications of the epistemic limits that democratic systems must confront. Taken together, Hayek's vast expanse of work possesses great evolutionary potential for the continued pursuit of the epistemic turn in economics and politics.

Bibliography

Arrow, Kenneth J. 1951. *Social Choice and Individual Values.* New Haven/London: Yale University Press.
Boettke, Peter J. 2012. *Living Economics: Yesterday, Today, and Tomorrow.* Oakland: Independent Institute.
Boettke, Peter J., and Christopher J. Coyne. 2009. An Entrepreneurial Theory of Social and Cultural Change. In *Markets and Civil Society: The European*

---

[3] Consider Hayek's claim from his Nobel lecture, "The Pretense of Knowledge" ([1974] 2016) that "If man is not to do more harm than good in his efforts to improve the social order, he will have to learn that in this, as in all other fields where essential complexity of an organized kind prevails, he cannot acquire the full knowledge which would make mastery of the events possible. He will therefore have to use what knowledge he can achieve, not to shape the results as the craftsman shapes his handiwork, but rather to cultivate a growth by providing the appropriate environment, in the manner in which the gardener does this for his plants."

Experience in Comparative Perspective, ed. Victor Perez-Díaz, 77–103. New York: Berghahn Books.

Boettke, Peter J., and Kyle W. O'Donnell. 2013. The Failed Appropriation of FA Hayek by Formalist Economics. *Critical Review* 25 (3–4): 305–341.

Buchanan, James M. 1954. Social Choice, Democracy, and Free Markets. *Journal of Political Economy* 62 (2): 114–123.

———. [1964] 1999. What Should Economists Do?. In *The Logical Foundations of Constitutional Liberty*, 28–42, Indianapolis: Liberty Fund.

———. 1969. Is Economics the Science of Choice? In *Roads to Freedom: Essays in Honour of Friedrich A. von Hayek*, 47–64. New York: Routledge.

———. [1979] 1999. Politics Without Romance: A Sketch of Positive Public Choice Theory and Its Normative Implications. In *The Logical Foundations of Constitutional Liberty*, 45–59. Indianapolis: Liberty Fund.

———. [1982] 2001. Cultural Evolution and Institutional Reform. In Federalism, Liberty, and the Law, 311–323. Indianapolis: Liberty Fund.

———. [1987] 2001. Market Failure and Political Failure. In *Federalism, Liberty, and the Law*, 276–288. Indianapolis: Liberty Fund.

———. [1989] 2001. On the Structure of the Economy: A Re-emphasis of Some Classical Foundations. In *Federalism, Liberty, and the Law*, 263–275. Indianapolis: Liberty Fund.

———. [1993] 2001. The Individual as Participant in Political Exchange. In Federalism, Liberty, and the Law, 185–197. Indianapolis: Liberty Fund.

———. 2005. Afraid to Be Free: Dependency as Desideratum. *Public Choice* 124: 19–31.

Buchanan, James M., and Roger D. Congleton. 1998. *Politics by Principle, Not Interest: Towards Nondiscriminatory Democracy*. New York: Cambridge University Press.

Buchanan, James M., and Gordon Tullock. 1962. *The Calculus of Consent: Logical Foundations of Constitutional Democracy*. Ann Arbor: University of Michigan Press.

Caplan, Bryan. 2007. *The Myth of the Rational Voter: Why Democracies Choose Bad Policies*. Princeton/Oxford: Princeton University Press.

Hayek, F.A. [1931] 1935. *Prices and Production*. London: Routledge.

———. [1937] 1948. Economics and Knowledge. In *Individualism and Economic Order*. Chicago: University of Chicago Press, chapter 2.

———. 1945. The Use of Knowledge in Society. *The American Economic Review* 35 (4): 519–530.

———. [1946] 1948. The Meaning of Competition. In *Individualism and Economic Order*. Chicago: University of Chicago Press, chapter 5.

———. 1948. *Individualism and Economic Order*. Chicago: University of Chicago Press.

———. 1960. *The Constitution of Liberty*. Chicago: University of Chicago Press.

———. 1973. *Law, Legislation, and Liberty, Vol.1: Rules and Order*. Chicago: University of Chicago Press.

———. [1968] 2002. Competition as a Discovery Procedure, *The Quarterly Journal of Austrian Economics* 5(3): 9–23.

———. [1974] 2016. The Pretense of Knowledge. In *Mainline Economics: Six Nobel Lectures in the Tradition of Adam Smith*, ed. Peter J. Boettke, Stefanie Haeffele-Balch, and Virgil Henry Storr. Arlington: Mercatus Center.

Katznelson, Ira, and Barry R. Weingast, eds. 2007. *Preferences and Situations: Points of Intersection Between Historical and Rational Choice Institutionalism*. New York: Russell Sage Foundation Publications.

Klein, Peter G., Joseph T. Mahoney, Anita M. McGahan, and Christos N. Pitelis. 2010. Toward a Theory of Public Entrepreneurship. *European Management Review* 7 (1): 1–15.

Landemore, Hélène. 2013. *Democratic Reason: Politics, Collective Intelligence, and the Rule of the Many*. Princeton: Princeton University Press.

Lucas, Robert E., Jr. 1976. Econometric Policy Evaluation: A Critique. In *The Phillips Curve and Labor Markets*, ed. Karl Brunner and Alan Meltzer. Amsterdam: North-Holland, Carnegie-Rochester Series on Public Policy.

Miller, Gary J. 1992. *Managerial Dilemmas: The Political Economy of Hierarchy*. Cambridge: Cambridge University Press.

Mises, Ludwig von. [1920] 1935. Economic Calculation in the Socialist Commonwealth. In *Collectivist Economic Planning*, ed. F.A. Hayek and Trans. S. Alder, 87–130. London: Routledge.

———. [1922] 1951. *Socialism: An Economic and Sociological Analysis*. New Haven: Yale University Press.

———. [1949] 1998. *Human Action*. Auburn: The Ludwig von Mises Institute.

Mueller, Dennis C. 2003. *Public Choice III*. Cambridge: Cambridge University Press.

O'Driscoll, Gerald P. 1977. *Economics as a Coordination Problem: The Contributions of Friedrich A. Hayek*. Kansas: Sheed Andrews and McMeel. Retrieved Liberty Fund's Online Library of Liberty.

Oakerson, Ronald J., and Roger B. Parks. 1988. Citizen Voice and Public Entrepreneurship: The Organizational Dynamic of a Complex Metropolitan County. *Publius: The Journal of Federalism* 18 (4): 91–112.

Olson, Mancur. 1982. *The Rise and Decline of Nations: Economic Growth, Stagflation, and Social Rigidities*. New Haven: Yale University Press.

———. 1993. Dictatorship, Democracy, and Development. *American Political Science Review* 87 (3): 567–576.

Ostrom, Vincent. 1980. Artisanship and Artifact. *Public Administration Review* 40 (4): 309–317. https://doi.org/10.2307/3110256.

———. 1987. *The Political Theory of a Compound Republic*. Lincoln/London: University of Nebraska Press.

———. 1993. Epistemic Choice and Public Choice. *Public Choice* 77 (1): 163–176.

———. 1997. *The Meaning of Democracy and the Vulnerability of Democracies: A Response to Tocqueville's Challenge*. Ann Arbor: University of Michigan Press.

Ostrom, Elinor. 1998. A Behavioral Approach to the Rational Choice Theory of Collective Action. *American Political Science Review* 92 (1): 1–22.

Ostrom, Vincent. 1999. Polycentricity (Part 1 and 2). In *Polycentricity and Local Public Economies*, ed. Michael D. McGinnis, 52–74 and 119–138. Michigan: University of Michigan Press.

Ostrom, Elinor. 2005. *Understanding Institutional Diversity*. Princeton: Princeton University Press.

———. 2010. Beyond Markets and States: Polycentric Governance of Complex Economic Systems. *American Economic Review* 100 (3): 641–672.

———. 2014. Do Institutions for Collective Action Evolve? *Journal of Bioeconomics* 16 (1): 3–30.

Ostrom, Vincent, and Elinor Ostrom. 1971. Public Choice: A Different Approach to the Study of Public Administration. *Public Administration Review* 31 (2): 203–216.

Ostrom, Elinor, and Vincent Ostrom. 2004. The Quest for Meaning in Public Choice. *American Journal of Economics and Sociology* 63 (1): 105–147.

Pettit, Philip. 2012. *On the People's Terms: a Republican Theory and Model of Democracy*. Cambridge: Cambridge University Press.

Polanyi, Michael. 1962. The Republic of Science: Its Political and Economic Theory. *Minerva* 1 (1): 54–74.

Riker, William H. 1982. *Liberalism Against Populism: A Confrontation Between the Theory of Democracy and the Theory of Social Choice*. San Francisco: Freeman.

Rubin, Paul H. 2001. Ideology. In *The Elgar Companion to Public Choice*, ed. William F. Shughart and Laura Razzolini. Cheltenham/Northampton: Edward Elgar.

Schumpeter, Joseph. 1954. *History of Economic Analysis*. London: Routledge.

Shughart, William F., and Laura Razzolini. 2001. *The Elgar Companion to Public Choice*. Cheltenham/Northampton: Edward Elgar.

Simmons, Randy T. 2011. *Beyond Politics: The Roots of Government Failure*. Oakland: The Independent Institute.

Smith, Adam. [1776] 1981. *An Inquiry into the Nature and Causes of the Wealth of Nations*. Ed. R. H. Campbell and A. S. Skinner. Indianapolis: Liberty Fund.

Smith, Vernon L. 2007. *Rationality in Economics: Constructivist and Ecological Forms*. Cambridge: Cambridge University Press.

Tullock, Gordon. 1966. *The Organization of Inquiry*. Durham: Duke University Press.

Tullock, Gordon, Arthur Seldon, and Gordon L. Brady. 2002. *Government Failure: A Primer in Public Choice*. Washington, DC: Cato Institute.

Wagner, Richard E. 1966. Pressure Groups and Political Entrepreneurs: A Review Article. *Papers on Non-Market Decision Making* 1 (1): 161–170.

White, Lawrence H. 2012. *Clash of Economic Ideas: The Great Policy Debates and Experiments of the Last Hundred Years*. Cambridge, MA: Cambridge University Press.

Winston, Clifford. 2006. *Market Failure vs. Government Failure*. Washington, DC: Brookings Institution Press.

Wohlgemuth, Michael. 2002. Democracy and Opinion Falsification: Towards a New Austrian Political Economy. *Constitutional Political Economy* 13 (3): 223–246.

10

The Reconstruction of the Liberal Project

Introduction

Prior to WWII—August 1938 to be exact—Hayek participated in a colloquium in Paris discussing Walter Lippmann's *The Good Society*. The organizers brought together the leading European scholars and intellectuals to meet and discuss with Lippmann the threats that the liberal order faced in the wake of the crisis of the Great Depression, and the rise of right-wing and left-wing authoritarian regimes. Organized by the French philosopher, Louis Rougier, the attendees included such established scholars as Raymond Aron (France), Ludwig von Mises (Austria), Michael Polanyi (Hungary), Wilhelm Ropke (Germany), and Alexander Rustow (Germany). It is perhaps important to note that Walter Eucken (Germany) was also invited but did not receive the necessary permission to leave Germany. Lippmann was the lone American and his book served as the basis for an intense discussion of the reconstruction of the liberal project in the wake of the challenges of collectivism, the problems with socialism, and the failure of classic laissez-faire capitalism. It is at this meeting that Alexander Rustow coined the term "neoliberalism," but I would suggest that readers do not read too much into that etymological fact for the

© The Author(s) 2018
Peter J. Boettke, *F. A. Hayek*, Great Thinkers in Economics,
https://doi.org/10.1057/978-1-137-41160-0_10

simple reason that the meaning of the term has evolved and remains so amorphous that it is near impossible for it to provide much conceptual clarity. Though critics continue to invoke the term to label political and policy trends they find unpleasant.

Though Hayek was in attendance, and a written record of the dialogue has survived, it appears he was not as active in expressing his opinions as others. But the enterprise had a profound influence on him. The Walter Lippmann Colloquium only met once, after the network of scholars assembled was unable to continue their work on the reconstruction of liberalism due to the advent of WWII. Scholars such as Mises were compelled by circumstances to engage in a harrowing escape from Europe to the USA to avoid capture and ultimate demise at the hands of the Nazis. Hayek would relocate to Cambridge with the rest of the LSE during the war, and would publish in 1944 *The Road to Serfdom,* as we have already discussed. Almost as soon as WWII was over, Hayek began his efforts to reconvene the network of scholars and intellectuals to discuss seriously the necessity of the reconstruction of the liberal project in the aftermath of WWII. This eventually led to the establishment of the Mont Pelerin Society (MPS) in 1947. Throughout its history, the MPS has sought to cultivate a constructive conversation among scholars and intellectuals about the challenges the liberal order faces. The vibrant conversation and intense debates among the attendees at MPS meetings focused on how to think about the challenges to liberalism, and more importantly, how to revise our understanding of true radical liberalism so it is an ongoing project that excites the imagination of scholars and intellectuals, and offers creative solutions to the pressing issues of the times.

What was true for the world in 1938, and for the world in 1947, is also true for us today in 2018. As a result, liberalism is in need of renewal. But it is important to stress that in my opinion, liberalism does not face a marketing problem; it faces a thinking problem. Too much time and effort has been put into repackaging and marketing a fixed doctrine of eternal truths, rather than rethinking and evolving to meet the new challenges. True liberalism today faces a serious problem from ideas emerging from a new generation of socialists on the left, and from conservative movements on the right. Both sides are fueled by populist rhetoric of a

primitive nationalism, and disillusionment born of discomfort from having to adapt to an ever-changing globalized world.

The challenges of a globalized world are not new, just as fear of the
"other" is not a new challenge to true liberalism. As Hayek pointed out
repeatedly, the moral intuitions that are a product of our evolutionary
past, which are largely in-group morals, often conflict with the moral
requirements of the great globalized society (see, e.g. Hayek 1979, appendix). We, as true liberal radicals, and in our capacity as scholarly students
of civilization, as teachers of political economy and social philosophy,
and as writers and public intellectuals, must aid in the cultivation of more
mature moral intuitions if the tremendous benefits of the great society are
to be sustained.[1] Left and right populism agitates against such an effort at
cultivating the sensibilities of the cosmopolitan liberal, and instead promotes parochial and in-group political thought and action. And both left
and right populism is based on poor economic reasoning.

The contemporary arguments deployed identify with traditional criticisms of the market economy based on inefficiency, instability, and
injustice, but, as in the past, cannot correctly identify the sources of
those social ills in the existing reality of our times. Just as the great economic voices for true liberalism in the post-WWII era, such as Hayek,
Friedman, and Buchanan, had to counter these arguments with careful
research and effective prose, so too must the current generation of true
radical liberals.

In the USA and the UK, the populist threat can be seen on both the
left and the right, as evident in the rhetoric of Bernie Sanders and Jeremy
Corbyn, respectively, and the populist electoral events of 2016 in the victory of Donald Trump in the US Presidential race as well as the Brexit
vote in the UK. Being anti-establishment should never be enough to
bring intellectual joy to a true liberal.[2] The progressive elite establishment

---

[1] See James Buchanan's "The Soul of Classical Liberalism" (2000). These calls are not for a change in human nature, but for a cultivation of an understanding and appreciation of how a change in the rules that govern social intercourse can channel our behavior into productive and peaceful interactions.

[2] The anti-globalization movement of the 2000s and the Occupy Wall Street protests in the wake of the global financial crisis of 2008 reflect the populist left, while the rise of the paleo-conservatives, paleo-libertarians, economic nationalists, and segments of the Alt Right movement represent the populist right. I am leaving out of the discussion the odious racial politics that is also intermingled here in the populist discussions of the USA and in Europe concerning immigration, refugees, and public policy.

in the Western democracies has indeed, as Hayek said in his Nobel Prize address, "made a mess of things" with economic policy and legislation that has undermined the rule of law (see Hayek [1974] 1989, 362). True liberals must be vociferous critics of the intellectual errors committed by the progressive elite, and the empirical consequences that such errors have brought in their wake. The dangerous alliance between scientism and statism that Hayek warned about must be first recognized, understood for the damage it has wrought not only to policy but also to science, and finally torn apart. Further, institutional safeguards must be introduced that provide effective resistance to this unhelpful alliance ever being forged again in the future. This requires hard thinking and careful research, and that is neither easy to do, nor easy to follow for the popular masses who too often become bored with nuance and subtleties of scientific and philosophical thought.

True liberal radicalism was always pulled on the nostril hairs of the pretentious and arrogant in positions of power who thought they could choose better for others than they could for themselves. Adam Smith ([1776] 1981, 478), for example, warned that:

The statesman, who should attempt to direct private people in what manner they ought to employ their capitals, would not only load himself with a most unnecessary attention, but assume an authority which could safely be trusted, not only to no single person, but to no council or senate whatever, and which would no-where be so dangerous as in the hands of a man who had folly and presumption enough to fancy himself fit to exercise it.

In this century, Ludwig von Mises was quick to remind his audience that: "It is impossible to understand the history of economic thought if one does not pay attention to the fact that economics as such is a challenge to the conceit of those in power" ([1949] 1998, 67). And, of course, F. A. Hayek diagnosed the consequences of *The Fatal Conceit* (1988, 76) and summarized the position of the liberal political economists when he stated: "The curious task of economics is to demonstrate to men how little they really know about what they imagine they can design."

True liberalism is a subtle and nuanced expert critique of rule by experts. It uses reason, as Hayek put it, to whittle down the claims of Reason. If liberalism is not successful in this effort to expose the pretense of knowledge, then those experts risk becoming tyrants over their fellows and destroyers of civilization (see Hayek [1974] 1989, 7). So, the populist critique of the establishment elite is not what constitutes the threat to a free society. It is the specifics of the populist program and its inward-looking policies, such as economic nationalism and protectionism, that stifle productive specialization and peaceful social cooperation. In some instances, they do not even want to see the gains from mutual trade pursued by neighbors who possess some degree of social distance that they find uncomfortable.

The true liberal mind-set, on the other hand, is one of cultivating and unleashing the creative powers of a free civilization. It is one that celebrates human diversity in skills, talents, attitudes, and beliefs and seeks to learn constantly from this smorgasbord of human delights.[3] Liberalism is, in theory and in practice, about emancipating individuals from the bonds of oppression. In doing so, it gives individuals the right to say NO (see Schmidtz 2006). But while saying no is critical to being able to break relationships of dominion, the positive program for liberalism is also about creating greater scope for mutually beneficial relationships, and thus the possibility for a free and willing YES in all acted upon social engagements. Economic liberalism is an argument grounded in the mutual gains from association that can be realized by individuals who are socially distanced from each other. These individuals can further benefit from cooperation with strangers as well as friends, and are able to turn strangers into friends through mutually beneficial commercial relationships. The liberal argument was based in part on the *doux-commerce*

---

[3] I still find one of the most persuasive statements of the underlying attitudes of a liberal society to be Steve Macedo's *Liberal Virtues* (1990), and of the institutional infrastructure that might follow to be Chandran Kukathus's *The Liberal Archipelago* (2003). The cultivating of mutual respect and dignity that a liberal order must entail does, as my colleague Tyler Cowen argued in *Creative Destruction* (2002), turn on the homogeneity of some beliefs at the rules level of analysis and heterogeneity at the within rules level. It is a question ultimately of the relevant margins that enable the operationalizability of cosmopolitan liberalism.

thesis, which is as much about civility and respect as it is about efficiency and profit.[4]

The liberal does acknowledge the right of others to hold parochial attitudes in their restricted sphere and the right to say NO to potential relationships of mutual cooperation, but they also recognize that this can only be possible within a *framework* of cosmopolitan liberalism. Saying NO in that context entails a cost that must be paid by the individual or group turning inward. They will bear the cost of foregoing the mutual gains from exchange, and thus the benefits of productive specialization and peaceful social cooperation. If, on the other hand, parochial attitudes grasp hold of the framework, which is what is currently at risk with this current populist threat, then those in power end up saying NO for the individual, and the creative powers of the free civilization will be curtailed and the growth of knowledge and growth of wealth will be equally stunted. Parochialism kills progress by forcing attention in-group, rather than allowing—let alone enabling—individuals in their quest to seek new ways to learn and benefit from others. Turning inward means turning away from pursuing productive specialization and peaceful social cooperation in the global marketplace.

"The goal of the domestic policy of liberalism," Mises wrote in *Liberalism* ([1927] 1985, 76),

is the same as that of its foreign policy: peace. It aims at peaceful cooperation just as much between nations as within each nation. The starting point of liberal thought is the recognition of the value and importance of human cooperation, and the whole policy and program of liberalism is designed to serve the purpose of maintaining the existing state of mutual cooperation among the members of the human race and of extending it still further. The ultimate ideal envisioned by liberalism is the perfect cooperation of all mankind, taking place peacefully and without friction. Liberal thinking always has the whole of humanity in view and not just parts. It does not stop at limited groups; it does not end at the border of the village, of the province, of the nation, or of the continent. Its thinking

---

[4] The work of my colleague Virgil Storr (2008) has developed this core thesis of liberal political economy in new and fascinating ways, and, in the process, drawn our methodological and analytical attention to foundational issues in the cultural science. See also Storr, *Understanding the Culture of Markets* (2012).

is cosmopolitan and ecumenical: it takes in all men and the whole world. Liberalism is, in this sense, humanism; and the liberal, a citizen of the world, a cosmopolite.

So how can there be any confusion on the relationship between liberalism and populism? True liberal radicalism has *nothing* in common with populist movements except a critique of the progressive elite establishment that has ruled the intellectual and policy world since WWII. And the liberal critique of the progressive elite is grounded in sound economics and the grand and honorable tradition of political economy; it is not born in disillusionment and angry frustration. The Mont Pelerin Society was founded to cultivate the conversation and perpetuate progress in *liberal* thinking for each new generation. That task remains our task, and we have to rise to the challenge.

Liberalism Is Liberal

The first job in that task, I would argue, is for the true liberal to reassert the fundamental liberal nature of true liberal radicalism to both friends and critics. Samuel Freedman published a subtle and sophisticated philosophical reflection on "Illiberal Libertarians" (2001), but his basic point was raised in a more popular treatment by Jeffrey Sachs in "Libertarian Illusions" (2012). After reading Sachs's understanding of libertarianism, there should be no doubt that extremely intelligent folks frequently misrepresent the classical liberal and libertarian position. Why would Sachs believe that "Compassion, justice, civic responsibility, honesty, decency, humility, respect, and even survival of the poor, weak, and vulnerable – are all to take a back seat." Did he read that in Adam Smith, in J. B. Say, in J. S. Mill, in F. A. Hayek, in Milton Friedman, in James Buchanan, or in Vernon Smith? Deirdre McCloskey, perhaps more than any other contemporary scholar, is really trying to set the record straight on these issues, but we need more voices to assert the firm commitment to liberal virtues in the classical liberal and modern libertarian project. Sachs needs to read McCloskey if he has not done so, and if he has read her to rethink his opinions on the libertarian project. However, those of us who share

McCloskey's commitments have to make it easy for folks like Jeff Sachs (or Samuel Freeman) to read our liberalism. We too often make it difficult due to certain habits of thought that crept into the liberal project during the second half of the twentieth century.

Simply pointing out what is wrong with others who read our works is not very helpful. We have to ask self-critically, how can our position be so misconstrued? What failures in thought and communication could we be committing? And to ask the even deeper critical question, what in our classic texts lead to this conclusion? Both Freeman and Sachs have more of a leg to stand on as they distinguish in their own ways between philosophical positions and practical positions on the one hand, and between classical liberalism and modern libertarianism on the other. What they are countering is, in their mind, a common fallacy which is to read modern libertarianism as a refinement and extension of classical liberalism. Libertarian, to many of us, is just a term invented after WWII due to the corruption of the meaning of true liberalism by the progressive establishment in the first half of the twentieth century—especially in the USA. This is how we see it, so their reading is jarring at first. Many would see Nozick, for example, as a modern restatement of Lockean liberalism; Hayek as a modern restatement of the liberalism of Smith and Hume; and Buchanan as a modern restatement of social contract theory and the project of the American founding fathers in constructing a representative constitutional democracy (see Boettke 1993, 106–31).

But not so fast, Freeman and Sachs contend. Liberalism is about basic human equality and seeing each other as equal. And, of course, they are right. But as they see it, libertarians place liberty above all other social values, and they argue for the sanctity of contracts above all else.[5] This could, and does in their reading, lead modern libertarians to hold rather illiberal positions. Rather than basic human equality and treating one another as equals, the commitment to property rights and freedom of contract can result in the exercising of dominion by some over others. Rather than

---

[5] Hayek (1960, 29), though, argued that: "Liberty is essential in order to leave room for the unforeseeable and unpredictable; we want it because we have learned to expect from it the opportunity of realizing many of our aims. It is because every individual knows so little and, in particular, because we rarely know which of us knows best that we trust the independent and competitive efforts of many to induce the emergence of what we shall want when we see it. Humiliating to human pride as it may be, we must recognize that the advance and even the preservation of civilization are dependent upon a maximum of opportunity for accidents to happen."

breaking the bonds of oppression, libertarianism can strengthen those bonds, and in fact, be responsible for the introduction of new bonds of oppression. We must admit that in the critique of the progressive establishment and its demands for encroachments on private property, freedom of contract, and freedom of association, libertarian writers have often taken a rhetorical stance that places priority of the sanctity of property and contract, a defense of tradition, and the parochial positions that many hold dear due to the accident of birth, family, and conviction. This conclusion may indeed follow as a consequence of freedom of association.

Hayek, however, cannot be accused of this libertarian caricature. "It is often objected that our concept of liberty is merely negative," Hayek admits, but this "is true in the sense that peace is also a negative concept or that security or quiet or the absence of any particular impediment or evil is negative. It is to this class of concepts that liberty belongs: it describes the absence of a particular obstacle—coercion by other men" (Hayek 1960, 19). What is more important for Hayek, however, is that liberty creates the institutional conditions that makes other social values possible, and therefore, liberty "becomes positive only through what we make of it. It does not assure us of any particular opportunities, but leaves it to us to decide what use we shall make of the circumstances in which we find ourselves" (Hayek 1960, 19).

It may be the case that, for whatever reasons, individuals hold parochial beliefs, but it does not follow, according to Hayek's rendition of liberalism, that it would allow such social values to be institutionalized into the political and legal *framework*. To do so would not only privilege in-group mores and practices, but also distrustfulness of out-group others, and is therefore illiberal. The rule of law, meaning the absence of political privilege, implies a limitation of such parochialism to social interaction between individuals and groups within a set of rules. However, the costs of holding such values is fully borne by individuals wishing to indulge such preferences, leaving them free to decide for themselves whether to forgo or accept the possibilities for mutually beneficial relationships with others of social distance, whether small or great.[6] Therefore,

---

[6] On the importance of the distinction between the general framework and particularly practices *within* the framework, see Nozick, *Anarchy, State and Utopia* (1974, 297–334). And within the framework, the critical question is the viability of exit as discussed in Kukathas (2003).

liberalism, which is indeed based on an institutional framework of private property and freedom of contract under the law, does not guarantee the complete elimination of such illiberal behavior. However, once we understand that private property, the institutional prerequisite for trade, gives rise to the *doux-commerce thesis*, which "cures destructive prejudices, and it is an almost general rule that everywhere there are gentle mores, there is commerce and that everywhere there is commerce, there are gentle mores" (Montesquieu [1748] 1989, 338). Ultimately, liberalism is liberal precisely because an institutional *framework* that follows from the consistent implementation of its general principles increases the cost of discrimination based on creed, gender, and race, and creates the conditions for civility, toleration, and respect to flourish.

Emphasizing the right to say NO has been deployed in some writings as a form of "litmus test" libertarian rhetoric that is particularly unhelpful for thinking about what rules of social interaction enable us to live better together than we ever could in isolation. The intellectual exercise of demonstrating logically the most *personally* obnoxious position one could hold with respect to liberal virtues and sensibilities from the non-aggression axiom, and then championing the "right" for people to hold that position, is not the same project as figuring out the rules of just conduct in a world where our bumping into our neighbors compels us to bargain with them so we can live together and pursue productive specialization and peaceful social cooperation.[7] The "litmus test" libertarian can take great pride in

---

[7] The bumping into neighbors metaphor is from Schmidtz's brilliant *The Elements of Justice*, as is the essential issue of the right to say NO to offered terms of exchange. Schmidtz, though, in my opinion, does not come close to committing the "litmus test" rhetorical error in social philosophical discourse. His is an inquiry in the moral sciences, and not an effort to "shock" and "test" his readers. That error is to be found in many other libertarian writers such as Rothbard, Block, and Hoppe. Hoppe's work on immigration, in particular, is a prime example of this error as well as blurring the line between the framework of society and individual behavior within a framework. This is why his work and this confusion between framework and individual action can inspire the odious Alt Right in Europe and the USA. The inquiry into how to square individual autonomy with human sociability, and the working out of social rules of engagement to resolve conflicts and enable cooperation, is a significantly different intellectual endeavor than attempting to deduce a complete system of applied ethics from the non-aggression axiom. This is not a marketing problem; it is a thinking problem—to pursue one precludes the other, and that choice has consequences for *thinking* in political economy and social philosophy. It is also an intellectual temperament issue and, thus ultimately, a reflection of the liberal mind-set or attitude. Illiberalism is a consequence of styles of thought.

being a contrarian and shocking readers, but this "pride" is a result of misconstruing the art of controversy in political economy and social philosophy. It is not a matter of marketing to say that we do not want to gratuitously "shock" readers, but instead want to "invite" them to an inquiry of mutual interest. Inquiry implies you are thinking, still in the process of learning, and finding joy in figuring things out. Shocking implies possession of truth and that joy is found in exposing errors and catching others engaged in presumed loose thinking. Inquiry requires ongoing hard thinking about complicated issues; shocking implies limited thinking on a topic and asserting your privileged understanding over others. Inquiry is a conversation among life-long adult learners; shocking is for children who are content with the simple and the silly. Those who shock could never be that comfortable with the liberal claim that out of the crooked timber of humanity, nothing straight can ever be made.

There are a multiplicity of reasons why the liberal espouses virtues of openness, of acceptance, of *toleration* above all else. As Mises wrote in *Liberalism*, "what impels liberalism to demand and accord toleration is not consideration for the content of the doctrine to be tolerated, but the knowledge that only tolerance can create and preserve the condition of social peace without which humanity must relapse into the barbarism and penury of centuries long past" ([1927] 1985, 34). Of course, Mises also argued that liberalism must be intolerant of intolerance. Those who seek to express their convictions through violence and disturbance of peace must be rebuked. The answer, however, is to be found in the Liberal principle of tolerance and the free flow of ideas and beliefs. If the Liberal principle of toleration makes it impossible to coerce others into one's cause, it is also impossible for other causes to coerce you. Even zealots, Mises reasons, must concede this point.

But the rhetoric of "litmus test" libertarians celebrates not the liberal virtues but the right of the individual to be closed, to reject, and to be intolerant. Rather than err in this rhetorical manner and waste intellectual effort in deriving a logical case for the right to be illiberal, I would suggest that serious thinking by true liberal radicals must emphasize the *positive aspects* of human sociability, of cooperation with those of great social distance, and of the civilizing aspects of commerce. The *doux-commerce* thesis from Voltaire, Montesquieu, and Smith needs modern advocates in addition to McCloskey that will address the questions of globalization, of immigration, of refugees, of the possibility for mutually beneficial exchange with those who think differently, who worship differently, who live differently, as well as the nuts and bolts issues that are tied up with worldwide commerce in monetary policy, fiscal policy, and international law.

Our modern understanding of the technical economics, the structural political economy, and deeper moral philosophy of Adam Smith is so flawed that the Scottish Philosophers' most basic common concern of creating the institutional conditions for a civil and compassionate society is lost in the rendering. Hume's focus on private property, the transference of property by consent, and the keeping of promises through contract are not rules that only benefit one segment of society at the expense of others, but instead form the general foundation for civil society and peaceful social cooperation. Smith's analysis of the wealth of nations is not ultimately measured in trinkets and gluttonous acts of consumption, but by a rising standard of living that is shared by more and more of the general population. It is an empirical matter as to which set of institutions best achieves that task. But the concern with raising the living standards of the least advantaged in society is never far from view in any careful reading of liberal political economy from Adam Smith to Vernon Smith. Going back to Jeff Sachs's caricature of libertarian economics, I am arguing he should know better, and so should others in philosophy, politics, and economics.

The difference in judgment between Hayek and Sachs is not one of philosophical concern with the least advantaged, but an empirical assessment of what system best provides "Compassion, justice, civic responsibility, honesty, decency, humility, respect, and even survival of the poor, weak, and vulnerable" (Sachs 2012). Throughout history, the liberal vision has sought to find a set of institutions that would produce a society of individuals who are free and responsible, who have the opportunity to participate and prosper in a market economy based on profit and loss, and who can live in, and be activity engaged in creating, caring communities.[8]

---

[8] The liberal vision, going back from Adam Smith ([1776] 1981, 135, 138) to Carl Menger ([1891] 2016) and Alfred Marshall ([1920] 2013, 594), Milton Friedman and George Stigler (1946, 10; Friedman [1962] 2002, 161–176; Stigler 1949, 1), and Gordon Tullock (1997) to Luigi Zingales (2012), have always been concerned with income distribution and inequality of income. The commonly oversimplified characterization by proponents and advocates is that economists working in the liberal tradition are inconsistent with public policy goals that are commonly associated with government intervention, such as the reduction of income inequality.

This ultimately is an empirical question. Empirical questions cannot be answered philosophically, but only through careful and thorough scholarship. And that means that we must push the conversation about compassion, justice, civic responsibility, honesty, decency, humility, respect, and a concern for the poor, the weak, and the vulnerable, beyond romantic poetry and to hard-headed institutional analysis. Compassionate concern for the least advantaged must always be disciplined by the analysis of how the institutional environment within which we live structures the incentives actors face in making decisions, and mobilizes the dispersed information that must be utilized in making decisions and learning from social interactions. Liberalism constitutes an invitation to inquiry into the rules of governance that enable us as fallible but capable human beings to live better together—to realize the gains from social cooperation under the division of labor. True liberal radicalism exalts liberal virtues, and those liberal virtues undergird the institutions of liberal political economy.

Populist Critique of the Establishment

The rise of the populist critique of the status quo in our time has multiple reasons—some in deep-rooted cultural frustration and disillusionment with the American Dream, others in frustration with policy choices that have made the perception of their lives less prosperous and less secure. To address a problem requires the admission of a problem. It is my contention that pointing out that these perceptions might not be the reality is perhaps not the most productive response. If problems exist, we should look for the institutional causes. Institutional problems demand institutional solutions, and liberal political economy has institutional solutions to offer.

The problem with the establishment elite in the democratic West is that the answer to social ills for over a century has been more government programs, and especially more government programs run by a trained policy elite who were largely immune from democratic feedback from the very populations these programs were designed to assist. Vincent Ostrom in *The Intellectual Crisis of American Public Administration* ([1973] 1989) detailed the transformation from democratic administration to bureaucratic administration during the Progressive Era. With this basic philosophical shift also came an institutional shift as the Progressive Era saw not only the rise of the regulatory state, but also the rise of the administrative state, and in particular independent regulatory agencies with trained experts at the helm. More recently, David Levy and Sandra Peart contend that this demand for—and more importantly, claim to—expert rule resulted in an argument for the *Escape from Democracy* (2017). The consequences, as Hayek identified in his Nobel address and discussed earlier in this chapter, were significant for the self-understanding of political economy, and the practical affairs of public policy and economic performance.

Unfortunately, the critique of the liberal order that the Progressives used to justify the shift from democratic administration to bureaucratic administration was treated by intellectuals as separate, and as such to be acceptable even if the proposed solution of expert rule was disappointing. The capitalist system was responsible for instability through industrial fluctuations, inefficiency through monopoly and other market failures, and injustice through income inequality and unfair advantages due to the accumulation of wealth. Today we find ourselves in a strange position, where populists critique the prevailing expert rule, but nevertheless believe the prevailing expert diagnosis of the problems that plague society, resulting in their disillusionment with the promise of progress from the prevailing expert public policies. The populist rhetoric argues that industrial workers are displaced by machines and lower cost foreign labor, whether through firms relocating overseas or immigrants competing with them in the domestic labor market. Not only do these immigrants cut into their standard of living; a subset of them, we are told, are criminals and terrorists who threaten their very safety and the safety of those they love. The populist rhetoric argues that the middle class and working-class population have been made to suffer through the irrational speculation of the investment bankers which destroyed the livelihood, the homes, and the communities of ordinary citizens. The world as we know it, they are told from various corners, including experts, is one of a privileged few, where monopoly power dictates the prices they have to pay, and monopsony power limits the wages they can reasonably expect from the market. In populist economic nationalism—of both left and right—only government intervention can serve as the necessary corrective, and we must restrict the free flow of capital and labor, counter monopoly power, and forcibly raise wages. Ironically, the populist criticizes the establishment elite in public policy, while still agreeing with its conclusions, which is to advocate for an increased role of the government to counter the social ills of instability, inefficiency, and inequality.

There is a fundamental contradiction in the populist critique of the establishment, both left and right, which is that government is failing them, but it is failing as it grows larger in scale and scope of activities. Yet, precisely because it is failing, it must grow in scale and scope to address the failure. Governments everywhere in the democratic West have grown bloated, and have deviated significantly from any constitutional principles of restraint. The progressive elite's critique of capitalism was grounded in a fear of the unhampered predatory capability of powerful private actors, but to curb private predation, they enlisted a powerful centralized public authority. In doing so, they enabled the possibility of wide-scale public predation. But while it may be acknowledged that the social ills that plague society manifest in public debt and inflation, it is not acknowledged they are tied to over-regulation, over-criminalization, over-militarization, and so on, which are other manifestations of an ever expanding scale and scope of governmental authority in the lives of citizens throughout the democratic world.

The truth is that the social ills that are faced throughout the world can be traced to this growth of government, which leads to the erosion of a contract-based society, the rise of a connection-based society, and the entanglement of government, business, and society. We have policies that do not promote competition, but instead, protect privileged individuals and groups from the pressures of competition. We have financial institutions that have been able to privatize their profits, while socializing their losses. We have governments (and their service agents) at the local to the federal level that face extremely soft budget constraints in fiscal decisions precisely because the monetary system places weak to non-existent constraints. Government over-reaches and over-steps everywhere and in everything so that pockets of liberalism provide growing freedom on some margins, while "the road to serfdom" is literally being manifested on other margins, such as mass incarceration in the USA and the biases evident in the criminal justice system. Again, government fails because it grows, and it grows because it fails.

The reconstruction of the liberal project must begin with a recognition of the problems that plague the societies of Europe, the USA, Latin America, and Asia. Under the influence of the progressive elite, the democratic countries have asked too much of government and, in the process, crowded out civil society, and constrained the market society. An answer is to be found in mechanisms to once more restrain the predatory capabilities of the public sector, and unleash the creative entrepreneurship of the private sector. This can be accomplished to some degree by convincing those in the progressive elite as well as those in the populist left and right that to engage in rigorous comparative institutional analysis, we must recognize that we are dealing not only with erring entrepreneurs but with bumbling bureaucrats. The main institutional differences are that erring entrepreneurs pay a price for their failures, and they either adjust in response, or some other entrepreneur will enter to make the right decision. There really is no direct analog to this with respect to the bumbling bureaucrat—once bumbling, they continue to bumble. Public sector activity seemingly just repeats the same errors over and over again, yet with the expectation of different results. Not much learning going on in that, at least not if the ultimate goal of ameliorating or eradicating the social ill targeted is to be achieved. This is most evident in our military affairs, but also, in other "war" metaphors deployed from the "War on Poverty" to the "War on Drugs" to the "War on Terror." It truly is the case that "War is the Health of the State," but these "Wars" are definitely not a reflection of true liberal radicalism.[9] Militarism, even in metaphor, is at odds with liberalism.

Cosmopolitanism as an Answer

My answers to our current challenges are simple ones. Let us begin at the beginning—which for the liberal is basic human equality. We are one another's equals. There should be no confusion on this point. And if you

---

[9] Among contemporary liberal political economists Christopher Coyne's work on military affairs is in my opinion the most insightful. See Coyne, *After War* (2008); *Doing Bad By Doing Good* (2013); and Coyne and Hall, *Tyranny Comes Home* (2018).

are an advocate of liberalism and you find yourself "standing" (meta-phorically or literally) alongside anyone asserting the superiority of one group over another, you should know you are in the wrong crowd. Liberalism is liberal. It is an emancipation philosophy, and a joyous cel-ebration of the creative energy of diverse peoples near and far. The liberal order is about a framework of rules that cultivates that creativity, and encourages the mutually beneficial interaction with others of great social distance—overcoming such issues as language, ethnicity, race, religion, and geography.

At a foundation level, no one is privileged over any other in recogni-tion of our basic humanity. As the great practical philosophical teacher in my life—my Mom—Elinor Boettke, used to say, "People are people," that is who we are, we just have to let each other live, and that is that.[10] We are fallible but capable human choosers, and we exist and interact with each in a very imperfect world. No one of us, let alone any group of us, has access to *the truth* from the Almighty Above, yet we are entrusted to find rules that will enable us to live better together than we ever would in isolation. We bump into each other and we bargain with one another to try to ease the pain of bumping or avoid the bumping in the future. But we must recognize that despite our basic human equality, we argue and we do not naturally agree with one another about how we live our lives.

So, in our bumping and bargaining with one another, it is critical to keep in mind that we will soon face severe limits on what we can agree on. In particular, we have little hope of coming to an agreement among dispersed and diverse individuals and groups over a scale of values, of ultimate ends that man *should* pursue. As Hayek put it in *The Road to Serfdom* (1944, 101): "The essential point for us is that no such complete ethical code exists. The attempt to direct all economic activity according to a single plan would raise innumerable questions to which the answer

---

[10] These words were spoken from the time I was growing up in NJ right outside of Elizabeth and Newark, NJ and with grandparents not far from Asbury Park, NJ and in the context of riots that nearly destroyed those cities for generations, and as a teenager in the 1970s, as sexual preference issues became hot-button topics among some extended family members, and later on in the 1990s and 2000s in discussing interracial and single-sex marriage and also reproductive freedom rights among women. "People are people, you have to let them live. Pretty common sense." Elinor Boettke (January 1, 1926–August 10, 2017).

could be provided only by a moral rule, but to which existing morals have no answer and where there exists no agreed view on what ought to be done." This is one of the reasons why the Progressive establishment's idea in public economics of a benevolent and omniscient social planner with a stable social welfare function who would easily direct public policy toward the "general welfare" is a nonsensical approach to political economy, as James Buchanan effectively argued throughout his career from his very first critique in 1949 of the "fiscal brain."[11] Yet, public economics in the tradition of Paul Samuelson and Richard Musgrave continued, and continues, as if this Hayek and Buchanan challenge was never made. And I should add, as if Kenneth Arrow had never demonstrated the impossibility of a democratic procedure for the establishment of a stable social welfare function. "We can rely on voluntary agreement," Hayek put it, "to guide the action of the state only so long as it is confined to spheres where agreement exists" (1944, 103).

If we rule out as impossible an all-inclusive scale of values on which we can agree, our public deliberation will be limited to a discussion of the means by which a diversity of ends can be pursued within society. We can, in essence, agree to disagree on ultimate ends, but agree about the way we can acceptably engage with one another in disagreement. We are, after all, one another's equals, and each of us must be accorded the dignity and respect as capable architects of our own lives. The liberal virtues of respect, honesty, openness, and toleration, all entail a commitment to a way of relating to one another, but not necessarily a commitment to agreement with one another about sacred beliefs or lifestyle choices, or what commodities we desire, or what occupation we want to pursue.

True liberal radicalism is about the *framework* within which we interact, and I want to suggest that the most critical aspect of a viable framework is that it can balance contestation at all levels of governance with the necessity of organizing collective action so as to address troubling

---

[11] See Buchanan, "A Pure Theory of Government Finance" (1949); also see Richard Wagner's *James M. Buchanan and Liberal Political Economy: A Rational Reconstruction* (2017) for a brilliant discussion of how this paper laid the groundwork for much of Buchanan's subsequent contributions to the field of political economy.

issues that cannot be adequately addressed through individual action.[12] Let me unpack that sentence. The first task in thinking through the viable framework is to determine what problems demand collective action, and what problems can be addressed by alternative forms of decision-making. Questions of the scale of government are not invariant with respect to questions of scope. As Keynes once remarked, you cannot make a fat man skinny by tightening his belt. Scope is about the range of responsibilities of government, while scale is about the size of the governmental unit. The growth of government discussed in the previous section is primarily targeted at scope, but that in turn, is reflected in scale.[13] Questions of scope are philosophical as well as practical. Though philosophical, there is an institutional component due to the very fact that even wishful thinking must be operationalized in practice, and that requires institutions and organizations.

Assuming we have solved these two structural problems of government—general, agreed-on rules about how we relate to one another and the delineated scope of responsibility and authority between local, state, and federal governments—we still have the problem of learning how to match citizen demand, expressions of voter preferences, and governmental policies and services. We have to postulate some *mechanism* for learning within the liberal order of politics that corresponds to the process that was identified within the marketplace. How do we get a sort of *learning liberalism* within this general structure?

In the marketplace, the learning is guided by prices and disciplined by profit and loss accounting. It is also fueled by the rivalrous competitive

---

[12] The troubling issues are the social ills that plague human interactions, such as poverty, ignorance, squalor. But the most troubling issue in designing the framework is the potential for the powerful to exert their influence over the powerless and establish rules that provide them with a permanent advantage. So both "within any system" and "about any system" of governance, we face trade-offs of eliciting agreement and curbing political externalities. If our liberal system of government is to institutionalize our basic human equality in our ways of relating to one another, then it must be designed so that neither discrimination nor dominion is permitted. Various classic works in the analytical tradition of political economy from a liberal perspective have tackled different aspects of these puzzles, starting, of course, with Hayek's *The Constitution of Liberty* (1960), Buchanan and Tullock's *The Calculus of Consent* (1962), Ostrom's *The Meaning of Democracy and the Vulnerabilities of Democracies* (1997), and Munger's and Munger's *Choosing in Groups* (2015).

[13] And central to the argument is that this expansion of scale and scope has pushed politics in the democratic West beyond the limits of agreement, and that this explains both the dysfunctions and the disillusionment.

process where one can be sure that if A does not adjust their behavior to learn from previous missed opportunity to realize the gains from trade or the realize the gains from innovation, then B will gladly step in to take their place. Can we get such contestation in the political process? It is not just a matter of contested elections, but contestation throughout the governmental process of service production and distribution. We cannot answer these questions without addressing the supply and demand of public goods, and thus, the political process within democratic society.

Obviously, the frustrations with the establishment elite are deep-seated for the true liberal radical just as they are for the populist on the left or the right. The status quo is neither desirable nor sustainable. The diagnosis of the reasons why the establishment elite has failed differ between the liberal and the populist, but the critique of expert rule is an area of overlap. The liberal project has a history that stretches back centuries, and the true radical liberal has always been frustrated. Constitutional constraints bend when they are meant to pinch, especially in times of war. Delineated authority and responsibility is violated all the time, and not always due to the unwarranted reaching of the federal into the affairs of the local, but in response to the state-elected official strategically interacting with duly elected officials from other states to form a political cartel to benefit local interest groups at the expense of the general population.

Hayek asked his audience in 1949 to allow themselves to be Utopian, and I think that is correct. As Hayek put it:

> We must make the building of a free society once more an intellectual adventure, a deed of courage. What we lack is a liberal Utopia … truly liberal radicalism … The main lesson which the true liberal must learn from the success of the socialists is that it was their courage to be Utopian which gained them the support of the intellectuals … Unless we can make the philosophical foundations of a free society once more a living intellectual issue, and its implementation a task which challenges the ingenuity and imagination of our liveliest minds, the prospects of freedom are indeed dark. But if we can regain that belief in the power of ideas which was the market of liberalism at its greatest, the battle is not lost (1949, 433).

Heeding Hayek's call, we need to envision a liberal system that respects the general rules of engagement, but structures an intense and constant competition between governmental units. Bruno Frey (2001) presented a vision of government without territorial monopoly. His idea of overlapping competing jurisdictions may be one such idea of how to cultivate a learning liberalism. Work by Edward Stringham (2015) provides another vision, and Peter Leeson (2014) yet another. What is common among all of these is that they make no recourse to axiomatic deductions from some non-aggression axiom. They instead offer arguments and evidence related to the operation of institutions and, in particular, the processes by which self-governance performs not only better than you think, but in many instances, better than any reasonable approximation for how traditional government would perform in the circumstances described.

Hayek throughout his career proposed a series of institutional suggestions to bind the monetary authority from engaging in the manipulation of money and credit, only to be met with frustration as his suggested method proved ineffective against the governmental habit. Perhaps then in the supply and demand of governmental goods and services, the governmental habit as well is a source of instability, inefficiency and injustice, and thus frustration. If so, the reconstruction of the liberal project in the twenty-first century may need to turn to utopian visions as laid out by writers I have mentioned. A humane liberalism, as well as a robust and resilient liberalism, may find its operationalizability in an institutional structure of overlapping competing jurisdictions, and in a public discourse that respects the limits of agreement on ultimate values, but insists on a general framework that exhibits neither discrimination nor dominion.

Conclusion

Liberalism is liberal. But to realize liberalism, it has to be institutionalized. That means a governance structure of general rules has to be at the forefront of the conversation. And that conversation is aided by the consequentialist reasoning of the discipline of political economy. What we have learned from this discipline is that there are great gains from pursuing productive specialization and peaceful cooperation among dispersed and diverse individuals. The greater the social distance, the more benefits we can realize in exchange, but also the more difficult it is to realize that exchange, given transportation costs, communication costs, and cross-cultural costs. In short, transaction costs were high, so the great expansion of wealth in the modern world was due to institutional changes that lowered transaction costs and made the development of exchange relations with distant others (distant due to social factors or geographic reasons). Liberalism was one of the main vehicles that made that lowering of the costs of exchange a reality. Its doctrines celebrated trade, gave individuals decision rights over resources, freed individuals from the bonds of serfdom, and separated science from religious dogma. It was a slow and onerous process, and liberalism certainly was not consistently applied. But the victory and spread of these ideas resulted in the unleashing of the creative powers of people across the globe.

Despite the obvious frustrations with the establishment elite, it is a simple fact that 2015 was the first year in all of recorded human history when less than 10% of the world's population were living in extreme poverty. What a miracle the modern world is. But this was realized in spite of the establishment elite's policies, and instead due to the power of economic liberalism even it is when restricted and constrained. The power of Smithian trade and Schumpeterian innovation simply offset and push ahead of the obstructions of government stupidity.[14] As Joel Mokyr (2016) likes to point out, there are tailwinds and headwinds, and as long as the tailwinds are stronger than the headwinds, progress is inevitable. Liberalism provides those tailwinds.

The challenge for liberalism in the twenty-first century is the same as in the past—there will be conservative forces that provide the headwinds. These conservative forces come in the form of the entrenched interests of the status quo establishment elite, and the populist movements on the left and the right, who while criticizing the establishment ironically demand more of the same policies in greater proportion—more government intervention, more regulation of industry, more restrictions on the movement of people, more restrictions on the flow of capital, and so on.

---

[14] See Boettke, "Pessimistically Optimistic" (2016) for a discussion of the play between Smithian and Schumpeterian forces for optimism and the stupidity of the governmental habit of obstructing the free flow of labor and capital and stifling entrepreneurial creativity and initiative.

There can be no alliance between the liberal and the populist precisely because populism is illiberal. The primitive nationalism exhibited in populist rhetoric is discriminatory, and it seeks not to limit power, but to put different people in power. The natural ally of populism is planning and militarism.

It has fallen on this generation of true radical liberals to stand up against the threats to basic human equality, to stand up against intolerance, to fear, to meddlesomeness. We must embrace Hayek's challenge and explore the philosophical foundations of a free society with a renewed excitement and invitation to inquiry. And we must, above all else, insist that liberalism is liberal in thought, in word, and in deed.

Bibliography

Boettke, Peter J. 1993. *Why Perestroika Failed*. New York: Routledge.

———. 2016. Pessimistically Optimistic. *The Independent Review* 20 (3): 343–346.

Buchanan, James M. 1949. A Pure Theory of Government Finance. *Journal of Political Economy* 57 (6): 496–505.

———. 2000. The Soul of Classical Liberalism. *The Independent Review* 5 (1): 111–119.

Buchanan, James M., and Gordon Tullock. 1962. *The Calculus of Consent: Logical Foundations of Constitutional Democracy*. Ann Arbor: University of Michigan Press.

Cowen, Tyler. 2002. *Creative Destruction: How Globalization is Changing the World's Cultures*. Princeton: Princeton University Press.

Coyne, Christopher J. 2008. *After War: The Political Economy of Exporting Democracy*. Palo Alto: Stanford University Press.

———. 2013. *Doing Bad By Doing Good: Why Humanitarian Action Fails*. Palo Alto: Stanford University Press.

Coyne, Christopher J., and Abigail R. Hall. 2018. *Tyranny Comes Home: The Domestic Fate of US Militarism*. Palo Alto: Stanford University Press.

Freedman, Samuel. 2001. Illiberal Libertarians: Why Libertarianism Is Not a Liberal View. *Philosophy and Public Affairs* 30 (2): 105–151.

Frey, Bruno S. 2001. A Utopia? A Government without Territorial Monopoly. *Journal of Institutional and Theoretical Economics* 157 (1): 162–175.

Friedman, Milton. [1962] 2002. *Capitalism and Freedom*, Fortieth Anniversary Edition. Chicago: University of Chicago Press.

Friedman, Milton, and George J. Stigler. 1946. *Roofs or Ceilings?: The Current Housing Problem*. Irvington-on-Hudson: The Foundation for Economic Education.

Hayek, F.A. 1944. *The Road to Serfdom*. Chicago: University of Chicago Press.

———. 1949. The Intellectuals and Socialism. *The University of Chicago Law Review* 16 (3): 417–433.

———. 1960. *The Constitution of Liberty*. Chicago: University of Chicago Press.

———. [1974] 1989. The Pretense of Knowledge. *American Economic Review* 79(6): 3–7.

———. 1979. *Law, Legislation, and Liberty, Vol. 3: The Political Order of a Free People*. Chicago: University of Chicago Press.

———. 1988. *The Fatal Conceit: The Errors of Socialism, the Collected Works of F. A. Hayek*. Ed. W. W. Bartley, III. Chicago: University of Chicago Press.

Kukathas, Chandran. 2003. *The Liberal Archipelago: A Theory of Diversity and Freedom*. Oxford: Oxford University Press.

Leeson, Peter T. 2014. *Anarchy Unbound: Why Self-governance Works Better than You Think*. Cambridge: Cambridge University Press.

Levy, David M., and Sandra J. Peart. 2017. *Escape from Democracy: The Role of Experts And the Public in Economic Policy*. New York: Cambridge University Press.

Macedo, Stephen. 1990. *Liberal Virtues: Citizenship, Virtue, and Community in Liberal Constitutionalism*. Oxford: Oxford University Press.

Marshall, Alfred. [1920] 2013. *Principles of Economics*. 8th ed. New York: Palgrave Macmillan.

Mises, Ludwig von. [1927] 1985. *Liberalism*. Irvington: The Foundation for Economic Education.

———. [1949] 1998. *Human Action*. Auburn: The Ludwig von Mises Institute.

Mokyr, Joel. 2016. *A Culture of Growth: The Origins of the Modern Economy*. Princeton: Princeton University Press.

Montesquieu, C.S. [1748] 1989. *The Spirit of the Laws*. Cambridge: Cambridge University Press.

Munger, Michael C., and Kevin M. Munger. 2015. *Choosing in Groups: Analytical Politics Revisited*. Cambridge: Cambridge University Press.

Nozick, Robert. 1974. *Anarchy, State, and Utopia*. New York: Basic Books.

Ostrom, Vincent. [1973] 1989. *The Intellectual Crisis of American Public Administration*. Tuscaloosa: University of Alabama Press

————. 1997. *The Meaning of Democracy and the Vulnerability of Democracies: A Response to Tocqueville's Challenge*. Ann Arbor: University of Michigan Press.

Sachs, Jeffrey D. 2012. Libertarian Illusions. *HuffPost,* January 15.

Schmidtz, David. 2006. *The Elements of Justice*. Cambridge: Cambridge University Press.

Smith, Adam. [1776] 1981. *An Inquiry into the Nature and Causes of the Wealth of Nations*. Indianapolis: Liberty Fund.

Stigler, George J. 1949. *Five Lectures on Economic Problems*. London: Longman, Green and CO.

Storr, Virgil H. 2008. The Market as a Social Space: On the Meaningful Extraeconomic Conversations that Can Occur in Markets. *The Review of Austrian Economics* 21 (2–3): 135–150.

————. 2012. *Understanding the Culture of Markets*. Foundations of the Market Economy. Ed. Mario J. Rizzo and Lawrence H. White, Vol. 31. New York: Routledge.

Stringham, Edward P. 2015. *Private Governance: Creating Order in Economic and Social Life*. Oxford: Oxford University Press.

Tullock, Gordon. 1997. *Income Distribution*. Boston: Kluwer Academic Publishers.

Wagner, Richard E. 2017. *James M. Buchanan and Liberal Political Economy: A Rational Reconstruction*. New York: Lexington Books.

Zingales, Luigi. 2012. *A Capitalism for the People*. New York: Basic Books.

11

The Hayekian Legacy

Introduction

F. A. Hayek published articles over seven decades, and across multiple
disciplines. This fact alone suggests the severe interpretative challenge of
understanding Hayek's work, as Bruce Caldwell has pointed out. There
are intellectual challenges that Hayek faced throughout his career—
methodologically, analytically, and ideologically—and there is the challenge to any scholar who hopes to make sense of Hayek's life work and
discuss his system coherently. How do all the pieces fit together?

It should be obvious that if there were no tensions in Hayek's work, he
would have been working with only simple explanations, as this would
have been the only way to ensure consistency over seven decades and
across several disciplines. But Hayek was a life-long learner, and certainly
no simple-minded thinker, so his work is necessarily full of interesting
interpretative conundrums, as you have no doubt experienced in reading
through my presentation of the evolution of the Hayekian research program in economics, political economy, and social philosophy. I would
argue, in fact, that while these conundrums, perhaps even inconsisten-
cies, do exist, there is also an underlying coherence to his work, which

© The Author(s) 2018
Peter J. Boettke, *F. A. Hayek*, Great Thinkers in Economics,
https://doi.org/10.1057/978-1-137-41160-0_11

can aid us in making sense of the various twists and turns that he made during his career. It is this coherence of the whole that enables us to see, in the tensions, a great evolutionary potential of Hayek's intellectual system for us *today*. Hayek's tensions give rise to a system full of intellectual promise for Hayekians to work on, and to develop in directions far beyond where Hayek may have been willing to go. In other words, his system is pregnant with ideas for the next generation of economists, political economists, and social philosophers.

This is how it should be if progress in science is to be made. As Vincent Ostrom argued in *The Meaning of Democracy and the Vulnerabilities of Democracies* (1997), progress in political economy can only come from the pursuing of anomalies, contradictions, and tensions. This should not be interpreted as a call for contradiction and confusion for their own sake. Clarity of thought and clarity of exposition in political economy should always be our goal, and we must remind ourselves that simple or basic economic reasoning applied to complex problems is not necessarily simple-minded. But simplistic stories and simplistic interpretations of the world do tend to undermine our quest to improve our human understanding. Again, Hayek's analysis was not simplistic, though I hope in the work you have just read that I was able to demonstrate that Hayek's thought was more often than not logically sound and his arguments were presented in a clear fashion. Just because "out of the crooked timber of humanity, nothing straight can ever be made," it does not follow that linear arguments and careful empirical examination should not be our goal. Kenneth Boulding, who was one of my graduate school professors, used to say, "Peter, the real-world is a muddle, and it would be a shame if we were crystal clear about it."

In the beginning of this book, I listed what I consider the ten common misconceptions of Hayek's thought, and hopefully, throughout the various chapters, I have effectively countered those and pointed you to a more accurate reading of Hayek's ideas, and a more productive way to conceive of the Hayekian research program in the social sciences and humanities. In what follows, I identify what I consider three critical tensions in Hayek's body of work that have been identified throughout our discussion, two of which I believe are resolved in a rather straightforward manner when you consider the details of his argument and properly contextualize his argument. However, the remaining tension does not have an easy solution. This will require serious work by Hayekians to perhaps tread into territory that Hayek himself was reluctant to pursue.

Tension 1: Technical Economists or Moral Philosopher

Hayek once remarked that though he was a technical economist, he always felt compelled to pursue questions with a philosophical bent due to the disputes he had with market socialists and Keynesian macroeconomists. One way to think about this "tension" in Hayek is to consider how a moral philosopher would fare in the age of economic scientism. Clearly, the broad philosophical questions that Hayek pursued in the 1940s and 1950s with such works as *The Road to Serfdom* (1944), *The Counter-Revolution of Science* (1952), and *The Constitution of Liberty* (1960) fit more with the classical political economy of Adam Smith than the modern technical economics of Paul Samuelson's *Foundations of Economic Analysis* (1947).

It makes sense for readers to see Hayek as a different specimen of economic scholar. So, the first interpretative tension in confronting Hayek is whether or not he is an economist or a moral philosopher. I believe this is precisely the wrong way to think about this issue, and thus the first tension in Hayek is really only an apparent tension, and not a real tension. Hayek was led to emphasize the institutional framework precisely because the evolution of economic theory in the 1930–1950 period increasingly ignored it, due to excessive formalism and excessive aggregation. The consequence of this was—and should have been perceived as—devastating for the theoretical progress of technical economics. Ignoring the institutional framework within which economic activity transpires is akin to ignoring basic scarcity and the constraints against which choices are made. An institutional antiseptic economics is not just limited in its explanatory power; it is an empty style of thought, even when this is presented in a technically competent manner.

Hayek's institutional turn coincided with his epistemological turn—both in the sense of what a science of society ought to look like if it takes dispersed knowledge and complexity seriously, and in the sense of how we are to talk about dispersed and distributed knowledge within that science to make theoretical progress in understanding the products of human action but not of human design. This project can be read back into Hayek's technical work in price theory, capital theory, and monetary theory, and again, into his work on competition as a discovery procedure and the evolution of institutions. The coherence in Hayek's project is grounded in his view of the subject matter of the science of economics at the idea of the coordination of economic activities through time between individuals within a context of productive specialization and peaceful social cooperation.

Tension 2: Evolutionary Emergence or Design Principles of Institutional Architecture

Hayek is best known for his evolutionary account of institutions, including not only the spontaneous ordering of market activity. Of course, Hayek's "Use of Knowledge in Society" (1945) is the classic statement of how the price system utilizes the dispersed knowledge within the economy to produce an efficient allocation of resources. In short, Adam Smith's famous "invisible hand" theorem received a modern restatement with the work of Hayek. In fact, much of the battle in economic theory during the twentieth century can be boiled down to whose, and which, restatement of the "invisible hand" do you see as capturing the essence of Smith's insight into how real-world markets coordinate economic affairs through time: Mises-Hayek-Kirzner or Arrow-Hahn-Debreu.

Critical to Hayek's analysis of the "invisible hand" was his view of market-generated prices, neither as summaries of previous costs nor as sufficient statistics to ensure competitive equilibrium, but as guides to the ongoing and ceaseless adaptation and adjustment of production and exchange. Moreover, also critical to Hayek's understanding of the price system was the role of the institutions within which economic activity takes place. Property and contract are key to market coordination, and so are money, social mores, profit-and-loss accounting, and language itself. The market society is, Hayek argued, a communicative system where property rights marshal the ordinary incentives of individuals, prices guide, profits lure, and losses discipline. Hayek argued that each of these critical institutions are the product not of deliberate design, but evolve through the spontaneous coordination of individual plans that constitutes the extended order.

In other words, Hayek's work is interpreted by many as suggesting that not only does the invisible hand work within a system of property, contract and consent, it works to provide the institutional framework *of* property, contract, and consent and all the subsidiary supporting institutions and practices that define and enforcement that institutional framework. Law itself is a by-product of evolutionary processes, and is to be contrasted with legislative dictums from central authorities, be they Kings and Queens, or Senators and Congressman.

This creates tension 2 in Hayek—that between evolutionary explanations of the basic institutions of society and the design of the institutional architecture of society through constitutional craftsmanship. In dealing with this tension, one must keep the following few points into consideration. First, the same Hayek who wrote about the twin concepts of evolution and spontaneous order, also wrote *The Constitution of Liberty* and *Law, Legislation and Liberty* (including the 3rd volume, which is full of design suggestions for an ideal constitution) (1973, 1976, 1979). Second, it must always be remembered that tracing back even to Carl Menger's presentation of spontaneous order of institutions in his *Investigations* (1996), a distinction was made between two types of orders—designed orders such as organizations, and spontaneous orders such as the organic institutions of language, law, mores, and markets. But Menger also stressed, just because these organic institutions owe their origin to spontaneous processes of evolution, this does not necessarily thwart any effort at *improvement* of their operation through the judicious use of man's reason.

Hayek often used the metaphor of the gardener in contrast with the engineer to communicate the switch in attitude required for the blending of spontaneous institutions with design principles. A good gardener does not allow the garden to be overgrown with weeds, and protects the garden from pests. So, a good gardener resists the *fatal conceit* of the planner, or the *arrogance* of the man of systems, but he also does not sit idly as his garden is overrun by weeds and pests. Of course, finding the right balance is not easy, but that is one of the reasons economic, political, and social institutions should build in mechanisms of contestation, and encourage experimentation and learning, rather than one-size-fits-all solutions and comprehensive plans of social engineering.

A similar tension with the issue of balancing between bottom-up gardening and top-down institutional design is seen in the work of Elinor Ostrom. For our present purposes, all that we have argued is just that Hayek did not demand complete passivity with respect to the emergent order. Yes, he adopted the Humean project of using reason to whittle down the claims of reason, but that does not simultaneously commit one to answering Hamilton's question in *Federalist #1* of whether our constitutions are a product of accident and force, or reflection and choice with the former rather than the latter. Good operating constitutions can be, and are, a product of reflection and choice. Nothing in the work of the author of *The Road to Serfdom, The Constitution of Liberty,* or *Law, Legislation and Liberty* should be read as denying the need for, and desirability of, a positive program for true radical liberalism.

The source of the confusion in Hayek's work on this issue derives from conflating the question of the origin of institutions, with questions of the development and improvement of institutions. Many of the most vital institutions in social order can emerge without central command, and covenants can indeed be formed without the sword. But development and improvement may require more conscious efforts at tinkering and piecemeal intervention. Remember the gardener versus the social engineer metaphor once more. A useful exercise would be to always counter Hayek's "Errors of Constructivism" with a close reading of "Why I am not a Conservative," for in these essays, Hayek clearly makes the argument that the social scientist must be free to question all of societies values, and to recommend changes for improvements. But Hayek stresses a basic epistemological point, which is just that the scientist can never step outside of the system and question all of society's values at once. Instead, they must take as given the vast majority of values and question specific values against this given backdrop.

Once we make this distinction between origins and development, the tensions between Hayek's emphasis on organic institutions that are not the product of human design, and the conscious actions of managers, legislators, and planners eases to a considerable extent, though of course not completely. As Hayek wrote in *The Road to Serfdom*, the question was never about planning or no planning, but who is going to plan and for whom is the planning intended.

When addressing this evolution and design tension in Hayek, it is important to properly place his most extreme statements about evolution in their proper argumentative context. He puts forth a bold thesis: man has reason because he followed rules, he does not have rules because he followed reason. The significance of this rests in Hayek's location in time of this argument, as discussed in the appendix to *Law, Legislation and Liberty*, Vol. 3 (1979). It is not a claim about modernity, or even antiquity, I would argue. It is an argument about our pre-human existence, and how group morality and then civilization emerged as in-groups began to interact with "others" and the extended order of trade and commerce evolved. These rules of just conduct are first tested in our in-group settings and through group survival. It is important to remember that nature is "red in tooth and claw" and that homo sapiens are not particularly equipped by nature to survive in isolation from one another. As Adam Smith argued in *The Wealth of Nations* ([1776] 1981), we stand at all times in constant assistance of our brethren even though in our lifetime, we have the time and opportunity to make but a few friends. We had to evolve rules of conduct not only for our in-group interactions with family and friends, but with other out-groups and sometimes distant strangers in order to benefit from the productive specialization and peaceful cooperation that generates wealth and generalized prosperity. A key idea to understand is that Hayek's choice of the term *catallaxy*, which is derived from Greek, meaning "to change from enemy into friend" (Hayek 1976, 108), was to describe a broader point about an extended marker order. The emphasis on exchange activity, rather than the pure logic of choice, reflects a deeper point about peaceful social cooperation under the division of labor, not atomistic maximization in a Robinson Crusoe economy. The theory of social cooperation under the division of labor, which was so vital to Mises's intellectual system, is just as critical to Hayek's system of thought.

Hayek's intellectual acquiescence to accident and force, I want to contend, is limited to our evolutionary heritage and particularly to our prehuman existence, where the survival of the group was the mechanism for the perpetuation of practices.[1] It was not, and should not be interpreted as, an argument for intellectual passivity in the face of inefficiency, instability, and injustice in the modern world. But the way those identified inefficiencies, instabilities, and injustices are to be dealt with is at the institutional level of analysis rather than within institutional manipulations of behavior of individuals and firms. In other word, institutional problems demand institutional solutions.

Tension 3: Moral Intuitions and Moral Demands

While Hayek is perhaps not guilty of naïve evolutionism and a passive form of functionalism, his identification of the in-group morality and its path dependency on our moral intuitions creates a critical tension in the liberal cosmopolitan project on which modern civilization depends. We are always living in two worlds at once, Hayek pointed out, and our inability to do so creates a situation where the promise of liberalism is universal, but the ability to realize liberalism can be experienced by only a subset.

There are many different ways that human societies can be organized, but only a few of those ways are consistent with individuals realizing the gains from productive specialization and peaceful cooperation that characterizes modern economic growth. Deirdre McCloskey is unique among contemporary economists in her argument that it is ideas that are the cause of modern economic growth. She has resurrected an older emphasis on ideas that can be found in the writings of Ludwig Mises, for instance in his *Liberalism* ([1927] 1985) and in *Human Action* ([1949] 1998), as well as Hayek's own emphasis on ideas in his works such as *The Road to Serfdom* and essays such as "The Intellectuals and Socialism." Ideas do, in

---

[1] This is also relevant for the discussions about group selection and Hayek's commitment to methodological individualism.

fact, have consequences. And as Keynes so eloquently put it at the end of *The General Theory* ([1936] 2016), the role of ideas should take priority over the role of vested interests in explanations of social order.

If the fundamental equation of political economy, as Charlie Plott (1991) has suggested, can be seen as Preferences + Institutions => Outcomes, then we have a choice to make in our explanatory strategies. Political economy can explain variation in outcomes either by stressing different preferences or different institutions. The problem with different preferences approach is that it does not really require much of a theoretical explanation as Hayek pointed out in *The Counter-Revolution of Science*. Reducing social explanations to bad people do bad things, good people do good things or dumb people do dumb things, smart people do smart things, may be true but it does not invite much interesting theoretical social science. More promising is to treat preferences as fixed, and vary the institutions under which they operate. As Buchanan puts it, same players, different rules, produce different outcomes. And this also gives us a window into rationality debates in the social sciences, which I will just briefly mention here without further elaboration. If you have a strong notion of rationality, analytically you can get away with a weak notion of institutions because all the explanatory work will be done by the rationality assumption. On the other hand, if you have a weaker notion of rationality, then analytically you will need to have a stronger notion of institutions because the explanatory work will be done through the impact of alternative institutional arrangements have on human behavior. Again, it is my contention that this weak rationality/strong institutions approach was a defining characteristic of mainline economics from Adam Smith to F. A. Hayek.[2]

While admittedly not the most philosophically sophisticated, perhaps the most analytically productive definitions of institutions is simply the informal and formal rules of the game and their enforcement in any given society. The small in-group moral intuitions influence the institutions of just conduct by raising or lowering the costs of enforcing the formal rules of the game. Ultimately, what is at question is institutional legitimacy. If

---

[2]On the relationship between rationality and institutions to understand human behavior, see Elinor Ostrom, *Governing the Commons* (1990, 25–26).

institutions face a legitimation crisis, then it becomes difficult for those institutions to form the background conditions for modern economic growth. In my reading of these literatures, it is not necessary to make an exclusive explanatory claim for ideas, institutions, and interests, but instead some melding of them with ideas having a causal role in initiating the process of modern economic growth. McCloskey's most important insight was that it was an ideas change that was required to experience modern economic growth. Ideas had to legitimize the institutions of property, contract and consent, and entrepreneurship and commerce in general for the great enrichment to take place. This remains true today.

If our moral intuitions derived from our in-group evolutionary past are allowed to trump the moral demands of the great society, then we will forego the great benefits of social cooperation under the division of labor. There is a constant tension, but perhaps while acknowledging this tension, we must also remember that Adam Smith wrote two books, and not one: *The Theory of Moral Sentiments* ([1759] 2010) and *The Wealth of Nations*, and that the critical point is to recognize how they can be reconciled, rather than in conflict with one another. This is what Hayek challenged us to think about when he said that we must learn to live in two worlds at once.

Conclusion

Let us end at the beginning—which, for the true liberal, is basic human equality. Hayek is an analytical egalitarian; he is not of course a resource egalitarian. This has tripped many people up over the years because they equate social justice with resource egalitarianism, so when Hayek critiques social justice, they believe he has abandoned concerns with justice and fairness. Not true, as the subtitle of *Law, Legislation and Liberty* suggests, Hayek's project was about restating and refining the liberal principles of justice and political economy. To the true liberal, we are one another's equals. The political economy question is what institutional configuration follows from recognizing each other as dignified equals. There should be no confusion on this point: Liberalism is liberal. We cannot allow our moral intuitions of in-group solidarity to delegitimize the moral demands of the "Great Society." The liberalism of Hayek is an emancipation philosophy, and a joyous celebration of the creative energy of diverse peoples near and far. The liberal order is about a framework of rules that cultivates that creativity, and encourages the mutually beneficial interaction with others of great social distance—overcoming such issues as language, ethnicity, race, religion, and geography.

Back at the beginning of this book, I pointed out that in the context of the discussion concerning *Exact Thinking in Demented Times* (Sigmund 2017), that there was the Vienna Circle's answer, and then there was Hayek's answer. The horrors of the twentieth century were the product of the lethal combination when the "Will to Power" was matched with claims to "Certainty by those in Power." This recipe for disaster remains so in those sad realities of inhumanity we are witnessing throughout the world as we begin the twenty-first century, such as Syria, Myanmar, Turkey, and Venezuela.

In contrast, at a foundation level, Hayekian liberalism argues that no one should enjoy a privileged treatment over others, in recognition of our basic humanity. We are fallible but capable human choosers, and we exist and interact with each in a very imperfect world. No one of us, let alone any group of us, has access to *the truth*, yet we are entrusted to find rules that will enable us to live better together than we ever would in isolation. We bump into each other, and we bargain with one another to try to ease the pain of bumping or avoid the bumping in the future. But we must recognize that despite our basic human equality, we argue and we do not naturally agree with one another about how we are to live our lives. Those moral intuitions from our evolutionary past and reinforced in our upbringing in the family must not be allowed to block our interactions with anonymous others and benefit from the "company of strangers"—to use the phraseology of Paul Seabright (2004).

In our bumping into, and bargaining with, one another, it is critical to keep in mind that we will soon face severe limits on what we can agree on. As humans, we argue with each other, we disagree constantly, we strategize, and we distrust. In particular, we have little hope of coming to an agreement among dispersed and diverse individuals and groups over a scale of values, of ultimate ends that individuals or groups *should* pursue. This is one of the reasons why theorizing with the aid of the assumption of a benevolent and omniscient social planner with a stable social welfare function that can easily serve as a guide to public policy for the "general welfare" is a nonsensical approach to political economy.

So, if we rule out as impossible an all-inclusive scale of values on which we can agree, rather than seeking agreement on the ends to be pursued, our discussion must be limited to a discussion of the means by which a diversity of ends can be pursued within society. We can, in essence, agree to disagree on ultimate ends, but agree about the way we can acceptably engage with one another in disagreement. We are, after all, one another's equals, and each of us must be accorded the dignity and respect as capable architects of our own lives. The liberal virtues of respect, honesty, openness, and toleration, all entail a commitment to a way of relating to one another, not necessarily a commitment to agreement with one another about sacred beliefs or life style choices, or what commodities we desire, or what occupation we want to pursue.

Besides balancing our moral intuitions with our moral demands, the machinery of governance must be established so that private and public predation are effectively curbed and peaceful social cooperation through commerce and community are encouraged and promoted. Such a solution requires institutional operations that are incentive compatible and mobilize the requisite knowledge for social learning. We have to postulate some *mechanism* for learning within the liberal order of politics that corresponds to the process that was identified within the marketplace. How do we get a sort of *learning liberalism* within this general structure?

In the marketplace, the learning is guided by prices and disciplined by profit-and-loss accounting, but it is fueled by the rivalrous competitive process where one can be sure that if A does not adjust their behavior to learn from previous missed opportunity to realize the gains from trade or the gains from innovation, then B will gladly step in to take their place. Can we get such contestation in the political process? It is not just a matter of contested elections, but contestation throughout the governmental process of service production and distribution. We cannot answer these questions without addressing the supply and demand of public goods, and thus, the political process within democratic society.

As we have seen in this survey, Hayek's contributions to economics, political economy, and social philosophy were not the product of intellectual dilettantism. Hayek's institutional and epistemic turn in the 1930s was made necessary by his fellow technical economists pushing into the background the very institutional framework within which the human behavior and commercial practices they hoped to illuminate in their studies had emerged. This is the point that Robbins made in *The Theory of Economic Policy* ([1952] 1965) when he argued that economic theory in Britain co-evolved with the institutions of liberalism such as property, contract, and consent. The fact that, absent this particular institutional framework, the human behavior and the commercial practices that would emerge would be radically different was ignored. This meant that among those with a reformers zeal, the belief quickly grew that radical transformation of the institutional framework, root and branch, was within their power, and certainly was their right as the heirs of philosophical radicalism.

Hayek's project is a challenge to the scientistic understanding of economics and political economy, and a rejection of constructivist rationalism in social philosophy. It is a project full of tensions, but also of great promise. This has not been a book primarily concerned with Hayek the man, but with Hayekian ideas and their evolutionary potential. It is my sincere hope that the reader will be inspired to go from here and explore in more depth the beauty of the logic of choice and the science of exchange; the explanatory power of market theory and the price system; the mysteries of money and capital; the urgent lessons to be learned from comparative institutional analysis of capitalism, socialism, and democracy; the analysis of the structure of politics and law of the liberal order of a society of free and responsible individuals; and ultimately, an appreciation of the liberal principles of justice and political economy for our time.

Hayek's ideas are not to be treated as settled doctrine, let alone as sacred texts. He was like us, merely mortal, and he expressed a pleasure in figuring things out, and invited us to muddle along with him on this journey of scientific discovery and philosophical reflection. We are all just trying to figure things out. The evolutionary potential of Hayek's ideas, I have argued, has not been exhausted. And, thus, let this book end with an invitation to inquiry into the science of economics, the art of political economy, and the implication of both for a renewed social philosophy for the twenty-first century.

Bibliography

Hayek, F.A. 1944. *The Road to Serfdom*. Chicago: University of Chicago Press.

———. 1945. The Use of Knowledge in Society. *The American Economic Review* 35 (4): 519–530.

———. 1952. *The Counter-Revolution of Science: Studies on the Abuse of Reason*. Glencoe: The Free Press.

———. 1960. *The Constitution of Liberty*. Chicago: University of Chicago Press.

———. 1973. *Law, Legislation, and Liberty, Vol.1: Rules and Order*. Chicago: University of Chicago Press.

———. 1976. *Law, Legislation, and Liberty, Vol. 2: The Mirage of Social Justice*. Chicago: University of Chicago Press.

———. 1979. *Law, Legislation, and Liberty, Vol. 3: The Political Order of a Free People*. Chicago: University of Chicago Press.

Keynes, J.M. [1936] 2016. *General Theory of Employment, Interest and Money*. New Delhi: Atlantic Publishers & Distributors.

Menger, Carl. 1996. *Investigations into the Method of the Social Sciences*. Auburn: Ludwig von Mises Institute.

Mises, Ludwig von. [1927] 1985. *Liberalism*. Irvington: The Foundation for Economic Education.

———. [1949] 1998. *Human Action*. Auburn: The Ludwig von Mises Institute.

Ostrom, Elinor. 1990. *Governing the Commons: The Evolution of Institutions for Collective Action*. New York: Cambridge University Press.

Ostrom, Vincent. 1997. *The Meaning of Democracy and the Vulnerability of Democracies: A Response to Tocqueville's Challenge*. Ann Arbor: University of Michigan Press.

Plott, Charles. 1991. Will Economics Become an Experimental Science? *Southern Economic Journal* 57 (4): 901–919.

Robbins, Lionel. [1952]1965. *The Theory of Economic Policy in English Classical Political Economy*. London: Macmillan.

Samuelson, Paul A. 1947. *Foundations of Economic Analysis*. Cambridge: Harvard University Press.

Seabright, Paul. 2004. *The Company of Strangers, Princeton*. Princeton University Press.

Sigmund, Karl. 2017. *Exact Thinking in Demented Times: The Vienna Circle and the Epic Quest for the Foundations of Science*. New York: Basic Books.

Smith, Adam. [1776] 1981. *An Inquiry into the Nature and Causes of the Wealth of Nations*, R. H. Campbell and A. S. Skinner (eds.), Indianapolis: Liberty Fund.

———. [1759] 2010. *The Theory of Moral Sentiments*. London: Penguin Books.

Appendix A: Scholarly Impact of Hayek's Work as Measured by Citations

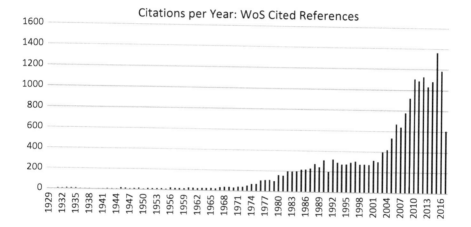

Citations per Year: WoS Cited References

© The Author(s) 2018
Peter J. Boettke, *F. A. Hayek*, Great Thinkers in Economics,
https://doi.org/10.1057/978-1-137-41160-0

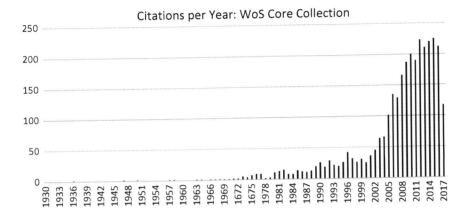

Citations per Year: WoS Core Collection

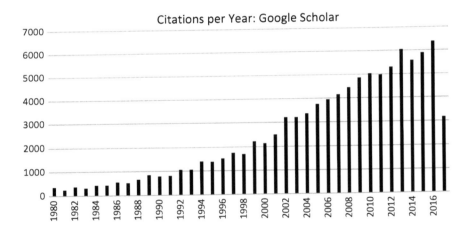

Citations per Year: Google Scholar

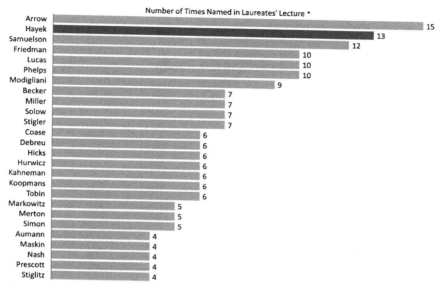

*This graph shows the number of times each Nobel Laureate has been mentioned in the "Prize Lecture" at the Nobel Prize ceremony.
Source: Skarbek (2009)

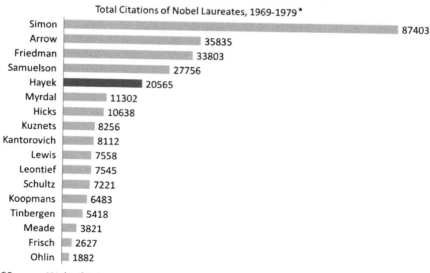

*Source: Web of Science (2018)

Appendix B: Top 20 Articles of the First 100 Years of the *American Economic Review*[1]

Alchian, A. A., & Demsetz, H. (1972). Production, Information Costs, and Economic Organization. *The American economic review*, *62*(5), 777–795.

Arrow, K. J. (1963). Uncertainty and the Welfare Economics of Medical Care. *The American Economic Review*, *53*(5), 941–973.

Cobb, C. W., & Douglas, P. H. (1928). A theory of production. *The American Economic Review*, *18*(1), 139–165.

Deaton, A., & Muellbauer, J. (1980). An almost ideal demand system. *The American economic review*, *70*(3), 312–326.

Diamond, P. A. (1965). National debt in a neoclassical growth model. *The American Economic Review*, *55*(5), 1126–1150.

Diamond, P. A., & Mirrlees, J. A. (1971). Optimal taxation and public production I: Production efficiency. *The American Economic Review*, *61*(1), 8–27.

Dixit, A. K., & Stiglitz, J. E. (1977). Monopolistic competition and optimum product diversity. *The American Economic Review*, *67*(3), 297–308.

---

[1] See Kenneth J. Arrow, B. Douglas Bernheim, Martin S. Feldstein, Daniel L. McFadden, James M. Poterba, and Robert M. Solow "100 Years of the American Economic Review: The Top 20 Articles," *American Economic Review* 101 (February 2011): 1–8.

© The Author(s) 2018
Peter J. Boettke, *F. A. Hayek*, Great Thinkers in Economics,
https://doi.org/10.1057/978-1-137-41160-0

Friedman, M. (1968). The Role of Monetary Policy. *The American Economic Review*, *58*(1).

Grossman, S. J., & Stiglitz, J. E. (1980). On the impossibility of informationally efficient markets. *The American economic review*, *70*(3), 393–408.

Harris, J. R., & Todaro, M. P. (1970). Migration, unemployment and development: a two-sector analysis. *The American economic review*, *60*(1), 126–142.

Hayek, F. A. (1945). The use of knowledge in society. *The American economic review*, *35*(4), 519–530.

Jorgenson, D. W. (1963). Capital theory and investment behavior. *The American Economic Review*, *53*(2), 247–259.

Krueger, A. O. (1974). The Political Economy of the Rent-Seeking Society. *The American Economic Review*, *64*(3), 291–303.

Krugman, P. (1980). Scale Economies, Product Differentiation, and the Pattern of Trade. *The American Economic Review*, *70*(5), 950–959.

Kuznets, S. (1955). Economic Growth and Income Inequality. *The American Economic Review*, 1–28.

Lucas, R. E. (1973). Some International Evidence on Output-Inflation Tradeoffs. *The American Economic Review*, *63*(3), 326–334.

Modigliani, F., & Miller, M. H. (1958). The Cost of Capital, Corporation Finance and the Theory of Investment. *The American Economic Review*, *48*(3), 261–297.

Mundell, R. A. (1961). A Theory of Optimum Currency Areas. *The American Economic Review*, *51*(4), 657–665.

Ross, S. A. (1973). The Economic Theory of Agency: The Principal's Problem. *The American Economic Review*, *63*(2), 134–139.

Shiller, R. J. (1981). Do Stock Prices Move Too Much to be Justified by Subsequent Changes in Dividends?. *The American Economic Review*, *71*(3), 421–436.

Appendix C: Hayek's Intellectual Family Tree

© The Author(s) 2018
Peter J. Boettke, *F. A. Hayek*, Great Thinkers in Economics,
https://doi.org/10.1057/978-1-137-41160-0

Intellectual Forefathers

Adam Smith
(Political Philosophy, Liberal Thought)
Carl Menger
(Marginalism, Subjectivity, Spontaneous Order)

Eugen von Böhm-Bawerk
(Interest Theories, Critiques of Marxism)
Friedrich Wieser
(**Direct Teacher**, Formal Similarity of Economic Problem, General Interconnectedness)

Ludwig von Mises
(Business Cycles, Economic Calculation, Methodology, Liberalism and Political Economy)

Intellectual Friends

Alchian – Buchanan -- Coase – Kirzner – North -- the Ostroms -- Vernon Smith

F. A. Hayek

Viennese Colleagues
Haberler, Machlup, Morgenstern, Popper

Hayek's Students

Chiaki Nishiyama, *The Theory of Self-Love*
Ralph Raico, *The Place of Religion in the Liberal Philosophy of Constant, Tocqueville, and Lord Action*
Ronald Hamowy, *The Social and Political Philosophy of Adam Ferguson*
Shirly Letwin, *Utilitarians and Fabians*
William Letwin, *The Advent of Scientific Economics (1660-1700)*
Joseph Hamburger, *The Philosophic Radicals*
Eugene F. Miller, *The Political Philosophy of David Hume*

University of Chicago

London School of Economics

Intellectual Foes

Neurath – Keynes – Lange – Samuelson – Grossman/Stiglitz

Vera C. Smith, *The Rationale of Central Banking*
Abba P. Lerner, *The Economics of Control*
Marjorie Grice-Hutchinson, *The School of Salamanca*
Bellikoth R. Shenoy, *Some Aspects of a Central Bank for India*
Ludwig Lachmann, *Capital Structure and Depression*
George L.S. Shackle. *Expectations, Investment, and Income*

Appendix D: Timeline of Hayek's Professional Life

- 5/8/1899: Hayek is born in Vienna, Austria
- 1914: World War I begins
- 1917: Joins a field artillery regiment in Vienna; sent to the Italian Front
- 1918: World War I ends; Hayek returns to Vienna and enrolls at the University of Vienna and studies philosophy, law, and economics
- 1921: Receives law degree from the University of Vienna
- 1921: Hired by Ludwig von Mises to work at the Office of Accounts (Austrian Civil Service) on the Treaty of St. Germain
- 1923–1924: Studies abroad in the United States of America (in New York, NY at Columbia University/NBER and at New York University, where he learned about modern statistical analysis of business fluctuations and compiled data on the Federal Reserve System)
- 1923: Receives his doctorate in economics from the University of Vienna
- 1925: Joins Ludwig von Mises's seminar in advanced economic and social theory (other participants include Haberler, Kaufman, Machlup, Morgenstern and Schutz)

© The Author(s) 2018
Peter J. Boettke, *F. A. Hayek*, Great Thinkers in Economics,
https://doi.org/10.1057/978-1-137-41160-0

- 1927: Mises and Hayek establish the Osterreichische Konjunkturfors Chungsinstitut (Austrian Institute for Business Cycle Research), Hayek serving as the first Director of the Institute; Morgenstern would serve as the second Director after Hayek moved to LSE in the 1930s
- 1929: Publishes *Monetary Theory and the Trade Cycle*
- 1929: Becomes Professor (Privatdozent) at the University of Vienna, where his first lectures were on the problems with underconsumption theories of industrial fluctuations
- 1931: Presents the "Prices and Production" lectures at Cambridge and the London School of Economics; Hayek's review of Keynes's *Treatise on Money* is published in *Economica*; publishes *Prices and Production*
- 1932: Appointed as the Tooke Professor of Economic Science and Statistics at the London School of Economics
- 1933: Publishes "The Trend of Economic Thinking" in *Economica*
- 1937: Publishes "Economics and Knowledge" in *Economica*
- 1938: Naturalized as a British citizen
- 1939: World War II begins
- 1939: Publishes *Profits, Interest and Investment*
- 1940: The LSE (and Hayek) relocates to Cambridge due to London bombings
- 1941: Publishes *The Pure Theory of Capital*
- 1944: Publishes *The Road to Serfdom*
- 1944: Elected a Fellow of the British Academy
- 1945: World War II ends
- 1945: Publishes "The Use of Knowledge in Society" in the *American Economic Review*
- 1947: Founding of the Mont Pelerin Society
- 1948: Publishes *Individualism and Economic Order*
- 1950: Appointed Professor of Social and Moral Sciences at the University of Chicago and joins The Committee on Social Thought
- 1951: Publishes *John Stuart Mill and Harriet Taylor: Their Friendship and Subsequent Marriage*
- 1952: Publishes *The Sensory Order* and *The Counter Revolution of Science: Studies on the Abuse of Reason*
- 1954: Publishes *Capitalism and the Historians*
- 1960: Publishes *The Constitution of Liberty*

- 1961: Appointed Distinguished Visiting Scholar at the Thomas Jefferson Center for Studies in Political Economy and Social Philosophy at the University of Virginia and delivers a series of lectures entitled "A New Look at Economic Theory"
- 1962: Retires from the University of Chicago, and is appointed Professor of Political Economy at the University of Freiburg in West Germany; delivers as his inaugural lecture "The Economy, Science and Politics"
- 1963: Delivers a series of lectures at the University of Chicago including "Economists and Philosophers" and an early version of "The Theory of Complex Phenomena"
- 1967: Publishes his collection of essays as *Studies in Philosophy, Politics and Economics*
- 1968: Retires from the University of Freiburg; takes Honorary Professorship at the University of Salzburg, Austria
- 1969: Appointed Flint Professor of Philosophy (a prestigious visiting position) at UCLA, where he teaches an undergraduate class on The Philosophy of Social Sciences and a graduate class on the unpublished manuscript of "Law, Legislation and Liberty"
- 1972: Publishes *A Tiger by the Tail: The Keynesian Legacy of Inflation* with Institute of Economic Affairs
- 1973: Publishes Vol. 1 of *Law, Legislation, and Liberty*
- 1974: Awarded the Nobel Prize in Economic Science and delivers his Nobel Lecture "The Pretense of Knowledge"
- 1974: Receives the Austrian Decoration for Science and Art (established by the National Council as an honor for scientific or artistic achievements by Federal Law of May 1955)
- 1976: Publishes Volume 2 of *Law, Legislation, and Liberty;* and publishes *The Denationalization of Money* with the Institute of Economic Affairs
- 1977: Receives Pour Le *Mérite* for Science and Art (a German and formerly Prussian honor given since 1842 for achievement in the humanities, sciences, or arts)
- 1978: Returns to the University of Freiburg
- 1979: Publishes Vol. 3 of *Law, Legislation, and Liberty* and publishes a collection of essays as *New Studies in Philosophy, Politics, Economics and the History of Ideas*

- 1983: Lectures at George Mason University on "The Rules of Morality Are Not the Conclusions of Our Reason"
- 1984: Awarded the Order of the Companions of Honor, United Kingdom (founded in June 1917 by King George V as a reward for outstanding achievements)
- 1988: Publishes his last book, *The Fatal Conceit*
- 1989: Collapse of Communism in East and Central Europe
- 1991: Receives the Presidential Medal of Freedom, United States of America (established in 1963 by President John F. Kennedy, it is the highest civilian award of the United States, recognizing those people who have made "an especially meritorious contribution to the security or national interests of the United States, world peace, cultural or other significant public or private endeavors")
- 3/23/1992: Hayek dies in Freiburg, Germany.

Author Index[1]

[1] Note: Page numbers followed by 'n' refer to notes.

© The Author(s) 2018
Peter J. Boettke, *F. A. Hayek*, Great Thinkers in Economics,
https://doi.org/10.1057/978-1-137-41160-0

Subject Index[1]

[1] Note: Page numbers followed by 'n' refer to notes.

Discrimination, 3, 12, 28, 210, 212, 214, 266, 275n12, 277
Division of labor, 11, 64, 81, 121, 123, 147, 163, 185, 186, 190, 205, 211, 219n9, 238, 251, 269, 289, 292
Doux-commerce, 261, 266, 267

E

Economic calculation, 22, 24, 30, 42, 89, 92, 121, 127, 144–146, 151, 162, 167, 181, 217, 237
Economic freedom, 32, 142, 143, 155, 200, 201, 211
"Economics and Knowledge" (Hayek), 25, 78, 81–88, 114, 132, 153, 169, 235, 238
Economics of Information, The (Stigler), 94, 96
Economic planning, 12, 22, 27, 30, 33, 120, 126, 135, 145, 149, 162, 170, 215, 232, 245
Economic Planning and the International Order (Robbins), 10, 22
Economic Theory (Becker), 21, 92n6
Efficiency
allocative, 103
Kaldor-Hicks, 125
market efficiency, 104, 131
Pareto, 188
static efficiency, 131
Emergence, 15, 28, 124–128, 135, 162, 164, 169–173, 180, 232, 243, 244, 264n5, 286–290
Emergent orders, *see* Spontaneous orders

End of Laissez Faire, The (Keynes), 20, 45n3
Entrepreneurship, 113, 243, 244, 272, 292
Epistemic institutionalism, xiii, xviii, 4, 11, 44, 72
Epistemic turn, 25, 81n4, 229, 232–239, 241, 244, 251, 252, 295
Epistemology, 80, 85, 107, 169, 285, 288
Equality, 176, 204, 215, 218, 221, 264, 272, 273, 275n12, 279, 292, 293
Equilibrium, 23–25, 23n4, 50, 79n2, 80–88, 91–94, 93n6, 96–100, 103, 105, 106, 108, 108n13, 109, 111–113, 126, 128–132, 136, 152, 167, 178, 180, 187–189, 230, 231, 234–236, 238, 241, 286
Evolution, xiii, xviii, xx, 2, 4, 28–30, 46, 127, 160, 161n2, 162, 174, 176, 178, 179, 186–188, 190, 192, 214, 219, 222, 232, 283, 285–287, 289
Exact Thinking in Demented Times (Sigmund), 31, 293
Expectations, xv, 10, 21, 41, 56n7, 82, 84, 105, 109–111, 110n16, 113, 188, 191, 206, 209, 250, 272
Externalities, 207, 208, 222, 240, 275n12

F

Fatal Conceit, The (Hayek), xviii, 28, 33, 67, 119, 137, 190, 212, 214, 260, 287

200–204, 205n4, 207–210,
208n5, 213, 215n6, 216, 217,
217n7, 219, 220, 231, 240,
241, 246, 248–250, 252, 258,
260–263, 260n2, 268–271,
269n8, 274, 275, 278, 294
Political economy, xi–xiv, xvi–xix, 3,
5, 6, 9, 11, 12, 15–17, 27, 30,
32, 39, 50–59, 61–65, 67, 70,
72, 80, 88, 92, 93, 120,
133–137, 136n8, 147–150,
155, 160, 161, 161n2,
163–166, 168, 174, 177, 178,
187, 192, 197–224, 228–232,
241, 246, 259, 260, 262n4,
263, 267–270, 267n7, 273n9,
274, 274n11, 275n12, 277,
283–285, 291, 292, 294, 295
Populism, 197, 210, 258, 259,
259–260n2, 261–263,
269–272, 276, 278, 279
Positivism, 233–234
Pretence of Knowledge, The (Hayek),
67
Prices, xiv–xvi, xviii, 6n5, 12, 20, 22,
23, 23n4, 25, 27, 30, 37–72,
78, 79, 83–94, 93n6, 96, 98,
99, 101, 103, 105, 106, 110,
111, 113, 114, 120–123, 125,
126, 130–133, 145–147, 153,
167, 171, 172, 175, 179, 181,
184, 204, 206, 208, 209, 216,
217, 217n7, 220, 221, 230,
235, 237, 239, 244, 248, 270,
272, 275, 286, 287, 294
Prices and Production (Hayek), 10,
19, 21, 124, 235, 306
Price system, xii, xvii, xix, 4, 20, 24,
30, 42–44, 45n3, 49, 50, 58,

68, 77–114, 120, 147, 170,
175, 204, 206, 235–237, 286,
295
Principles of Economics (Menger), 17,
165
Private property, 22, 24, 28, 87, 88,
90, 112, 121n3, 122, 129,
135, 145–147, 162, 167, 181,
186, 191, 200, 211, 212, 231,
232, 238, 265, 266, 268
"Problem of Social Cost, The"
(Coase), 77n1, 173
Progressivism, 210, 213
Property rights, 12, 28, 87, 101,
121n3, 123, 147, 152n1, 162,
164, 167, 168, 170, 176, 192,
200, 209, 264, 287
Property-rights economics, 168, 170,
192
Public choice economics, 168,
239–241
Pure Theory of Capital (Hayek), The,
4, 22

Q

Quantitative Easing and Operation
Twist, 46

R

Rational expectations, 21, 109, 110
Rationality
constructivist, xvi, 27, 153, 175,
295
ecological, 153
Reason, xvi, xviii, 1, 1n1, 25–27, 49,
63, 69, 77, 79, 80, 90, 103,
124, 126, 128, 133, 142,

Made in the USA
San Bernardino, CA
22 April 2020